PAWN ON A CHESSBOARD

PAWN ON A CHESSBOARD

From Minesweepers to Mayfair

Leslie Jackson

The Book Guild Ltd
Sussex, England

First published in Great Britain in 2001 by
The Book Guild Ltd
25 High Street,
Lewes, Sussex
BN7 2LU

Typesetting in Times by
Keyboard Services, Luton, Bedfordshire

Printed in Great Britain by
Bookcraft (Bath) Ltd, Avon

A catalogue record for this book is
available from the British Library

ISBN 1 85776 591 5

For inspiring me to write my memoirs, I dedicate this book to my five grandchildren

> *Marc*
> *Sophie*
> *Daniel*
> *Jessica*
> *Natalie* – *who, as a student of graphic design at Leeds Metropolitan University, designed the dust jacket*

CONTENTS

ACKNOWLEDGEMENTS

In writing about events that have taken place over my lifetime –
a period of 80 years – not only have I drawn on my memory where
I was personally involved, but I have been assisted by many
Institutions and other sources to enable me to highlight my own
small part in events that were played out on a much wider stage.
Among those to whom I would like to express my appreciation
for their help are The Bank of England; The British Petroleum
Company Ltd; The Naval Historical Branch of the Ministry of
Defence; The Royal Naval Patrol Service Association, Lowestoft;
The Institue of Chartered Accountants in England & Wales;
HarperCollins publishers for permission to reproduce the 'love
poem' from Leo Mark's book *Between Silk and Cyanide*;
W Foulsham & Co Ltd publishers and Harry Ludlam co-author
of *Out Sweeps*; *The War at Sea* by Captain N Roskill DSC, RN,
published by HM Stationery Office; The British Boxing Board of
Control; Tesco Plc; Hospitality Action (HCBA); The Municipal
authorities of the City of Brno; First Garden City Heritage
Museum; The Archivist of The Honourable Society for the Inner
Temple; The Czechoslovak Embassy; U-Boot-Archiv, Cuxhaven,
Germany.

I would like to pay a special tribute to my family and particularly
to Jillian for her support and encouragement, without which this
book might never have seen the light of day.

1

Days of Wine and Photos

My entry into the world was precipitated by a bomb dropped by a Zeppelin a short distance from the City of London Maternity Hospital. It probably added to the hostility that my mother was already experiencing in the ward where she was regarded with suspicion, as the only languages at her command were Rumanian and Yiddish. Rumanian was incomprehensible and Yiddish sounded like German to the Cockney nurses. They might have thought my mother was a spy, irrespective of the fact that spies do not usually have babies whilst on the job. If the bomb dropping on that fateful day in January 1917 was intended to get me, it failed miserably. The enemy was to have another go some 22 years later. But that is another story.

My father was born in 1879 in Jassy, a prominent town on the border which Rumania shares with Moldavia. He met my mother when he was 21 and she was 18. They married in 1902. Their engagement photograph shows a handsome couple: Marcus dark-haired and with a moustache which he cultivated and retained throughout his long life, Clara a natural blonde with a wasp-waist which she was destined to lose as it expanded in proportion to the size of her family.

Marcus, who was an accomplished winemaker, bought a country tavern where he made and served his wines and my mother cooked. In a country where illiteracy amongst the peasantry was the norm, he showed early promise of his future success by being appointed the local Inspector of Weights and Measures. It is more than likely that he was self-taught as secular

1

education was not available to a Jew and it would in any case have been rare for a professing Jew, such as my father, to have been appointed to an even minor government post.

The tavern prospered and three sons were born – Harry in 1903, Cyril in 1905 and Joe in 1908. Then my parents took a bold and brave step. My father had a passion for education and he was determined that his children should grow up in a more equitable and just society than the one in which he had spent his own childhood. The tavern was sold about 1910 and the family moved to the Belgian city of Antwerp, where Marcus took up an entirely new career and became a commercial photographer. I have not been able to discover how or why he chose this particular trade. It might well have been his love of travelling, which he was now enabled to indulge – an interest which he never lost. He became fluent in French, German and Italian in addition to Yiddish and his native Rumanian. His intuition – I can think of no other explanation – led him, after living in Belgium for four years, to move once again. The family took passage on the last ship to leave Ostend for England, arriving on 1st August 1914, and made their way to London. Germany invaded Belgium the very next day. Forty-eight hours later England declared war on Germany and World War I had begun.

I look back and try to comprehend the manifold problems with which my parents, seeking refuge, must have been confronted with on arrival in England with their three sons all under ten years of age. My father was resourceful but his knowledge of English was minimal. Passports were not in use and I doubt whether he had any documentation from the Rumanian authorities. On entry to England via the port of Harwich he was questioned by the immigration officials.

The family name was Janoviçi, written with a cedilla under the 'c'. When speaking, the letter 'j', as in the German language, converts to a 'y', so that the name took on an entirely different pronunciation from the written form. It was pronounced 'Yanovitch'. Even to this day I find it very confusing. It took only a few moments for this spelling to be entered on to a document and from then onwards and, for nearly half a century, my parents and their children acquired a new identity. In my early youth this varied slightly over the years, according to the whim of an official or head-teacher as either Yanovitch, Janovitch and even Yenovitch. All these variants have appeared, at one time or another, on my school reports and examination certificates.

Making their way to London with their possessions packed in just a few valises they were contacted by a Jewish relief organisation which arranged for them to be accommodated in the West End of London. For the removal of any doubt, I should point out that it was not in Mayfair or in the vicinity of Park Lane but in Poland Street. Mostly inhabited by immigrants from central and eastern Europe, Poland Street lies to the south of Oxford Street, an unattractive neighbourhood devoid of even a solitary tree.

The accommodation offered was in a building known as The Shelter, and so far as my family was concerned it lived up to its name. My parents were so grateful that they had escaped the fate of being overrun in the German invasion that they accepted the cramped living conditions with good grace. Within weeks my mother, who was an accomplished needlewoman as well as being a superb cook, came to the notice of Mrs Model, one of the luminaries in the refugee organisation. She volunteered to act as a wet-nurse to Mrs Model's grandchild, so my family were rehoused in the upper part of a small early-Victorian house built on two floors. It comprised two rooms and the tiniest of kitchens. There was no bathroom and only one internal toilet to be shared with the family occupying the ground floor. The wooden staircase, devoid of any linoleum, was scrubbed daily by my mother and the woman who lived below us, taking it in turns. It was a typical slum property but, within the constraints imposed on them, kept scrupulously clean by the two ladies. It was to this abode that my mother brought my dear sister Pauline when she was born almost a year after our parents' arrival in England. The family now consisted of six souls.

As an alien, although a friendly one, my father was not subject to conscription. This did not, however, prevent him from volunteering for the armed services only to be rejected as having

3

'trench-feet' despite his never having got nearer to Flanders than his pre-war sojourn in Antwerp.

He needed a job and his knowledge of wine now served him in good stead enabling him to find employment in the cellars of Justerini & Brooks, an old-established firm of wine merchants. This firm, who gave its name to the J&B brand of Scotch whisky (after being acquired in more recent times by Grand Metropolitan plc), occupied cellars in Bond Street. Casks and hogsheads of fine wine imported from the great chateaux of France were bottled and labelled for the all-important English market in these cellars. It was only after the Second World War, taking their cue from Château Mouton Rothschild in Pauillac, a commune of the Bordeaux wine region, that the premier wine houses started to bottle their product on their own estates and ship it to England in wooden cases. As a cellarman, my father would have handled bottles which, if available today, would be worth a king's ransom. I hope he obtained the job on merit alone, despite the tidal wave of sympathy for 'brave little Belgium', the first country in Europe to have been invaded by the Kaiser.

The war dragged on, with terrible losses and suffering on both sides. Life, with the ensuing shortages, would have been far from easy for the working class, although there was a great labour shortage resulting from the mobilisation of millions 'called to the colours'.

Marcus, the devoted father of four children, must either have been careless or a super optimist when, in January 1917, I arrived on the scene – an additional mouth to feed. He gave me the name of Lazarus. I have always wondered why. No other member of the family bore a name even remotely resembling it. I subsequently could only associate it with the brother of Mary of Bethany in the story related by John in his Gospel where he describes how Lazarus died and was brought back to life. I find it difficult to believe that this miracle had any influence on the choice of name for my parents' fourth son. My father, a devout Jew, had probably never read the Gospels. His Bible ended with the Prophets, and the New Testament was for him a 'no-go area'.

Because of my dislike for the name, I tried to find a logical answer for its choice that would excuse my parents for the misery it was to cause me throughout my school days. My theory ran as follows. My maternal grandfather was called Eliezer and had been named after the trusted servant of the Patriarch Abraham, who had been despatched to find a bride for Isaac, his first-born. The shortened form of Eliezer, probably a nickname of endearment, was Lazar. I can visualise Marcus, still with a limited command of English, going to register his newborn son. The registrar asks him the name. 'Lazar,' replies my father. This was a new one for the registrar. Biblical names have always been popular and the registrar could well have been a biblical scholar able to recite the Gospels by heart! At weekends when he was not registering the births of little boys, he might have toiled away as a Sunday school teacher. Mindful of the fact that he was dealing with a foreigner who could not be expected to know the nuances of the English tongue, he adds the letters 'u' and 's' to Lazar and laboriously writes 'Lazarus Yanovitch'. How was he to know that, years later, young bullies would cause their schoolmate such unnecessary heartache. Perhaps it is some comfort to me that it was at this time that the house of Battenberg felt it advisable to anglicise their name to Mountbatten. I wonder what Prince Louis would have done if he had been saddled with the name Lazarus?

At eleven o'clock on the morning of 11th November 1918 the guns finally fell silent, and in the following summer a vast victory parade was held through the streets of London. My very first memory, and one which made a very great impression on me, is of sitting on my father's shoulders amongst the crowds lining the Pall Mall approach to Buckingham Palace, hearing the regimental bands and staring with astonishment and delight at the seemingly endless ranks of marching warriors who had fought on the Allied side – our side – the winning side. I was two and half years old.

The peace was not to be celebrated for long. A virulent form of influenza swept across Europe and claimed as many victims, 20 million it is reported, as four years of the most terrible war ever fought. Our family did not escape. A brother, born a few weeks after the Armistice, succumbed in 1919 aged only nine months. Noah, named after my paternal grandfather, is reunited with our mother Clara in a cemetery in Streatham in South London, surrounded by the small graves of children similarly struck down.

Economic conditions after the war and in the early twenties were depressed. For four years the economy had been geared up to providing the hardware to prosecute the war regardless of the human and material cost. Millions of men on being demobilised were thrown inevitably on to a labour market which was not geared to absorb them.

The war had been financed through immense borrowings; at home by open-ended War Loans at $2\frac{1}{2}\%$ and $3\frac{1}{2}\%$, and from the United States who, not having entered the conflict until March 1917, had been very happy to bankroll our war effort – but at a price. The National Debt soared. Although only a single decade had passed, the world of 1920 seemed, by contrast, a whole century away from 1910, the year that King George V had ascended the throne to rule over an Empire 'on which the sun never sets'.

My boyhood was probably little influenced by the cataclysmic changes that were taking place in society. I played in and wandered around the streets of our neighbourhood – feeling very safe and very secure. I recall the milk being delivered by a horse-drawn cart and the milkman filling the jugs we handed to him, from a large copper urn. On Sundays, above the sound of church bells, came the call of the muffin man, who would announce his arrival with a small hand bell. It was a common sight to see poorer children with bare feet, whilst mine were shod in laced-up boots – shoes had not yet 'arrived'. One of my chores was to take cakes that my mother had prepared to the bakers to be cooked in their coal-fired ovens. It was not until my father imported a cooking range from Germany that we became self-sufficient; needless to say, it too burned coal. Any French baker will still swear that these ovens turn out the best bread. Our home was lit by gas, with the gas mantles requiring frequent replacement. They were made of a very fine filament-like cotton and had to be handled with great care as any break in the material rendered them useless. The gas supply was monitored by a meter which had an insatiable appetite for shillings (5p).

Our neighbours were small shopkeepers and artisans. The father of my closest friend was a military tailor who specialised in making riding breeches for cavalry officers. He was an out-worker for a firm in Savile Row, the Mecca of bespoke tailors; he would walk to his employer's showroom, about a quarter of a mile away, with a clutch of completed breeches under his arm. I would wander into the small living room, which doubled up as a workshop, and watch him and his eldest son sitting cross-legged on their large cutting table whilst they hand-stitched the garments. I loved to visit a brewery depot and watch the dray horses, coming in from their day's delivery round, being brushed down and fed with a bag of oats. Even to this day I can conjure up the sweet smell of the amalgam of stout and ale mixed with the strong aroma of the stables.

There was a gap of nine years between me and my next older brother so I came in for a certain amount of favouritism, particularly from my father. He would take me on outings to Hampton Court by double-decker bus – the upper deck being open to the sky. We would sit upstairs and when it rained we would cover our laps with an oiled canvas sheet. The buses in their red livery were operated by the General Omnibus Company and were the same models that had been pressed into service during the early years of the war to transport infantry right up to the French front lines.

I started to attend an infants' school at the age of three and recall being taken there, holding the hand of my sister Pauline who, although only two years older, was considered adult enough to be responsible for her young brother. Apart from being warned not to take sweets from a stranger, it was considered perfectly safe to walk the half-mile to school without a parental escort.

Our school was named Pulteney Street Infant's School and was situated in Berwick Street market in the heart of Soho, a fascinating and compact area which displays its origins and kaleidoscope of cultures at every turn. Geographically it is bounded by some of the major streets of London: Regent Street to the west; Oxford Street to the north; Tottenham Court Road to the east and Shaftesbury Avenue in the south. Honeycombed with narrow streets and alleyways, it has for the past 300 years been home to numerous waves of refugees, political as well as economic. The houses, strung out in terrace form, are architecturally undistinguished, particularly those built during the reigns of George III and Queen Victoria. Who used to live in these houses? Craftsmen, writers, poets, revolutionaries, pimps and prostitutes – Bohemians all. So many cultures, so many nationalities. Some streets were dominated by Italians, others by the French. There is even a Greek Street, which runs at right angles to Old Compton Street, one of the most diverse thoroughfares of the area. The Chinese had not yet arrived in force but today they are the dominant ethnic group, with Chinatown the most colourful part of Soho.

This territory became my playground. I came to know every nook and cranny, the distinctive aroma emanating from each restaurant – even the composition of their menus. The fashionable ones, such as Gennaro's where every lady diner was given a red carnation on arrival, Quo Vadis and, of course, Kettners founded in 1867 by Auguste Kettner, chef to Napoleon III. The stalls in the open-air market displayed a huge variety of fruit and vegetables and at the end of the day's trading there was always an apple or a banana, bruised or slightly damaged or just past its sell-by date, as a prize for a young scamp.

Soho not only supported its many nationalities in the material sense, it also provided spiritual nourishment. Churches were there in profusion, the spectrum ranging from Anglican and Catholic through to Greek and Russian Orthodox. On Sundays, their bells would ring out. Not in unison. Heaven forbid. That was only one of the many differences which contributed so attractively to the patchwork of Christian observance. I knew of no mosque. There were no Arabs. Neither was there a temple to Buddha, the Indians not yet having discovered Soho. The Chinese, if they prayed at all, did so above their restaurants, where they invariably lived. But there were synagogues. These ministered to the differing degrees of orthodoxy of the large Jewish population.

My father, who on the question of religion was the family decision-maker, joined not one but two synagogues. One was situated in Soho Square on the top floor of a substantial stone building reached by endless flights of stairs. It was called Bet Hasepher – a literal translation from the Hebrew is 'House of the Book'. The other was the Talmud Torah in Manette Street, a small alleyway off the Charing Cross Road well known for its proliferation of bookshops. My attendance at this synagogue, which I preferred to the other one for no reason other than I hated to climb all those stairs, began at an early age. Not only was attendance with my father compulsory every Sabbath morning, but I was enrolled in the Sunday school and received additional lessons once a week from an elderly and bearded rabbi in reading and translating the Bible and the prayer book from Hebrew into English. This was carried out on a one-to-one basis which I disliked immensely. Not only did I miss the company of other five-year-olds but I was on the receiving end of many a clip around the ears from this partriarch whenever I made an error in my reading. I envied my sister Pauline, who was exempted from this form of mental torture. She was even excused attendance on Saturday mornings. She did, however, join me on festival days and I look back with nostalgia to the annual Day of Atonement, Yom Kippur, when it was incumbent on adults, those more than 13 years old, to fast for 24 hours. Mother would prepare two parcels of food to sustain Pauline and me for the long day ahead, a day to be spent praying for forgiveness for all the sins committed during the previous year. The parcels, tied up in large squares of white linen, were our picnic to which we eagerly looked forward each year.

Marcus, who had spent the war years working in the Old Bond Street wine cellars, now decided to return to photography. The hobby of taking snapshots was in its infancy. Cameras were without the sophistication of zoom lenses, automatic focusing and built-in exposure meters the refinements that are taken for granted today. The most popular model was the simple Brownie box camera. Even at a price of 5 shillings (25p), a camera was considered a luxury and not an essential item to be taken on holiday. Instead there was the peripatetic cameraman carrying his 'instant' camera on a wooden tripod from beach to beach or from fête to fête. The camera was known as an 'instant' camera because its exposures took no more than five minutes, after being immersed in a small tank of hypo solution, to be developed onto tin plates. The cameraman would fit the photograph, measuring about 3 by 2 inches, into a decorative cardboard mount to be sold for a sixpence (2½p). These cameramen were to be found in every English seaside resort, funfair and outdoor sporting event. Marcus did not aspire to walking the sands of Bournemouth or Bridlington – he had a wider horizon. Doing his own market research, he discovered that whilst the camera was made in England, the most reliable tin-type films came from a factory in Nijmegen, Holland.

His knowledge of languages now stood Marcus in good stead. Arriving at the Nijmegen factory and finding common ground with the manufacturers, he was able to secure the sole-agency for the British Isles for their product. He was now in business.

Nijmegen and Arnhem were to become famous some 25 years later as the scenes of the desperate battles fought by the Airborne Division to capture strategic bridges over the Rhine. Had the operation succeeded, the war would have been shortened by many months. In the event it ended tragically – a bridge too far.

The immediate post-war years were traumatic ones for the German Weimar Republic. Germany had lost a war which it had inflicted on Europe, and now faced retribution from the Allies, who were in no mood to be magnanimous in victory. The Treaty of Versailles not only saddled Germany with a vast bill for reparations but redrew the map of Europe by breaking up the German heartland and Empire.

By the autumn of 1923 inflation raged and was completely out of control. Reichmarks had become virtually valueless. Recognising a window of opportunity in this otherwise parlous state of affairs, Marcus made regular trips to Germany, buying such diverse products as mouth-organs, wallpaper, clocks, and textiles, all at less than their cost of production. Importing them into England proved very profitable. Frequently, I was taken by my mother to meet him at Liverpool Street Station on his return from Europe via the Hook of Holland. It was not unknown for Pauline and me to make our own way to Victoria Station when he travelled on the cross-Channel ferry from Dover. I loved the bustle of the stations: the steam from the powerful coal-burning locomotives and the myriads of porters pushing barrows full of luggage belonging to the boat-train passengers. Although Marcus' trips involved only short absences from home, he invariably brought Pauline and me a present – a doll for her, a model train for me and sweets for us both. On one occasion there was something really special – a suit of clothes. My father told me that the Germans were short of virtually every commodity and had begun to make *ersatz* (imitation) cloth suits for boys out of recycled paper. To my great excitement, he unwrapped one. It fitted me reasonably well and I wore it several times until I was caught out in the rain when, to my great embarrassment and consternation, it became *papier mâché* and dissolved!

To further illustrate the dire effects of inflation on the German man-in-the-street he would tell me of his experiences of buying simple things such as a newspaper, which each day would cost double or treble the price of the day before; how an empty wine bottle could be sold a week later for more than it cost when it was full. In one transaction he was told by the wholesaler of some fancy goods which he was interested in buying, that he would prefer payment to be in food rather than in foreign currency. A barter deal was struck involving 24 loaves of bread brought over from London; the decisive factor being that the bread would be baked with white flour, which the Germans had not seen for months.

Britain had suffered grievous losses in the war. A whole generation – the 'flower of its manhood' – had been killed or maimed. The material cost was of equal magnitude. Reserves of gold and foreign currencies had been decimated to ensure survival. Victory, when it finally came, had not come cheaply. There was, however, one saving grace that distinguished us from our main ally, France. We had not been invaded and our countryside had not been devastated. Had the Kaiser entertained the illusion of crossing the Channel, the Royal Navy would have turned his dream into a nightmare. After the Battle of Jutland at the end of May 1916, the final assessment of which was to be debated over the following decade, the German Grand Fleet never again posed a real threat to our coasts nor did it challenge our domination of the English Channel.

Gradually the war weariness was left behind and in its place came a resolve to show the world that Britain was still great and could call on the support of a loyal and mighty Empire. And so in May 1924 an Empire Exhibition was opened on a greenfield site in Wembley, previously an outlying suburb to the north west of London. In order to bring the public to this almost rural area, the Underground was extended from central London linking Baker Street to a newly built station facing the exhibition grounds. Once again Marcus recognised a business opportunity. He negotiated with the organisers the exclusive photographic rights for the exhibition. Knowing that the scale of operation would be beyond his limited resources he decided to grant licences to other photographers on condition that they purchased their photographic material from him. The plan worked. I was taken many times to the exhibition. It was a whole new world, with each country having its own hall or arena. Imagine the excitement of a seven-year-old who had never before ventured further than a bus ride from home, visiting a Maharajah's palace, being thrilled by a real American rodeo and delighting in the spectacle of the scarlet-uniformed Canadian Mounties. To cap it all there was a gigantic funfair with a death-defying scenic railway and all the side-shows which children have always loved. The public adored it and came in their thousands. With their attendance came prosperity.

In the autumn of 1925, Clara gave birth to the last of her progeny – a daughter. At the first Thursday morning prayer service at the local synagogue she was duly blessed and given the name of Frances. The small ceremony was accompanied by the traditional shower of almonds, raisins and sweets which, on my hands and knees, I rescued from the synagogue's tessellated floor.

Marcus judged that the time was now opportune for the family to move out of the crowded streets of the West End to a more salubrious part of London. He was faced with a great dilemma. He had frequently discussed a move with my mother but she was adamant that, despite the cramped living accommodation, she did not wish to move, being loath to leave behind her extensive circle of friends with a similar Central European background. She also enjoyed living in the heart of one of the best shopping areas in the world, with its numerous departmental stores, Galeries Lafayette in Regent Street being her particular favourite. I recall accompanying her to the store on one occasion when she needed to replenish her stock of face powder, which she had specially compounded to suit her fair complexion.

Resourceful as ever, my father arranged for Clara to go on an extended visit to Rumania to see her mother and younger sister Rachelle. Taking advantage of her absence and with a little help from an estate agent in Highbury Corner, he purchased the lease of No. 19 Alwyne Road – a four storey victorian house in Canonbury on the estate of the Marquess of Northampton.

2

A Great Injustice

The transition from Dufors Place to Alwyne Road in Canonbury was a cultural shock in reverse. I had never lived in a house with a garden and here we had two. Being the end property in what was in effect a cul-de-sac, there was not only a lawn in front but half an acre of cultivated garden at the rear sloping gently to the bank of a river with crystal-clear water. A majestic weeping willow with its boughs trailing into the river was neighbour to an ancient mulberry tree which in late summer was laden with large juicy berries. It was my job to pick the mulberries for Clara's jam making although her favourite fruit for preserves was really the quince. For the sum of one pound a resident could obtain a fishing licence from the New River Company Ltd., an organisation which had been incorporated in the late seventeenth century charged with the task of providing London with clean drinking water. As I was the only one in the household interested in fishing, I doubt if the fee was ever paid. The river was stocked with bream, carp and perch, and for two years I carried on an unequal duel with an enormous pike. It would remain motionless, sheltering under an overhang of the river bank, and then dart out to midstream, returning with its catch impaled on the sharpest teeth of any fish I know. Summer followed summer without success. On one occasion it broke my rod and on another pulled it right out of my hand. My ingenuity was no match for the pike's strength and guile and I have never angled since.

The new house brought out latent talents in the family. It had a cellar which Marcus began to use for winemaking and storage. In the early autumn he would take me to Spitalfields fruit and vegetable market situated in the East End of London. In the early eighteenth century, Spitalfields had been settled by Huguenots, French Calvinistic Protestants, fleeing from persecution in a predominately Catholic France. They were craftsmen and silk weavers and the area still retains some fine examples of their homes. However, the fruit market had established itself towards the end of Queen Victoria's long reign and it was here that we came to buy grapes for our wine. Marcus was a knowledgeable buyer and when he had completed his purchases he would call a taxicab and load up the luggage compartment next to the driver with crates of Greek or Cyprus grapes each weighing about 10 pounds and costing half a crown. This worked out at about $1\frac{1}{2}$p per pound. Then home to Canonbury, where an oak hogshead awaited the grapes. The barrel had been prepared by Marcus, using a sulphur stick to ensure that it was sterile and thoroughly cleaned from the vintage of the previous year. Into the barrel went the grapes, and the fermentation, aided by some added sugar, commenced.

When the process had reached the pressing stage, the grapes would be ladled into a wooden wine press which he had bought in Paris. Winemaking became a communal chore and the whole family took a turn on the bar which wound the spiral screw and released the juice to run into large enamelled basins, leaving behind a concentrated cake made of grape-skins and pips. My brother Cyril, whose hobby was gardening, soon discovered that the grape-cake had organic fertiliser properties and spread it over the flower beds. I thought that horse manure was better, plentiful and free of charge. As there was always an abundance in the streets around us, I was deputed to go out with a shovel and a bucket and bring in the harvest dropped by the dray horses, whose carts were still the most common form of delivery by the local dairyman, coalman and butcher who 'waited' on families.

Today our winemaking methods might be considered crude, but they did work. Bottling, corking and sealing, we produced about 200 bottles each year of a reasonable quality *vin de table*, which were stored in racked bins in the cellar, with the occasional explosion reminding me that winemaking was not without its hazards. Not only was the family self-sufficient in wine but we rapidly acquired a widening circle of friends who would arrive with an empty bottle and leave with 75 centilitres of Château Marcus. Strictly speaking it was illegal to make wine without a licence and paying a fee to the Customs & Excise. A disgruntled housemaid used this omission as leverage to improve her wages. Her blackmail failed and she left, only to be immediately replaced by another maid who received the standard wage of £13 per annum including board and lodging.

The larger the garden the more one notices the impact of the four seasons. Each one brought its own distinctive pleasures and pursuits for a boy growing up in a happy family environment. Winter meant making bonfires of leaves that only a few weeks earlier had given shade and beauty. The days were short and I planned ahead and stored up all the boys' magazines to be read during the Christmas holidays – preferably in bed. Top of the list was *The Wizard*, followed closely by *The Magnet* with tales of Billy Bunter and his pals. For a penny one could buy a cut-out sheet of buildings and figures, and Pauline and I would spend our Sundays making a model theatre and acting out a play which we made up as we went along.

The Sabbath, Saturday in our case, was observed in the Jewish Orthodox manner. Attendance at synagogue was mandatory; the afternoons were whiled away reading or playing some innocuous game. No writing, no card games, no playing of music, no shopping or handling money, no cooking fresh food or turning on or off of lights. All these were forbidden under the strict rabbinical interpretation of the Biblical injunction that on the Sabbath 'no manner of work' should be done. My father was very strict in these matters and woe betide me if I stepped out of line.

Summer was my favourite season. I lazed in the garden, swinging on a hammock. Sadly this did nothing to prepare me for the Admiralty issue which was awaiting me a decade later on. I fished our river and helped Cyril in the garden, but he came to rely less on me and more on Bert. Bert came every Thursday, complete with his scythe and whetstone, and mowed the lawn. He wore baggy brown corduroy trousers tied at the waist by a knotted cord and gathered at the ankles with bicycle clips. A red and white spotted handkerchief was wound around his neck which he constantly used to wipe his face, the texture and colour of tanned leather, and to mop the sweat off his brow. He was fond of telling me that he only came to work for us 'for me beer and baccy'. He was paid half a crown (13p) for a morning's work but the cost of beer was only 2p a pint and an ounce of pipe shag-tobacco little more. I would help by raking the mown grass and building up the compost heap.

I was nine years of age when the trade unions called a general strike and brought the country to a standstill. No trains ran. There were no buses. No letters were delivered. The coal mines shut down and the country was in crisis. I recall a cart pulled by a shire horse loaded with hundredweight sacks of coal coming into Alwyne Road. At great risk of being attacked as a strike-breaker, the coalman bellowed his usual call 'coal, coal, coal' but instead of a shilling he had doubled the price to a florin. My mother told me to buy one bag and to tell him to pitch the coal directly into the coal shed. With the 112-pound hessian bag of coal carried easily on his shoulders, his head and neck protected by a stiff black leather hat, the coalman obliged. The strike lasted for about 12 days before it was broken by the government. The untold damage it did to industrial relations and the legacy of bitterness it left behind is remembered to this day – more than 70 years later.

It was now time to sit for the compulsory 11-plus school examinations to progress from a primary school to secondary education. The school leaving age was 14, but the successful candidate for a place in a grammar school could look forward to remaining at school and being educated up to the age of 18 preparatory to entering University. I remember those early examinations well, particularly an essay in which I described a copse of silver birch trees as 'the ladies of the woods'. It was the ambition of most children to win a scholarship to a grammar school, but very few free places were awarded. Fees were normally in the region of two guineas (£2 10s) a term – a sum so high that I was reasonably content to accept a free place at

Barnsbury Central School for Boys; my sister Pauline had entered the girls' school a year earlier. Not to be outdone by its peers, our school boasted a coat of arms and, as is usual with such pretentiousness, it bore a motto which read *'noblesse oblige'*. During my schooldays no-one ever translated this for me and it was only later on in life, when I had every reason to heed its advice, that the significance of the phrase took on a special meaning – 'rank and position imposes obligations'. My school curriculum was similar to a grammar school but with a vocational bias. The classical languages of Latin and Greek were not taught. Instead I learnt book-keeping, shorthand and typewriting – skills that later on in life I found more useful than the ability to translate Horace and Virgil.

Once I had survived the initial bullying with its overtones of anti-Semitism, I was reasonably happy at my new school. I had to fight my corner; this frequently ended in a nosebleed which I always tried to conceal from my parents. On one occasion my mother discovered a bloodstained shirt and to my great embarrassment my father stormed up to the school and remonstrated with the headmaster.

I worked diligently but I was only an average student. I was punished with the cane once and was frequently set a hundred lines. My school reports suggested that I might possess some hidden talents because they always ended with the phrase 'could do better'. I must have discovered them in my penultimate year at school and was appointed a prefect, exchanging my bright red cloth cap for a handsome black velvet one with the monogram BCS (Barnsbury Central School) embroidered in silver wire thread. I enjoyed the privileges and prestige of being a prefect, feelings that I was not to experience again until I was commissioned into the Royal Naval Volunteer Reserve about ten years later.

Meanwhile father's photographic business was thriving with his invention of the Jano-While-U-Wait camera which pre-dated the Polaroid camera. The Jano was designed for the professional studio photographer and printed straight onto postcards within five minutes of exposure. They were exported around the world, particularly to the African countries. I soon made a collection of stamps taken from the envelopes containing orders emanating from the Gold Coast, Sierra Leone, Tanganyika, Nyasaland and Northern and Southern Rhodesia – names that have now passed into history. The countries are still there but with new names and no longer part of the British Empire. Achieving Independence has proved of dubious value to all but their rulers.

Since early boyhood I had developed a quirk of independence. I did not want to be given presents or hand-outs. I felt the need to buy things for myself using money I had personally earned. I resisted my parents buying me toys – whenever I could I acquired them by barter. For example, a stamp album would be a fair exchange for a pair of secondhand football boots. Comics and magazines were never bought from a newsagent but swapped with friends. Consequently when the time arrived to sit the School Certificate of the Oxford University Local Examination Board I was able to pay the examination fee of two guineas from my own modest earnings derived from addressing envelopes for a local charity.

The examination took place in November 1932 in a vast hall in Somers Town in the vicinity of Kings Cross Station. I was examined in ten subjects – mathematics, French, English, commercial subjects, art, physics, chemistry, mechanics, geography and history – the latter being my favourite and strongest subject and for which I had been awarded the school prize. I still remember one of the art test papers – a still-life group of an earthenware jug surrounded by different kinds of fruit. The examinees were seated in long lines of desks, very close to one another, each with a small personal easel. Immediately in front of me sat a novice nun who made a habit of tossing her head back on each occasion that she judged the perspective with an upheld pencil. As a result her veil would envelope my drawing board and I would have to throw it back. After several clearances I brought this to the notice of the invigilator, who had me moved to a safer zone.

The results came out in February – I was devastated. I achieved credits only in English, mathematics, French, commercial subjects

19

and art. I failed to get a credit in English history the paper about which, when I had come out of the examination room, I had felt most confident. The curriculum had covered the 100 year period 1815 to 1914 – a really momentous century. I had, I thought, written in masterly fashion on the policies of Disraeli and Gladstone. I had learnt most of the Acts of Parliament passed during the period, including the one that had puzzled me for two whole terms – The Incitement to Murder Bill. I kept wondering what Bill had done in 1832 to deserve such a fate. I had become an authority on the Corn Laws. Palmerston and Pitt were almost related to me – I got to know them so well. I was as sympathetic to the plight of the Puddletown Martyrs as I was to the soldiers in the Crimean campaign. The examiners obviously had not found sufficient material of merit in my 14 pages of foolscap to give me a credit pass. In my lifetime I have sat for countless examinations and I still equate the result of this one in my youth, with great injustice.

I was not due to leave school until the end of the summer term of 1933. The absence of a Sixth form to prepare one for university entrance meant that there was no structured curriculum to hold my interest. I decided to learn German, although it was a language not taught at the school. For 2p I was able to buy a second-hand German grammar and acquired a rudimentary knowledge of the language. Having mastered the Gothic print I could translate simple sentences into English. My next preoccupation was the choice of a career.

For some years I had shared a desk with a boy whose hair was the colour of burnished copper. In all those years I had never addressed him by his name of Henry as he always responded to his nickname of 'Ginger'. We became bosom pals and we shared the same hobby. We both had become avid stamp collectors and made regular Saturday afternoon trips to the numerous philatelic shops in the City of London. We would take the tram from Highbury Corner, get off at Finsbury Circus and slowly stroll down Moorgate to the Bank of England. Saturday afternoons in the City were tranquil and free of the traffic that on weekdays clogged every street. En-route we would stop and window-shop.

As we had no money with which to buy, the fact that all the stamp shops were closed for the weekend fitted our impecunious state admirably. One day a burnished brass plate diverted my attention from admiring a collection of airmail first-day covers. It read *Gregory, Tomkins & Co. Chartered Accountants*. I turned to Ginger, who was looking enviously in the shop window at a block of four unfranked penny blacks. Pointing to the brass plate I blurted out, 'That's what I'm going to be.'

'Chartered Accountant,' he slowly read out aloud. 'What do they do?'

'I don't know,' I replied, 'but doesn't it sound grand?'

I was 15 years of age and I had decided on my future.

My brother Cyril was a very sensitive and kind person and, although 11 years older, he was always ready to support my ambitions. At the time, he was working as an assistant to a Mr Zahariya, who practised dentistry from a surgery in Shaftesbury Avenue. It was in the era before registration and qualification when a person could practise without having first graduated from medical school.

Cyril befriended me and would take me to the cinema. I laughed at Charlie Chaplin, Buster Keaton and Laurel and Hardy. I was thrilled by Tom Mix and all the cowboy and Indian films, but it was the old war films that moved me most, particularly the classic *All Quiet on the Western Front*, a film directed by Lewis Milestone of the book written by Erich Maria Remarque. As a special treat Cyril took me to the New Gallery cinema in Regent Street to see a film called *Mare Nostrum* – Our Sea. Italian-made, it extolled the exploits of the Italian Navy in the Mediterranean in the First World War. On another occasion, over an August bank holiday weekend, I experienced my first sea voyage when I accompanied him to Dublin. We took the overnight ferry from Fishguard, crossed the Irish Sea and landed at Bray, a small seaside resort close to the city. I fell in love with Dublin and its Georgian architecture, although I found it upsetting to see the outward signs of extreme poverty as one moved away from the main thoroughfares. Boys of my own age were running barefoot and ragged amidst the shells of buildings destroyed 'in the troubles' that had preceded the setting up of the Irish Free State in 1921, six years previously.

Cyril now dedicated himself to getting me started on a career. To qualify as a chartered accountant necessitated being articled to a practising chartered accountant for a term of five years. It was customary for accountancy firms to require the payment of a premium, which varied in amount according to the size and prestige of the firm. Premiums would normally range from 250 up to 500 guineas for a firm as well known as Price Waterhouse. My brother had a friend, recently qualified and now in his third year in public practice. After an interview I was told that he would be pleased to offer me articles for the 'nominal' sum of £50, equal to about £5,000 at today's values. I endeavoured to convince Cyril that one day I would get articles on merit alone and I was relieved when he agreed to drop his negotiations with his friend.

Taking myself off to a City employment agency, I was sent to a set of barristers' chambers which had a vacancy for a junior clerk. Kings Bench Walk in the Inner Temple was probably built during the reign of George I and No. 11, near the Embankment, was at the end of a long terrace of austere four-storey buildings overlooking Temple Gardens. It was early summer. The sun shone from a cloudless sky and the courts had not yet started the long vacation. As I walked down Kings Bench Walk young barristers dressed in shirts and white flannel trousers instead of black court gowns drifted past on their way to a game of tennis.

I entered the much worn stone-paved hallway of No. 11 and looked at the panels bearing the names of the sets of barristers painted in white on jet black panels. I had an appointment with Mr Arthur Henderson Jnr. I climbed a flight of uneven stone stairs to the first floor and with some trepidation knocked on a door which was opened by a man in his early forties who introduced himself as the senior clerk. He briefed me on the vacant situation telling me that the Set was run by two clerks, a junior and himself. If I was successful, my duties would commence at 9 a.m., in-augurating the day, in winter, by lighting the coal fire in the small grate laid the night before by the charwoman. I would be required to make tea or coffee, answer the telephone, speak to the clerks of instructing solicitors, and type the Opinions dictated by any one of our barristers. It would be my task to mark up the reports of cases in the different law books for easy reference in court, to which I would accompany counsel, carrying his wig and gown in his bag slung over my shoulder – red as a reward for merit given by King's Counsel to his junior or blue for a junior barrister. In court during the trial I would sit behind him handing over the law books as he called for them. I would be paid £1 per week with two weeks' holiday per annum.

I could not imagine a more agreeable job and I was on cloud nine until, carrying a shorthand notebook, I was summoned into the room occupied by the head of chambers – Arthur Henderson. I now began to feel like a schoolboy summoned to appear in the headmaster's study. The room was sparsely furnished, each wall being lined with shelves of law books all bound in identical brown calf leather, gold-blocked on the spine with the year of publication. I subsequently discovered that they contained the reports of cases heard in the High Courts of Justice. The bound volumes of law reports covered centuries of litigation. Other shelves held textbooks on different subjects – libel, taxation, land tenure, divorce and, of course a set of Halsbury's *Laws of England* – the indispensable working tool to be found in the library of every legal office in the land.

On Mr Henderson's desk was a pile of briefs, neatly folded A3 parchment, bound with red tape. Prepared by solicitors, each one told the story of the action on which the barrister would base his case or give his written opinion.

Mr Henderson, who had not yet taken silk and become a King's Counsel, put me at ease. He questioned me on my school work, looked at my final term's report with my headmaster's testimonial and seemed impressed that I could do shorthand as well as being able to type. He then dictated a long paragraph from a book on constitutional law that was lying on his desk and told me to go away and type it and bring it back to him. As I sat at an old Underwood typewriter I really became apprehensive and nervous.

Many of the words were completely new to me and I had to make a guess of several of the shorthand outlines for legal terms and phrases. I must have transcribed the dictation to his satisfaction as I was engaged to start immediately as junior clerk to the chambers. They really must have been desperate for a tea-maker.

I learnt that Mr Henderson bore the same name as his illustrious father, the Rt. Hon. Arthur Henderson, who had been the Home Secretary in the first Socialist government the country had known, in 1924. Mr Henderson, the Cabinet minister, was an avowed pacifist and a strong opponent of rearmament. In the House of Commons he was an adversary of Winston Churchill who was vehement in his endeavour to alert the country to the threat of a militant Germany headed by its new Chancellor, Adolf Hitler, and to urge rearmament. 'My' Mr Henderson, who always added the abbreviation 'Jnr.' to his name, had been born in Newcastle-on-Tyne in 1893. He had read law and economics at Trinity Hall, Cambridge, and was the author of a standard textbook on *Trade Unions and the Law* as well as a treatise on industrial law which he had written jointly with Sir Henry Slesser KC, the previous head of our chambers, who had handed over to Arthur when he was appointed Lord Justice of Appeal after the Socialist victory in the 1929 election.

Although I found myself at the opposite end of the political spectrum to my employer and his father, I was somewhat overawed by these personages. I had never met Sir Henry Slesser, who had been called to the Bar of the Inner Temple in 1906. My senior clerk, a mine of information and anecdotes about his previous employer, told me that on his appointment as Solicitor General in the Labour victory of 1924 he had been duly knighted. He shocked his wife when phoning to give her the news by saying, 'Henry Slesser is no more...' He paused and then added, '*Sir* Henry is born...' As Solicitor General, Sir Henry would have shared the duty of prosecutor for the Crown with his colleague the Attorney General.

I was more then delighted when, soon after joining the Chambers and in the process of cleaning out a cupboard, I came across a pile of briefs gathering dust, all headed *Rex v* —; it was like opening Pandora's box. Over the following weeks I read them all, but with a sense of guilt such as one might have if caught reading a soft pornographic magazine. I was just 17 years old and a closed closet had been opened. Here in plain unadorned English I was inducted into the seamy side of life in the raw, the breakdown of society resulting in cases involving murder, incest, rape and brutality in many forms. Had I possessed the literary skill I would have found the plots of several thrillers and novels in those dusty briefs.

Mr Henderson's personal practice was far less glamorous. He was the standing counsel for the Labour party and much of his work was of a political nature devoted to labour issues and complex workman's compensation awards. I never had to attend court with him as most of his work was done in chambers. I could see little evidence of his earning more than a modest living at the Bar in contrast to the great advocates of the day who, supplanting the stars of screen and football pitch, quickly became my heroes. They were the celebrities of the mid-thirties, lionised by society as they argued their cases – whether for the prosecution or defence it did not matter – in the many *causes célèbres* in which they appeared. It could be a murder case, a contested society divorce, or a well publicised libel. At the Criminal Bar there were the two adversaries, Patrick Hastings and Norman Birkett, and the great legal luminary Stafford Cripps, later to become Chancellor of the Exchequer in the first post-war Labour government. Their earnings became a legend and pictures of them were rarely out of the newspapers. My particular favourite was Norman Birkett and I would read all his speeches and the skilful cross-examination of witnesses. Of course he did not always win his cases and there was one, I remember, where he appeared in defence of one of those accused, along with Leopold Harris and his gang, in the notorious fire fraud prosecution. It became the longest running case heard at the Old Bailey up to that time and although Birkett's client, a fire assessor, was found guilty, Birkett's masterly cross-examination no doubt resulted in a lesser sentence than the man might otherwise have received. In the event it was three years' penal servitude, and in those days penal servitude really meant *penal.* In 1946 Sir Norman, as he was to become, together with Sir Hartley Shawcross, were our joint prosecutors at the Nuremberg trial of the chief Nazi war criminals.

Although the leaders at the Bar earned princely fees, there was very little work for the great majority of barristers no matter how well they had done at Oxbridge. The proven formula for success was to have a father or an uncle as a practising solicitor. One of the 'names' on the door of my set was that of Arthur Jaffé. During my year he only visited once; I thought he was eccentric and quite a character. In his sixties, he had practised at the Irish Bar as well as in England and had made his name, and no doubt his fortune, in cases involving the payment of reparations by Germany after their defeat in 1918. One of the major companies involved was the chemical and armament colossus IG Farben Industries.

In fee terms my most successful barrister was Mr Edward J.C. Neep. A King's scholar at Westminster School, he specialised in patent law and I frequently accompanied him to the Patent Office in Chancery Lane. During my year he was briefed by British Celanese in the series of epic battles they fought against Courtaulds, who claimed breach of their patents in the manufacture of rayon and other synthetic yarns – nylon was still to be discovered. The stakes were very high and this was reflected in the size of the fee marked on his brief – 1,000 guineas (always guineas and never pounds) with 100 guineas a day retainer. One would need to multiply these sums by a factor of at least 50 to bring them up to today's real value. The case of Courtaulds v Celanese raged in the High Court as well as in the Court of Appeal for several years, finally ending with a victory for Courtaulds in the House of Lords. Although the chemistry and the points of law at issue were completely over my head, I could not fail to be excited by the gladiators in the case, although 'my' man, fighting for British Celanese, was on the losing side.

At the opposite end of the earnings scale was Eric Falk, a recently called barrister. His family business was Falk Stadelman, a major manufacturer of gas mantles, a small but essential piece of equipment that before the era of electricity enabled gas produced from coal and coke to be transformed into domestic and street lighting. The arrival of *any* brief for him was a cause for jubilation even if it was worth no more than two guineas for an appearance in a magistrate's court.

3

On My Way

I had set myself a limit of one year in the Temple before testing the market to see whether I could be offered articles without paying a premium. In the *Daily Telegraph* I spotted an advertisement inserted by a firm of chartered accountants in Paternoster Row in St Paul's Churchyard. They wanted an articled clerk. I applied and was invited to an interview. My year in chambers had given me confidence and poise. I was not, however, prepared for the ensuing ordeal.

Paternoster Row lay off Ludgate Hill in a maze of narrow lanes, no more than the width of a cart, with two and three-storey buildings on either side. The properties all dated back to the rebuilding of the City of London after the Great Fire of 1667, which followed on the heels of the Plague that had decimated the populace the previous year. There at the top of Ludgate Hill was Christopher Wren's masterpiece – St Paul's Cathedral. My destination was No. 16, the offices of Scott Mitchell Boswell-Phillips & Company. I was to be interviewed by Mr Boswell-Phillips, CA. To admit that I was caught off balance would be an understatement. Mr Boswell-Phillips was as dour a Scotsman as one was likely to meet south of the border and his extreme Glaswegian accent turned his conversation into mumbo-jumbo. I had to get him to repeat his questions several times over whilst my mind raced to translate what he was saying into English. Unlike Mr Henderson, he was not all impressed with my typing and shorthand skills – 'we employ girls to do that,' he said disparagingly. I had already decided that he was going to turn me down, when unexpectedly I was offered the job, with the prospect of indentures to qualify as a chartered accountant. I was to be paid £1 per week, the same as I had started with in the Temple the previous year. I accepted.

Mr Scott Mitchell, the senior partner, also a Scot from Glasgow, could not have been more different from his colleague Boswell-Phillips. Possibly because he had been cast in a completely different mould I grew to like him. He was stockily built, with a keen sense of humour, unlike the taciturn Phillips, who had a lean and hungry look. I could even understand Mitchell's Glasgwegian-speak and rarely had to ask him to repeat a sentence. He was a lay Methodist preacher. I had a standing order every Friday afternoon to buy him a stiff white wing collar at Austin Reeds, size 17$\frac{1}{4}$, into which he would change before setting off to deliver a sermon in the country. He had married a Miss Alice Pickering, whose family publishing firm, Pickering & Inglis, was one of the City's leading booksellers of bibles and evangelical texts. Paternoster Row, in the shadow of St Paul's had, since Elizabethan days, been the home of numerous book publishers and Pickering & Inglis had established their large shop and offices there during the reign of Queen Victoria. As the accountancy offices adjoined their shop, I could not but help feeling that Scott Mitchell had succeeded in marrying 'the girl next door' and, to keep the business within the family, our firm had been appointed the company's auditors.

Little time elapsed before I discovered that there were no less than four separate and autonomous professional bodies whose members were entitled to call themselves 'chartered accountants'. The largest and most prestigious was the Institute of Chartered Accountants in England and Wales, incorporated by Royal Charter in 1880. There was also the Institute of Chartered Accountants of Ireland, the Association of Chartered Accountants of Edinburgh, as well as the Society of Chartered Accountants in Glasgow. I felt trapped when I discovered that Scott Mitchell Boswell-Phillips were members of the Glasgow society. I would have to take their examinations, which, although held in London, would include papers in Scottish law and practice. Having come so far, I was determined to see it through even when I was told that my School

Certificate from Oxford University would not exempt me from the society's preliminary examination, and that I would need to have a credit in higher mathematics together with statistics. Apparently the society accorded a high degree of importance to statistics, which also featured in their intermediate professional examination. I decided to enter for the external matriculation of London University by studying at home in the evenings after returning from the office in Paternoster Row. I struggled with differential and integral calculus for six months and sat the examination in my five chosen subjects. One sunny November morning I raced down to the university buildings in Bloomsbury and there on the pass sheet was my name. I was on my way – or so I thought.

One episode that occurred during my service with Scott Mitchell Boswell-Phillips is unforgettable.

I had to work on alternate Saturdays until 1 p.m. It was no hardship as I enjoyed the calm that would settle on the City in complete contrast to the frenetic activity of every weekday. It was Friday 30th December, and in anticipation of the end of Pickering & Inglis's financial year the following day, I called next door to see the company secretary. I told him that as I intended reconciling his cash books with the bank statements the next morning, would he be good enough to have them written up to date, ready for me. The cash book was in two volumes: one for money received and paid into the bank, the other for cheques drawn. Each book was specially printed for the company with 24 analysis columns, as the receipts, in particular, were diverse. From my previous experience of conducting the audit I knew that a major source of income was from the sale of Gospel tracts and bibles printed by the British & Foreign Bible Society, the market leader in this field. Pickering & Inglis's customers were the missions and evangelists spread all over the world. Payment was by international money and postal orders, which could be easily cashed. Each day brought a mail bag filled with orders from missionaries who had established a toe-hold in the remotest parts of the globe; the envelopes bearing the stamps of China, Africa, India and the South Pacific Islands.

The sun shone that Saturday morning as I made my way by bus

to St Paul's. Arriving at the corner where Paternoster Row meets Ludgate Hill, my entry was obstructed by a barricade manned by a City policeman who towered over the force's minimum height requirement of 6 feet. Through the barricade I could see that Paternoster Row was blocked by fire engines and criss-crossed by hosepipes. The bible shop had been on fire during the early hours of the morning and smoke was still rising from the shattered shop front. I explained my business and was allowed to enter the premises. The damage was limited, but in what remained of the secretary's office I could see the safe with its door wide open and the charred remains of the account books and hundreds of bills and invoices forming a funeral pile in the middle of the room. Ever since the Great Fire of London in the seventeenth century, whenever a fire took place within the City's boundaries it had to be investigated at an inquest in a coroner's court in the same way as a homicide. The verdict the following week was 'arson by a person or persons unknown'. Unknown? Hardly! The secretary, a pillar of the Church and a Sunday school teacher, was missing, had left home and could not be traced. The top priority now was to reconstruct the cash books and I was allocated this task of forensic accounting. It took me nearly three months to piece it all together and to determine that the defalcations amounted to more than £1,000, equivalent to about £100,000 by today's standard. In due course the secretary surrendered to the police, was tried at the Old Bailey for arson, not fraud or theft, and sentenced to three years' imprisonment. Pickering & Inglis, in accordance with their code of Christian ethics, refused to press charges and I heard that they re-employed the secretary on his discharge from prison.

I found office routine boring as I slowly became the equivalent of today's pocket calculator – a human adding machine. There was some compensation in that constant repetition and practice sharpened my mental arithmetic and rewarded me with a dexterity with figures that enabled me to add up long columns with speed and accuracy, a skill which has stood me in good stead throughout my life.

I became friendly with Eric Ellis, who was in his second year of articles. Coming from a working-class home and reliant entirely on the nominal wages being paid to him, he had to watch every penny he spent. He lived in one of the outer suburbs and had found that he could make a very substantial saving by travelling to London on a workman's ticket. This meant him arriving at King's Cross railway station about 6.30 in the morning, two and a half hours before our office opened, time which he spent in the station waiting room completing a study paper before posting it to the correspondence college. We decided that our friendship was sufficiently strong that it could survive our taking a holiday together. Both of us being impecunious students, we decided that a week spent walking in the Cotswolds was as ambitious a vacation as we could afford. We fixed a budget of £4 and started to save.

We were Shakespearean fans and habitués of the Old Vic theatre, built in 1818 in the reign of George III, where for a sixpence we could occupy a wooden bench-seat in 'the gods' and get a bird's eye view of the remote stage. I cannot forget the thrill of seeing Laurence Olivier play Hamlet. Seated on a stool at the edge of the stage and almost in the orchestra pit, he would smite his forehead with a clenched fist and start on his soliloquy 'To be or not to be, that is the question'. In one term, I came to see the play three times and joined in the thunderous applause at the end of each performance, applause which has reverberated down through the years until, as Lord Olivier, he passed away in 1989 at the age of 82. As a Shakespearean actor, we will never see his equal.

The departure date for our meticulously costed holiday arrived and, clad in khaki shorts and matching shirts with rucksacks on our backs, we each bought a third-class return ticket from Paddington to Oxford. The cost was five shillings (25p) for the 100-mile round journey. Oxford was to be the starting point of our Cotswold odyssey which would end in Stratford-on-Avon, Shakespeare's birthplace. Arriving in the city of dreaming spires, we spent the day looking at the colleges. As it was vacation time friendly lodge porters allowed us to wander at will across the grassy quadrangles into ancient candlelit chapels and view Jacobean panelled dining halls hung with the portraits of masters, rectors, provosts or principals long departed. I could not help but feel envious of the gilded youths who had the good fortune to study in those cloistered surroundings. What a contrast to my own routine, which involved working for nine hours in a city office to be followed by an evening lecture and a session of study at home which frequently extended into the early hours of the following morning. I was not to know then that 50 years later I would come to live in Oxford.

We had obtained a list of youth hostels. The one in Oxford had been recommended and for the sum of a shilling (5p) we were able to spend the night in a sleeping bag and awake to the sound of birds heralding a bright summer morning. Our first 'leg' was a walk to Banbury, a distance of 17 miles through the heart of Oxfordshire's rolling landscape, its innumerable villages boasting Norman and Tudor churches and meandering cobbled lanes lined with thatched cottages whose doors were framed by rambling roses. We chose an inn for a night's stay and after a bout of serious negotiation were offered a room that the two us could share for five shillings, to include a supper of cheese, pickles and a freshly baked cottage loaf. The room, which had been newly redecorated, had chintz curtains and was sparsely furnished but our interest was focused on the large pitcher and basin that stood on the marble-topped washstand. My feet, unused to my new boots or to walking more than a few miles let alone 17, felt as if they were on fire, and a large blister was forming on my left heel. We asked for the pitcher to be filled with cold water and as soon as the landlady had left the room we both rolled down our thick socks and immersed our feet in the wide basin – what bliss; it was a process we repeated several times before slipping into bed between lavender scented sheets, in complete contrast to our previous night in the youth hostel.

The next two days saw us walking at a leisurely pace through Chipping Norton and Moreton-in-Marsh, those lovely market towns each with its old open-sided wool exchange built of Cotswold stone, and along the Fosse Way, the old Roman road that led to our destination. To arrive in Stratford-on-Avon on foot made us feel like pilgrims. In one sense that is what we were, except that instead of Jerusalem it was the newly-built theatre on the banks of the Avon that we had come to see. The Shakespeare Memorial theatre had only recently been opened and had already established an international reputation for its own theatre company. Finding that the cost of a ticket would break the bank, we had to forgo watching the Royal Shakespeare Company and instead spent the afternoon sun-bathing on the terrace of the theatre whilst watching the swans and ducks float idly past. For the time being we could only dream of the day when we would be able to afford the best seats in the theatre.

It was time to start our return journey which was by way of Stow-on-the-Wold and Upper and Lower Slaughter, names that sounded whimsical to two Cockneys whose occasional forays into the countryside were limited to visiting Hampstead Heath on a bank holiday. We had fallen in love with the Cotswold counties of Oxfordshire, Gloucestershire and Warwickshire and in later years I was to revisit them time and time again, discovering gems like Bourton-on-the-Water and the Little and Great Tew. Making our way through picturesque Burford we arrived back in Oxford, where we caught a train that puffed its way through the Thames Valley, stopping at every halt, until it reached London.

On returning from my holiday to the office in Paternoster Row my priority was to complete the application form for indenture. Duly signed by Mr Scott Mitchell and accompanied by my birth and matriculation certificates, they were submitted to the Society of Chartered Accountants in Glasgow for registration. Their response was curt and in the form of a questionnaire:

'Why does Mr Lazarus Janovitch want to qualify for membership of this Society?'
'What connection does Mr Janovitch have with Scotland in general and Glasgow in particular?'

I was shocked, and so I thought was Mr Mitchell, but in the event he left me to fight my own battle without any practical support from the firm.

I replied civilly, giving sound practical reasons for my

application. Their response was to return my certificates. I remonstrated with the secretary of the society both in correspondence and on the telephone to Glasgow, but to no avail. They refused to register me as a student and I had no right of appeal. Rightly or wrongly I attributed their attitude to anti-Semitism. My friend Eric Ellis, who was also a Sassenach, had not experienced any problems with his registration despite the fact that he had no 'Scottish connections', being descended from a long line of Cockneys. In fact no questionnaire had been sent to him and his registration had come through automatically.

It was 1936, and I was an angry 19-year-old. I felt humiliated and discriminated against but determined to fight on and secure those elusive articles. I decided not to risk a repetition of ethnic discrimination and after a lot of heart-searching decided that I should anglicise my name. I told my father and he raised no objection. I had no experience of how one changed one's name legally, so I called in to the Solicitors Law Stationery shop in Chancery Lane, who were pleased to sell me a Change of Name form for a shilling (5p). Following the notes at the back of the form, I duly completed it and advised all and sundry that henceforth I would be known as 'Leslie Jackson'. Within a week I had been interviewed and engaged by Wilson Bigg & Co., members of the Institute of Chartered Accountants in England and Wales, the premier accountancy body. Within one month I had signed articles, my principal being the senior partner, Hugh Alexander Robert James Wilson – known to the staff and to generations of students by his initials H.A.R.J.

The firm's offices were at No. 16 Coleman Street, off London Wall and a stone's throw from Moorgate, the haunt of my stamp collecting days, and close to the Hall of the Institute of Chartered Accountants, where I would attend lectures. Wilson Bigg & Co had a relatively small accountancy practice but it was unique in that the two senior partners owned the pre-eminent accountancy correspondence college known to thousands of students as Foulkes Lynch and had acquired the publishing rights of the Spicer & Pegler textbooks which were standard reading for every student. Both Wilson and his colleague Walter Bigg, as students, had been placed first in their respective final examinations and been awarded the gold medal of the Institute. Bigg specialised in auditing and cost and works accounting, whilst H.A.R.J. was an authority on executorship law and taxation. I was overjoyed at my luck in having joined such illustrious company and I settled into the office routine without any problems. It was, however, made abundantly clear to me at the very outset that I was expected not only to work hard in the office but to achieve a high examination standard as a student. I was confident I could do both, and proved it at my Intermediate examination in 1938; when I was awarded a Certificate of Merit by the Institute, being placed 13th out of a total of 650 students who sat the examinations.

4

A New King and a New Office

I was born during the 26-year-long reign of King George V, who was crowned in 1911, a year after the death of his father, King Edward VII. King George was the last monarch to have reigned over the British Empire whilst it was at the pinnacle of its size and power – an empire so vast that it embraced several continents and included Canada, India, Australia and much of Africa. In the assembly hall of my old school there hung a large Mercator map of the world with the British Empire coloured in red which bore the slogan 'The British Empire – an empire on which the sun never sets'. Each year during the month of May the school celebrated Empire Day with innocuous activities including dancing around the maypole. Empire Day was very popular with school children as it meant that a half-day holiday would be granted.

Shortly after my nineteenth birthday the 70-year-old king died, not in one of the palaces but in his own home in Sandringham. I will never forget that cold grey January day when I joined a seemingly endless queue and waited for hours to enter ancient Westminster Hall to pay homage to our King, lying there in state. His four sons, Edward Prince of Wales, Albert Duke of York, Henry Duke of Gloucester and the youngest, George Duke of Kent, had the previous night been standing vigil at each corner of their father's catafalque. It must have been a most moving sight.

The monarch's eldest son Edward, who had achieved notoriety as a playboy, was immediately proclaimed King and arrangements were put in hand for his coronation at the end of the year. He assumed the title of Edward VIII but was to reign for only 325 days before abdicating prior to the coronation that was being planned for him. I recall vividly the newspaper reports of his liaison with Wallis – Mrs Ernest Simpson – and the 'quickie' divorce rushed through for her. Everyone in the land seemed to become involved in the constitutional crisis, the Prime Minister Stanley Baldwin, the Archbishop of Canterbury and most of the bishops of the Church of England, of which the King was the titular head. People took sides. Some favoured a morganatic marriage as a solution, others thought the King should go. Finally the newspaper headlines screamed 'ABDICATION', which was followed by a last sad farewell speech broadcast to the nation. The Greek tragedy had come to an end. In the dead of night, at 2 a.m. on 12th December 1936, the destroyer HMS *Fury* sailed from Portsmouth alone and without the customary escort carrying the ex-King, in future to be known as the Duke of Windsor, into exile.

My sister Pauline was a secretary at Crockfords, an exclusive bridge club occupying prestigious premises in Carlton House Terrace overlooking Pall Mall. I was delighted when she told me that her employer had given permission for me to view the coronation procession of the new monarch, King George VI, from a balcony in their lovely Queen Anne building. The weather was sunny and warm on the morning of 12th May 1937 as King George VI and Queen Elizabeth left for their coronation ceremony in Westminster Abbey. I could not have been in a better position to watch them progress to the Abbey and return up the Mall to Buckingham Palace. My invitation also extended to a participation in an epicurean lunch (the club employed one of the best French chefs in London). As the day drew to its close I felt privileged to have seen the start of a new reign – that of a monarch whose dignity in office earned him the respect and affection of all his people.

Paternoster Row, although strictly within the City boundaries, lying as it does east of Temple Bar which acts as a meridian dividing east from west, did not enjoy the unique City atmosphere I now found in Coleman Street, which was well and truly within the 'square mile' of the City proper. Its heart lay in a box bounded on one side by the Royal Exchange, the other by the Bank of England, then the Stock Exchange and finally the Mansion House, the official residence of the Lord Mayor of London. Streets were busier here, traffic denser, taxis harder to get, whilst scores of bank messengers in smart livery and top hats would be carrying millions of pounds worth of bearer bonds in their satchels for delivery to the stockbrokers and banks concentrated in Throgmorton and Threadneedle streets. There were no street robberies and the term 'mugging' had not yet been invented. At every street corner stood a newspaper boy selling the *Evening Standard* and the *Evening News*, both available in different editions throughout the day, starting at ten o'clock in the morning. Their respective posters displayed the latest headline and each newspaper was priced at one penny. Everyone was dressed formally. My outfit was a dark blue suit, white shirt, stiff starched collar and striped tie. A hat was mandatory and I sported a black bowler and carried a tightly furled umbrella. Any departure from this strict dress code would bring a reprimand from the office manager. On Saturdays the rules were relaxed and a navy blue blazer with grey flannel trousers was *de rigueur* – and *no* bowler hat!

I was kept busy in the office working mainly on the audits of companies based in London. I remember being instructed that for the next ten days I would be working at Boake Roberts, a company that manufactured essences, colours and flavours for the food industry. I became really excited when I was told that their factory was in Stratford, and as I could now afford a ticket at the Memorial Theatre, I looked forward to seeing some Shakespeare performed. My hopes were soon dashed to the ground when it transpired that my destination would be in the east London district of Stratford-atte-Bow and not Stratford-on-Avon in Warwickshire. It was only a threepenny bus ride away through the grim streets of Whitechapel and past evil-smelling glue and soap factories.

An audit I found enjoyable was that of Jamesons Chocolates. Their factory was at Edmonton in the north-eastern part of London. To get there I would take a train from Liverpool Street Station and change onto a bus at White Hart Lane – the home of

Tottenham Hotspur Football Club. On one occasion with Tim, a fellow articled clerk, we arrived at Liverpool Street to find that the best connection was the Newmarket train. At the platform barrier was a notice 'beware of cardsharpers' and half obscuring it stood a statuesque figure dressed in the robes and feathered plumes of a Zulu warrior shouting, 'I've gotta n'orse; I've gotta n'orse'. It was my introduction to 'Prince Monolulu', one of the greatest, certainly the most colourful, betting tipster on or off the race track. He was selling his tips for the day's racing at Newmarket.

Tim and I duly climbed into a carriage which was already occupied by three men. One, an Indian, had a bandage around his head, another was balancing a small attaché case on his lap, whilst the third was almost hidden by the newspaper he was reading. No one spoke until the train began to pull away from the platform, when the man with the attaché case produced three cards from his pocket and placed them face down on his case. Addressing the Indian gentleman, he said, 'Go on sir – find the lady.' Tim and I watched fascinated whilst each time he dealt, 'the lady', namely the queen of hearts, was revealed. We both noticed that that particular card had one of its corners creased and appeared easy to spot. By this time the newspaper reader was wagering five pounds on each quick deal and the dealer looking up asked us if we would like to wager. After quickly consulting Tim I said, 'Yes, for ten shillings.' He refused, saying it was not enough. Nothing daunted and knowing that we were on to a certain win, Tim said 'all right then, three pounds.' He pointed to a card and handed over the money. Mister Attaché Case dealt the cards fast as we drew into the platform of White Hart Lane. It was now revealed that the creased corner had transferred itself magically from the queen of hearts to the ten of spades. It was only then that we realised that we had fallen for the oldest confidence spoof – the three card trick. The arrival at our destination stopped us starting a fistfight with, no doubt, disastrous consequences for us both as it was only then that we realised that the three ostensible strangers in the carriage were in fact a gang. We stood on the platform numbed with Tim saying, in despair, that the three pounds was his bed-sitter rent for a month and what was he to tell his landlady?

Manfully I promised that I would pay my half of the bet by six weekly instalments of five shillings. This was of little consolation to Tim and proved to be the end of our friendship.

Jamesons Chocolates was owned by two brothers and they allowed us to use their private office whilst auditing the books. Their major customer was F.W. Woolworth & Co. Ltd. and the sales ledgers had to be checked for every consignment to each regional branch. The work was monotonous, relieved only by the opportunity to taste the variety of chocolates which were laid out on tables to test their shelf-life at room temperatures. When our fondness for these test chocolates was finally discovered, we were banished to a loft in the factory where we had to rest our ledgers on bags of cocoa beans in a temperature that rarely fell below 100°F.

Another of the firm's clients was A.E. Symes & Co. Ltd., builders specialising in developments on behalf of municipal authorities. They built libraries and town halls, as well as public swimming baths. Their head offices were in east London. Taken off another audit, I was sent down post-haste to their offices when the directors had become aware that the company secretary/accountant had gone absent without leave. I had acquired a taste for forensic accounting and looked forward to acting as a detective. We had a suspect, but was there a crime? My auditing studies had led me to the conclusion that it was not the custodian of the petty cash float one had to watch, but the officers of the company whose transactions would often be uncontrolled and not normally subject to scrutiny.

It transpired that a local authority had returned a statement from the company disputing the balance shown, claiming that they had made a stage payment of £5,000 several months earlier which had not been deducted. Symes's alarm bells rang and Wilson Bigg & Co. sent me down to carry out an investigation. I suspected a common form of fraudulent accounting known as 'teeming and lading'. This is practised by a bookkeeper who, having misappropriated a cheque, would endeavour to cover up the defalcation by allocating or splitting subsequent cheques received in order to place them to the credit of those accounts that had been raided. This type of theft called for a high degree of effort and concentration to keep the fraud going over a long period without detection. Eventually the web of deceit would break when the perpetrator lost his nerve, suspecting that discovery was imminent.

My first step was to circulate all customers with an up-to-date statement taken from the company's sales ledger showing how much they owed and asking for an immediate verification. I then endeavoured to match up the amounts paid into the bank with the sums credited to the sales ledger accounts. There were numerous variations between the names on the retained bank pay-in book and the accounts which had been credited. Which entries were correct? Only by inspecting the original copy of the pay-in slip retained by the bank could I make a judgment. I went to see the bank manager, who pointed out that it would be a monumental task for the bank to sieve through the pay-in slips for a whole year, but they would give me every assistance if I was prepared to tackle the job. I was. The outcome was verification beyond dispute that £20,000 had been stolen and a successful criminal prosecution followed.

I was enjoying my work and studying hard, frequently into the small hours of the morning. I joined the Chartered Accountants Student Society of London and in 1937 won the annual essay prize, writing on the subject of 'valuation of stock in hand and work-in-progress'. I still have the essay; it is in my handwriting which I am surprised has changed so little over the years. I attended the annual general meeting of the society, sitting at the back of the hall. Just before the meeting concluded I was asked to propose a vote of thanks to the Chairman, Lord Plender. The doyen of the accountancy profession, Lord Plender had qualified in 1884, the year in which the Institute had been granted its royal charter. He was the senior partner of Deloitte Plender Griffiths now incorporated in Deloitte Haskins and Sell. I was completely unprepared and about to say 'no thank you, ask someone else', when an inner voice prompted me 'go on, have a go'. I stood up and in a tremulous voice thanked his lordship for presiding over the meeting. It was my very first foray into public speaking. There is a lot to be said for being metaphorically thrown in at the deep end without warning as a way to overcome one's initial fears. I was to have this confirmed five years later when I was appointed to command one of his Majesty's minesweepers.

I had responsibility for another client for whom I had to prepare the annual accounts. It was for me an unusual type of business – a stud farm owned by a Mr Kenneth O. Peppiatt. Now Mr Peppiatt was no ordinary mortal. He was none other than the Chief Cashier of the Bank of England and, as such, his signature appeared on every banknote ranging from the common ten shilling note up to the rarely seen £1,000 specimen. A banknote is in effect a promissory note which in the smallest of print bears the inscription: 'I promise to pay to the bearer on demand the sum of . . .' followed by the signature of the Chief Cashier.

One might well ask what would happen if the holder of, say, a ten-pound note confronted the Chief Cashier and demanded that he keep his promise. What would he pay with? Other banknotes, similarly signed? And then where would it all end? Before 1931, the year that we left the gold standard, one could demand payment in gold sovereigns when gold traded at a fixed price of a little less than £4 per ounce. The Bank of England was required by Parliament to have the total of the banknotes in circulation backed by holdings of gold bullion stored in its vaults. No doubt, in order to keep a check on the amount of paper money that was being printed and circulated, the Bank Charter Act of 1844 obliged the Issue Department of the bank to publish its accounts every week in the *London Gazette*. Currently through this source we are made aware that there is now £23 billion of paper money floating around. Only a fraction of this is covered by our gold reserves – the shortfall is known as the Fiduciary Issue, which is backed by other securities – other bits of paper. There is no hope, therefore, of being able to exchange a ten-pound note for gold, even for a little gold dust, especially now that the price of gold, which fluctuates daily, is in the region of £174 per ounce.

Mr Peppiatt and his wife enjoyed living on their farm at Beaconsfield in Buckinghamshire breeding and raising horses. Alas the stud farm made no money. In fact, year after year, it showed a loss. Fortunately for my client, there was a happier outcome to this venture when I was able to reduce his income tax liability each year by setting off the loss against his £3,500 salary from the bank, which must be equivalent to at least £200,000 today. My ambition, which I had formulated at that time had been to earn the princely sum of £1,000 per annum and I am today reminded of a ditty I used to recite from Gilbert & Sullivan's opera *The Pirates of Penzance*:

> When I was a lad I served a term
> as office boy to an Attorney's firm.
> I cleaned the windows and I swept the floor,
> And I polished up the handle of the big front door.
> I polished up that handle so carefullee
> That now I am the Ruler of the Queen's Navee.

My version was:

> When I was eighteen or so
> I started on a term of articles of clerkship
> With a posh accounting Firm.
> I drank so much coffee as I played at Matador
> That now I am a partner with my name upon the door.

As a young man I lost no opportunity to see the D'Oyly Carte Opera Company play Gilbert & Sullivan. My tastes were very simple and sometimes derided by my elders in that I had no time for Italian opera; I revelled in the music of Ketelbey and loved to delve into the collected poems of Rudyard Kipling.

My lecturer in contract law was a young barrister named Sebag-Shaw whose fee from Foulkes Lynch for a lecture was the nominal sum of two guineas. On one occasion I approached him to borrow a Spicer & Pegler textbook on mercantile law, which he was pleased to loan to me. I am ashamed to say that it took me 40 years to return it. When I did (offering my abject apologies) at a dinner at the Connaught Rooms where he was the guest of honour, he graciously inscribed it with the words 'to Leslie Jackson – a student of mine who showed promise and went on to fulfill his potential'. He signed it 'Lord Justice Sebag-Shaw' and handed it back to me. It occupies pride of place on my bookshelves.

It had been a year I could never forget. It should have been for me an *annus mirabalis*. It was the year that I had left school and started my first job in the Temple with all the enthusiasm and idealism of a boy of 16. Two shattering events were to take place that turned it into a personal *annus horribilis*. On 30 January 1933 Hitler had come to power as Germany's Chancellor, inaugurating a reign of terror for Europe's Jewry, and on the 1st of July 1933 my mother, Clara, had died. The first of July had been a blazing hot day, but for me there was a total eclipse of the sun. As I wept for her short life – she was only 56 years old – I thought how unjust and cruel life could be. The last words she spoke to me through her sobs as I stood at her bedside the day before she died was to express her sorrow that she would not be spared to see her daughter Pauline married in synagogue (under the Chupah, the bridal canopy). She had completely devoted her life to her children.

My mother was a very special person. One can have numerous brothers and sisters, and aunts and uncles galore but only one mother, the person who endured pain to give you birth and throughout her life did everything in her power to shield you from pain. It was only when she was gone for ever that I was able to appreciate her worth and how much she had meant to me. I have already written of how she had arrived in England as a refugee with three small children: without a home, with no knowledge of the language or of English customs – just a foreigner in a country about to be engulfed in a war which would change its social and economic fabric for ever. A devoted wife to a handsome Rumanian who had no money and no job.

I loved my mother and she returned my love. She would ask me to accompany her when she shopped for food, an outing to which I always looked forward. Invariably it was to the street markets of the east End of London. Mr Sainsbury was operating only small shops devoted to the sale of butter, bacon, cheese and

45

eggs. His shops did not feature on mother's shopping list. The founder of Tesco was just getting into his stride and building up the chain of grocery stores that was to develop into the country's largest group of supermarkets. It was not so many years since Jack Cohen had been demobilised from the army as a private and, using his gratuity to purchase a barrowload of canned food, coined his motto 'pile it high, sell it cheap'. Marks & Spencer was still trading as The Penny Bazaar and did not sell food in their shops. For my mother, the magnet was Petticoat Lane in the East End, where there was a cornucopia of food and delicacies that formed the bedrock of a cuisine founded on the observance of the Jewish dietary laws, the laws that have added a new word to the English language – 'kosher', which the Oxford dictionary translates as 'genuine, correct, legitimate'.

Once a week, usually on a Thursday after I had come home from school, or on a Sunday morning, we would catch the tram to Petticoat Lane in Whitechapel armed with several large fish bags made of yellow raffia. The streets would be thronged with shoppers jostling one another on the crowded pavements as they bargained and bought from the stalls. There was a bonhomie about it all, good humour and friendly banter between stall holders and customers that was unique to this melting pot of European immigrants.

One could watch the bakers twisting lengths of dough into the traditional challah (bread baked specially for the Sabbath) and bagels, those round bread rolls with a hole in the middle which are made from a special dough which has to be boiled prior to baking. There was the fishmonger who sold live Spiegel carp imported from the fishponds of Holland, which my mother would stuff and boil. Pike was a great favourite with the family. She would in some magical way fillet the long fish, leaving the almost transparent skin intact. After finely chopping the flesh, seasoning it and adding ground almonds, she would stuff it back into the skin and sew the fish up with fine cotton to be boiled in a tasty bouillon. When it was cool the fish would be cut into inch-thick slices and served with wedges of lemon and a horseradish sauce to which beetroot had been added. This was the traditional gefullte fish. The ritual slaughter of chickens went on all day long and one would select a plump hen from a cage, have it weighed with one foot attached to a spring-loaded scale and pay for it at the rate of 4p a pound. It would then be taken to the *shochet*, the religious slaughterman, to be humanely and ritually killed. There were the stalls selling the wide variety of root vegetables considered to be essential to the preparation of chicken soup – referred to jocularly as the 'penicillin' of Jewish cuisine. We would both return home with me carrying as many of the bags as my mother would permit.

It was an era before the emergence of convenience foods and I enjoyed watching her make her own pasta. Enormous sheets of dough as large as the kitchen table were rolled out to paper thickness and then, with the precision and speed of a machine gun, she would cut it into fine strips, making vermicelli for the chicken soup. Her *kreplach* – ravioli – was my particular favourite.

How tempting were her biscuits and cakes, which varied according to the time of the year and the festivals being celebrated. She would make soft cheese from milk specially set aside to turn sour and ferment, then filtered through cheesecloth to separate the curds from the whey. The resultant cheesecake was mouth-watering. I can only marvel at the flavoursome food which she was able to produce from her very basic kitchen, without the benefit of all the labour-saving devices and gadgets considered essential in the modern kitchen.

5

Friends

Outside the office I was the youngest of a small coterie of staunch friends whose attachment to one another was to last a lifetime. In the case of two of us this has extended to more than 60 years. We were diverse in character and, as they will be referred to frequently in these memoirs, I feel that I should describe my friends in greater detail. The oldest one is George – George Revonetz, now Dr G.G. Richardson, Ph.D, MSc, C.Chem, FRSC, MIM, FNCRT to give him his full title! When he came into my life as a teenager, and became a relief teacher at my Sunday school at the Dalston Road Synagogue, I was ten years old. One of a large family, he was a neighbour of ours in Canonbury. His parents, carrying George in their arms, had left Antwerp on the eve of the outbreak of World War I on the same ship as my own family. He did not exactly detest sports, but the only physical activity I knew him to engage in was weight-lifting. His girth probably mitigated against the former but fitted in well with the latter. What attracted me to him was his intellect and, despite his youth, the confident manner in which he would demolish contemporary shibboleths.

I enjoyed attending Sabbath services at our synagogue and for a time, and until my voice broke, sang in the choir. At other times I would sit in the same pew with George, who would give me a running commentary on the weekly Bible reading. When the story of the creation was read at the beginning of the book of Genesis, he would turn to me and say, 'You can't believe that. The earth wasn't created in six days. It took millions and millions of years.' Whilst I thought this was sheer heresy, I was thrilled to think that this genius of 15 was not above imparting such a revelation to a mere 10-year-old. I adopted him as my mentor and he exerted a great and beneficent influence on me during my teens.

George attended the Central Foundation Boys' School, a grammar school otherwise known as Cowper Street, adjoining City Road and within 100 yards of the hospital in which I had been born. It was in the top league of London schools because of the consistent academic success of its scholars, particularly in mathematics and the sciences. George was about to take his matriculation and hoped to win a place at the Imperial College of Science to study chemistry. He duly matriculated but was denied the all-important government student grant. Having been born in Belgium and his father not having become a naturalised British subject, George was a foreigner and as such not entitled to free higher education. We all thought it was an outrage. Our other friends less academically gifted than George would be eligible as soon as they had gained their Higher Schools Certificate.

George's father was a skilled jeweller whose wages were just sufficient to maintain his family and he could not afford university fees for his eldest son. Undeterred, George took a day job and, after passing his intermediate degree, enrolled for a Bachelor of Science (Honours) degree in chemistry at Birkbeck College, which he attended in the evening. He continued to tell me all about his studies and his lectures and the *conversaziones* he had attended. When I asked him what *conversaziones* were and what part he played in them, he would say, somewhat dismissively, 'Oh, you know, *soireés* given by a learned society.' I really was impressed. He sat his finals and the examinations extended over a fortnight. Meeting him by chance on the penultimate day of his exams I asked him why he wasn't in the examination hall. He explained that right up to the previous day he had been satisfied with his performance but in his physical chemistry paper he felt he had fallen short of his best and rather than get an upper second and not the First he had set his heart on, he had walked out of the exam room and intended to sit it again the following year.

Provided it was written down, George could learn anything. At 16 he had added Esperanto to the several other languages in which he was fluent and began to teach it to me. He was not a misogynist but he was the only one of our group who showed no interest in girls, that is, until he started an evening course in public speaking. In his class he discovered Victoria, a stunning brunette. He fell head over heels in love and insisted on giving me an inventory of Vicky's divine attributes. He wanted to learn how to dance and had bought a book entitled *Ballroom Dancing for the Beginner.* Would I help him? And so it was that, holding a chair as a surrogate Victoria, he waltzed, quickstepped and foxtrotted around our dining room clutching the book in his free hand and following the diagrams that illustrated the footsteps of the dance. My contribution to the learning curve was to wind up the gramophone and keep changing the 78's. He never learnt how to do the tango – our repertoire of records did not include any Spanish or South American tunes.

Now that Vicky had come into his life and his contemporaries were all graduate physicists or chemists, I saw less and less of George but more and more of John, who was a few months younger than me. John had a great zest for living but, despite having a very high IQ, he eschewed any semblance of a formal education and was the very antithesis of George, who had introduced him to me. We became as close as brothers.

John came into my life by walking through the window of the front lounge of our house in Highbury New Park, a street of very fine Victorian homes in North London to which we had moved from Canonbury. Up to the end of World War I, it had been enclosed by gates and guarded by porters dressed in coachman's livery. The post-war years had not been kind to the neighbourhood. The gentry had moved away and shopkeepers and the lower middle class had taken over. The houses still retained some of their original grandeur being set well back from the wide avenue which, when Queen Victoria was still a slip of a girl, had been planted with plane trees now towering majestically on each side of the road.

The boy stepping over the windowsill into the lounge was taller and slimmer than I was. With a broad smile lighting up his sun-tanned face he held out his hand with the words, 'I'm Johnny;

50

we're going to be friends.' He wasn't like any other of my school friends. He had already acquired a maturity and polish that belied his 16 years and I experienced an immediate empathy with him. Coming from a broken home, he had been banished to a boarding school near Brighton where he spent six miserable years. This experience had killed off any interest he might have had in further schooling. He was now living on the opposite side of Highbury New Park with his elderly Uncle Reuben and Aunt Manya, both of Russian origin and childless. He was quite fond of them both and in return for his keep, he not only undertook to keep the garden at the rear of the house duly watered but would every night, but never on a Saturday, walk out his aunt's yapping Pekinese. On Saturday night he walked out with a two-legged companion. His charm and courtesy endeared him to everyone, particularly the girls.

John had just started work as a trainee in the offices of the Ingersoll watch company, which manufactured a range of low-priced pocket and wrist watches. Not long after our first meeting he presented me with a wrist watch which I identified from newspaper advertisements as coming from their five shilling range. Welcome as the gesture was, I felt very diffident about accepting such a gift from my new friend telling him that he did not need to spend his money on me. He dismissed my protest, saying that it did not cost him anything as he had got it at work. The end of his first week coincided with the end-of-the-month stocktaking and he had been directed to the storeroom and instructed to 'take stock'. With a mischievous grin he told me that when he took the watch he was only carrying out his orders. I was speechless but accepted the gift.

He introduced me to his tailor, who had a small shop in Stoke Newington High Street. Above the fascia there appeared the slogan 'Admired, Desired if by M. Summer attired'. The slogan seemed made-to-measure for John. The tailor's standard price for a bespoke three-piece suit (jacket, trousers and waistcoat) was four pounds, at which level I had no option but to remain loyal to Montagu Burton, the Fifty Shilling Tailor.

One day I accompanied John to see Mr Summer under the

impression he was attending for a fitting of a new sports jacket that he had mentioned to me some weeks previously. Experience had by now taught me not to be surprised at anything John did but still I was unprepared for the shock of seeing the tailor handing him a half-finished garment, not of brown Harris tweed, but of black barathea. It was the top half of an evening dress suit. My pal wanted to cut a dash with his latest girlfriend and thought that an evening dress suit with white tie and tails would do the trick. He coolly informed me that dinner jacket with a black tie was the accepted dress at formal dinners *only* when there were no ladies present, a type of function that held little interest for him at the present time.

Shortly after our first meeting he introduced me to Fred Saville, a fellow employee who worked in the company secretary's office. His background was seemingly light years away from both of ours. He had been to a public school, a minor one he would admit bashfully, but all the same a public school. His family had farmed in Lincolnshire for generations but his father had lost all his money in Farrows Bank, which had crashed in 1920. He now lived with his mother and two sisters in genteel poverty in the garden flat of one of the big houses in Highbury New Park. The very diversity of our upbringing could well have been the main ingredient in an association that was to make us inseparable. Throughout our lifetime we never had a quarrel. We were never jealous or envious of one another. We were good friends.

I was growing up in a fast-moving epoch, with history in the making. I could not help but think that I was a participant in some game of chess; but a part so small and insignificant that I would liken it to a pawn that is moved at will by some Grand Master across a giant chessboard.

The newspaper headlines left one in no doubt that there was trouble ahead. Almost on a daily basis Adolf Hitler would make threats against the neighbours of his German Reich. As a demagogue he had no equal. I would listen on the wireless to his ranting speeches at the Nuremberg rallies which, rising in a screaming crescendo, would be answered by a tumultuous roar of *Sieg heil* from his adoring supporters massed in their tens of thousands in the stadium. If I was listening to these hysterical diatribes, so were tens of millions of Germans – his *Herrenvolk* – and they went along with what he was saying. They agreed with him. They must have been willing partners in the overall strategy of subjugation, and I still dismiss subsequent denials as 'white-wash'. His constant theme was that Germany needed *lebensraum*, more living space for all ethnic Germans. It mattered not whether they were in Austria, Czechoslovakia, in the 'Polish corridor' or in Alsace Lorraine. It mattered not if they had been settled for centuries in those territories – he intended to expand Germany's frontiers to embrace them all.

In England the most frequent topic of conversation, displacing the traditional comment on the weather, became 'What do you think of the international situation?'

When I was a boy I was an avid reader of stories about the Great War, which had ended just before my second birthday. Through these books I had followed the rape of Belgium and the flight of the refugees from the Uhlans, the dreaded German cavalry wearing spiked helmets and wielding curved sabres. I had read eyewitness accounts of the great battles in France at Ypres and the retreat of the Old Contemptibles from Mons, the slaughter on the Somme where 20,000 British troops had died on the first day of battle, the mud of Passchendaele, the horror of the trenches in Flanders and the infantry's dread of 'going over the top'. As I grew up I made up my mind I would never become a soldier – the very thought of having to stick a bayonet in someone was anathema to me. And yet I knew in my heart that war was inevitable and that I needed to find an answer to the unpalatable question of what I, as a very ordinary citizen, ought to be doing about it. How did I prepare myself both mentally and physically? I was not alone in thinking along these lines. John, Fred and I spent hours debating the various options, which ranged from doing nothing at all and just waiting to see what happened, to joining the Air Force or the Royal Navy. We even considered registering, when the time came, as conscientious objectors.

A fellow articled clerk always seemed to have a streaming cold, this being most pronounced on a Monday morning. As he was sneezing vociferously one day, I happened to remark on it and he told me that, having joined the Royal Air Force Voluntary Reserve, he was spending his weekends flying planes with open cockpits and kept catching cold. No sooner had he got over one by Thursday, than he would catch another as soon as he went up again over the weekend. I eliminated one of the options. I was not going to join the Air Force.

Fred and John were keen on the Navy. We enjoyed spending weekends punting on the upper reaches of the Thames at Windsor and Cookham, but I knew nothing about boats. I had only been on a ship on one occasion and that was my trip on a ferry across the Irish Sea to Dublin. Nelson was one of my heroes and remains so to this day, but his blood did not course in my veins and I looked upon myself as the archetypal landlubber. The arguments put forward by my friends in favour of joining the Navy had nothing to do with maintaining England's maritime supremacy, nothing to do with the battles of Trafalgar or Jutland; they had no desire whatsoever to emulate Sir Francis Drake or Admiral Beatty. They only talked about the girls. Whistling the tune 'All the Nice Girls Love a Sailor', they took great pains to paint a rosy picture of the three of us spending our two-week annual summer holidays on one of His Majesty's ships. We would call in at exotic harbours where the ship's company would be fêted. We would be made more than welcome in Skegness, Scarborough and Southampton, places bursting with girls. We had been told this on good authority and had seen the statistics!

Meanwhile storm clouds continued to gather across Europe as 1938 was ushered in and, although I was about to celebrate my coming of age, I was in no mood to have a twenty-first birthday party. Events were moving fast and it seemed to me that our government's response, under the premiership of Neville Chamberlain, was at best half-hearted. Mussolini had invaded Abyssinia and Eritrea some two years earlier, to be punished by the League of Nations only with the imposition of ineffective economic sanctions. The following year the German air force had taken an active part in the Spanish Civil War, their bombing raids being in the nature of a dress rehearsal for the main drama yet to be played out on the world stage.

On Saturday morning 12th March, the world was plunged into crisis as newspaper headlines focused on the news that Germany had invaded Austria and the threatened *Anschluss* had become a reality. We three friends held our own crisis meeting. We did not debate for long. We would join the Navy – if it would have us.

We knew that the headquarters of the London Division of the Royal Naval Volunteer Reserve was based on board HMS *President*, which was moored close to Blackfriars Bridge. A sloop built in 1918 as a 'Q' ship to fight U-boats, *President* was originally named *Saxifrage* (a herbaceous plant, also known as London Pride). Taking a tram along the Embankment we arrived at the ship's gangplank which was guarded by a naval rating. We were not allowed to go on board but were informed that recruiting took place at 6 p.m. on Tuesdays. In common with millions of our fellow countrymen we had spent an anxious weekend and Tuesday could not come fast enough. When it did, in company with 50 other prospective recruits, we went aboard to be subjected to a rigorous medical examination and a searching enquiry into our background and the reasons for wanting to enlist in the Senior Service. I thought it diplomatic not to mention girls. A chief petty officer explained that the Admiralty had chosen the London Division to train signalmen of which there was an acute shortage. Many of them would, in the event of war, serve as teleprinter operators on capital ships such as battlecruisers and aircraft carriers. No trenches. No bayonets. I was hooked.

The first hurdle was to pass the medical examination, which was conducted by a young surgeon lieutenant, the red band on the sleeves of his naval jacket separating the two wavy gold lace stripes indicating his specialisation. Not only did the number of gold stripes vary according to the rank of the officer, but if they were straight he would be Royal Navy, if wavy Royal Naval Volunteer Reserve, known affectionately, and sometimes derogatively, as 'the wavy navy'. Whilst waiting for the result of my medical I was told that new entrants became ordinary seamen and were considered to be the lowest form of marine life. They would be instructed in every aspect of seamanship and after passing an examination would be trained as signalmen. Obligatory drills took place every Tuesday and Friday evenings and it was mandatory to spend a minimum of two weeks every year on a sea-going ship of the Fleet. It was then that we would be able to enjoy the delights of Skegness, Scarborough and Southampton! There were no financial rewards but on being mobilised on the eve of war we would receive a bounty of five pounds. After a long period of waiting and nail-biting, all three of us were passed medically fit and accepted as ordinary seamen. Of the fifty would-be sailors only 12 passed. We later found out that the majority had failed because of impaired eyesight, particularly colour-blindness. It was essential that a signalman enjoyed perfect vision as he had to differentiate between hundreds of different flags of every colour in the spectrum.

I had now crossed the Rubicon and there was no turning back, but there remained an even greater test of my resolve. I had to tell my father. In common with most orthodox Jewish families, Friday night was dedicated to the coming Sabbath. We would sit down, *en famille*, to a traditional supper at a table covered with a starched white linen tablecloth, enhanced by a pair of silver candlesticks – heirlooms which had been used regularly by generations of our family. Blessings on the challah bread and wine would be recited before supper was served and, led by my father, we would later sing the grace after meals. It was inconceivable that Marcus would ever countenance a break with this tradition. It was therefore with some trepidation, despite my having two months previously attained my majority, that I told him the following morning, before leaving for the office, that I had joined the Navy. His reply was spontaneous: 'Bless you, my son.'

I went on, 'But I will have to do my drills on a Friday night.'

'Well,' he said, 'we will have to keep your dinner warm for you until you come home.' I could have cried with the emotion of the moment as I knew what a conscious effort must have gone into his ready acceptance of the situation.

56

Only the previous day Hitler had marched into Vienna at the head of his troops; if he had his way no Jews in England would live to celebrate the Sabbath.

6

Learning the Flags

Life was very hectic, certainly not glamorous but intense. I continued with my accountancy studies for the final examination. Twice a week I changed into my sailor's uniform of blue serge bell-bottomed trousers and jumper, and was taught everything a seaman needed to know about a ship, particularly a warship: how to tie knots, splice a rope, drop anchor and pick up buoys, the points of the magnetic compass, the workings of small-bore rifles and pistols and the complexity of 4- and 6-inch guns. I learnt how to form fours and to drill shouldering arms and, to my horror, with a bayonet fixed to the short Lee-Enfield rifle. After three months I was examined in all these maritime skills and martial arts and passed out as an AB – an able-bodied seaman. The time had now arrived for me to acquire the skills of a signalman. Throughout this training period our trio had been in unison but Fred now declared a preference for qualifying as a gunner rather than as a signalman. He decided to postpone making a final decision until we had completed our first sea-going exercise. We made plans to take our two-week summer holiday at the end of July and were drafted to HMS *Furious*, an aircraft carrier berthed in Devonport dockyard. John was delighted, as the Ingersoll company had a shop in neighbouring Plymouth and he had spoken to the manageress about the possibility of our visiting the town. She promised to find two friends so that we could all go out together. She would show us the town and we could go to a dance – and the rest was up to us! The *raison d'être* for preferring the Navy to the other services was now proving itself.

One fine Saturday morning at the end of July, clad in our best uniform with gold badges and carrying our kitbags over our shoulder we boarded the *Devon Belle* Pullman train at Paddington Station. His Majesty's Government had provided us with a travel voucher to Plymouth and a meal ticket for one shilling and sixpence (9p). We found seats in the third-class dining car, having dumped our kitbags in the guard's van. Our adventure and, hopefully, a summer holiday were under way. We studied the menu and made our selections but our obvious pleasure was short-lived. The train had no sooner pulled away from the platform than the dining car attendant, standing over us menacingly and gesticulating with his thumb, said, 'Get out! I'm not having Matelots in this carriage.' We pleaded with him and brandished our meal vouchers, to no avail. As we slunk away to find seats in another third-class compartment the irony of the situation dawned on us. This was class discrimination in the raw. We wanted to serve our country but the Great Western Railway did not want to serve us.

Arriving in Plymouth we made our way to the dockyard and to the berth where HMS *Furious* was tied up to the quay. I had never seen such a big ship before. She had been launched at the end of the Great War but had not seen service as a heavy cruiser, for which she had been designed. Converted into an aircraft carrier, one of the very first of her class, she was later to take on a vital role in establishing superiority over an increasingly powerful German Navy, much of it built in secrecy and in defiance of levels laid down in the Anglo-German Naval Agreement of 1935.

We marched proudly up the gangway at the head of which sat a Royal Marine who directed us to the ship's police office, where a chief petty officer master-at-arms interviewed us. Having told him that we were reservists joining the ship for training, he asked for our names and service numbers and entered them on individual cards. He then asked if we were 'T' or 'G'. These letters stood for Temperance or Grog. We were already aware that every sailor below the rank of commissioned officer was entitled to a tot of rum each day or to receive threepence in lieu if electing to be 'Temperance'. In unison we answered 'G'. Turning to me, he then asked for my religion, to which I replied 'Jew'. Seemingly taken aback, he looked up sharply, turned to John and repeated the same question, to which he received an identical answer. Throwing his pen on to the desk and not attempting to hide his anger and disgust he exclaimed, 'What's this, an *effing* invasion?' There was a malicious edge to his voice which only resumed some semblance of normality when Fred confirmed that he was C. of E. In all the seven years I was to spend in the Royal Navy this was the only overt anti-Semitism I encountered but at the time it made a deep and painful impression on me.

Having been issued with hammocks, we made our way below decks down numerous steel ladders and along a labyrinth of corridors divided up by watertight bulkheads. We eventually arrived in the signalmen's mess. It was Saturday afternoon and a cursory look around convinced us that the mess deck was deserted. On closer examination we could see sailors sleeping under tables, tucked up in odd corners or below the oak benches which served to seat them when eating at the refectory-type tables. As the ship's bell struck the afternoon watch they seem to come to life, and we were able to introduce ourselves as we sat at a long table whilst large aluminium teapots, slices of bread an inch thick accompanied by slabs of butter and jars of plum and apple jam appeared as if by magic. I found carrying on a conversation extremely difficult. Sentences were constructed by interspersing the odd noun or verb between four-letter words all beginning with the letter 'f'. I quickly gave up and resorted to asking a series of questions and was astonished at the youth of these sailors, most being aged between 16 and 19. I was to learn that on entry into the Navy the lowest rank was that of boy seaman second-class rising to boy seaman first-class. To these youngsters I was already old. I was 21.

Tea over, there was a burst of activity to change into No. 1's – our best suits – and prepare for shore leave. The No. 1 suit is traditionally made by a naval outfitter ashore at the sailor's own expense. The 'tiddly suit', as it was affectionately known, was made of fine serge and tailored to hug the body skin-tight. Unlike the normal workday uniform issued free by the purser's department, it sported badges woven in gold wire instead of being embroidered in red cotton. The trousers were exceptionally wide at the bottom and flared. Instead of regulation boots, black shoes could be worn.

We had only experienced four hours of service life but we were more than ready for our long-awaited tryst with the Manageress of the Ingersoll watch company shop in Union Street. We were dressed in our finery, but we observed that officers leaving the ship were not in naval uniform. They were, however, uniformly dressed in either a sports jacket or blazer, grey flannel trousers, brown brogue shoes and wore a 'pork pie' hat which, combined with the cane walking-stick that they carried, marked them out as superior beings.

We walked jauntily through the dockyard, down the main roads of endless shops and public houses catering for naval ratings and literally bounced into the Ingersoll shop. Full of bravado we asked for Sarah Jones, who duly appeared from a small inner office. She was an attractive blonde in her early twenties. As we made our introductions I noticed a distinct lack of warmth in her welcome. She soon made it clear that she had no intention of joining us that evening or, for that matter, any other evening during our stay in Plymouth. 'Sailors!' she exclaimed in a broad Devon accent. 'Me and my friends would be dead in this town if we were seen out with *sailors*.' We began to wonder whether we had joined the right Service. Perhaps if we had come dressed as Commanders of the King's Navee our reception would have been less frigid. We departed, utterly crestfallen. There was going to be no visit to the Palais de Danse and we were left to find our entertainment in Plymouth without female company.

Saturday night in Devonport with the Fleet in harbour was rowdy, with the pubs packed to their swing doors and doing a roaring trade. Units of naval police patrolled the streets wearing armbands, their trousers tucked into whitened gaiters, swinging short batons as they marched in a phalanx of four ready to deal with any sailor who stepped out of line. Feeling that we were in hostile territory we adjourned to a nearby cinema and returned early to the ship to spend our first night in a hammock. I did not sleep a wink but it seemed that in no time the loudspeaker above my head was broadcasting a bugle call followed by a sing-song announcement that I deciphered as 'wakey wakey, rise and shine.' It was six o'clock in the morning. None of us felt like shining but literally fell out of our hammocks and made our way bleary-eyed to the very basic ablutions which were built into the fo'c'sle.

Church service was held on the flight deck and the sound of a choir of more than 1,000 sailors singing the Navy's hymn 'Eternal Father, strong to save,' remains with me to this day. I so loved the harmony and the lyrics that throughout the war, and particularly if we were in a tight spot, I would sing it quietly to myself and was comforted by the words written by William Whiting more than a hundred years ago: 'O hear us when we cry to thee for those in peril on the sea.'

The ship carried a crew of 1,500 sailors, together with airmen belonging to the Fleet Air Arm and a detachment of about 100 marines. I felt quite overwhelmed as each day we continued our signal training under the tutelage of a chief yeoman of signals and we learnt how to live as sailors.

The Navy is a force of specialists. On entry, every rating must learn basic seamanship before being selected for one of the many different categories of personnel essential to the operation of a warship. There were wireless telegraphists, stokers, gunners, torpedomen, divers, anti-submarine operators, engine room artificers, stewards, cooks, paymasters, masters-at-arms and, of course signalmen, all specialists and trained to a high degree of proficiency. Of all these I considered signalmen to be an elite group and was happy that I had been drafted into this arm of the Service. Before the era of radio telegraphy, visual signals had been the only means of communication between ships at sea as well as between ships and the shore. One has only to think of Nelson's message to the fleet before the battle of Trafalgar, which was expressed in a hoist of flags on HMS *Victory*: 'England expects every man to do his duty', probably the most momentous battle-cry in English history.

There was a different flag for each letter of the alphabet, and each flag had its own meaning. One would denote 'I have a pilot on board', another would mean 'my speed is — knots' or 'turn — degrees to port or starboard', whilst a flag I would later on use very frequently was one indicating 'there is a floating mine'. There were code books to decipher and semaphore to be mastered so as to be able to send or receive a message transmitted at 25 words a minute. And then there was the Morse code. At sea in time of war, except when in action, radio silence between ships was mandatory. Messages would be flashed in Morse with a hand-held Aldis lamp or a large shuttered lamp that could have a range of 20 miles. At night, so as not to reveal one's position to the enemy, the winking light would come from a small box lantern resembling a Brownie camera with the tiniest of apertures.

I relished the opportunity of acquiring this expertise.

I returned to the office and the daily routine of work by day and study by night, interspersed with my naval drills. As the year 1938 dragged on, the international situation continued to deteriorate. In times of great tension between nations, actions can be taken and warnings given which, short of an ultimatum, is calculated to send a clear signal to the other side that the current position was considered to be untenable and if not remedied could lead only to war. One such signal would be a partial mobilisation of armed forces. Wednesday 28th September was such a day and the Royal Navy and the naval reserves were mobilised. Full of foreboding, I rushed down to HMS *Chrysanthemum* moored at Blackfriars Bridge and joined my comrades who were flooding in from their homes or offices. Some were dressed in uniform whilst others had had no time to change and were in 'civvies'. We stood around listening to the radio bulletins and conjecturing what the next move on the chessboard would be. In the House of Commons the Prime Minister was speaking to a full House packed not only with Members of Parliament and Peers of the Realm but with the Gallery taken over by foreign diplomats.

The House was in a very sombre mood as Chamberlain recounted his meetings with Hitler and Mussolini during the months leading up to the mobilisation: His visits to Berchtesgaden,

Hitler's hideout in the Bavarian Alps, and the undertakings and assurances that he was given, only to have them broken. He would now make one last effort for peace. Next morning whilst I waited on board HMS *Chrysanthemum*, the Prime Minister made his very first flight by air, taking off for Munich to meet Hitler and his ally Mussolini, where he was joined by Daladier, the French Prime Minister. The following day Chamberlain returned and landed at Heston, the forerunner of Heathrow airport. He emerged from the aircraft and at the top of the steps facing the assembled news reporters, stood waving a piece of paper proclaiming that he had brought 'peace with honour'. The Navy was stood down. I returned home, somewhat wiser and a little richer by having been given a large new five-pound note. Two days later Hitler's troops marched into the Sudetenland – part of Czechoslovakia.

War had been averted. The 'phoney' peace had begun.

The New Year brought no relief or reduction in the tense world situation. On the contrary almost every day brought a new and unpleasant surprise as Hitler's appetite, whetted by his success at Munich, grew even more voracious. He extended his grip on Czechoslovakia by annexing Bohemia and Moravia. Mussolini, intent on keeping up with his fellow dictator, was also on the expansion trail and grabbed Albania whilst signing a pact with Hitler containing secret protocols. I shared the hope of millions of Englishmen that at long last Britain would now rearm in earnest against the fateful day which we felt must come – the Day of Judgment if not Armageddon itself.

On the diplomatic front Britain was locked in protracted negotiations with the Soviets for a treaty of non-aggression. At home, trenches were being dug in Hyde Park and communal air raid shelters built. Individual households were recommended to construct an Anderson shelter made of corrugated iron in their garden and, if they had no garden, to place a steel-framed Morrison shelter in their home. The whole population was issued with gas masks.

I continued with my naval drills and together with my two friends started to discuss our summer holidays. John was intent on spending his fortnight in Jersey. Fred was indecisive. This left me as the only one electing to do his sea training. I chose the two weeks ending on 29th August 1939.

I was posted to HMS *Southampton*, lying in the Humber at Immingham. I was excited at the prospect of joining the Fleet, even in my very humble capacity as a signalman. The ship was one of our latest 6-inch gun cruisers and with her sister ships *Glasgow*, *Edinburgh*, *Sheffield* and *Belfast* made up the powerful Second Cruiser Squadron. She flew the flag of Vice Admiral Sir Edward Collins, who two months earlier had been promoted and knighted on board by the King on his return crossing of the Atlantic with Queen Elizabeth following their much acclaimed State visit to Canada.

Arriving in Immingham, little more than a fuelling base for the Navy and a short distance along the Humber estuary from Grimsby, I found the drabness of the town in sharp contrast to the brightness of the summer day. The sight that thrilled me had nothing to do with the topography or, for that matter, the weather. It was the sight of the whole Home Fleet lying at anchor in the river. Its combined might was mind-blowing. This was the country's first line of defence and the only offensive force it had ready for immediate action. There, glistening in the August sunlight, were the floating legends – the battleships *Nelson* and *Hood* and the aircraft carrier *Ark Royal*. Squadrons of cruisers and destroyer flotillas seemingly without number. I felt proud to be part of the show.

Going out into midstream in a pinnace, I duly joined the ship – only to find myself going ashore again a few hours later, having been encouraged by several of my new mess-mates to join them in spending the last few hours of freedom, before sailing, in making whoopee in Immingham's desolate Lincolnshire docks. We would be able to spend the night ashore and catch the last liberty boat at six o'clock the following morning. I was naïve and ignorant of the antics of sailors when let loose ashore. I found the streets teeming with Navy – civilians seemed to have fled to safety. Public houses were crammed, with the overflow, in varying stages of inebriation, hanging on to lamp-posts for support whilst singing 'Nellie Dean'.

After spending the night in a filthy hostel, a genuine dosshouse for down-and-outs where I did not once close my eyes, believing that I had fallen into a Sweeney Todd trap, I, with the others, staggered out bleary-eyed into the early morning sunshine and was ferried back to our ship in one of *Southampton*'s fast pinnaces. At midday we raised anchor and, leading our squadron, we made for the open sea. We had been briefed that we would be on war manoeuvres and that ships of the Second Cruiser Squadron were to emulate the German pocket battleships *Deutschland* and *Admiral Graf Spee* by steaming up to the North Cape, turning round past the Lofoten Islands and at full speed penetrate the defensive line held by the rest of the Fleet strung out across the North Sea to the Norwegian coast. The comparison between the *Southampton* and a pocket battleship was not very encouraging for us. Their main armament was 11-inch compared with our 6-inch guns. Our armour had been sacrificed in the interest of greater speed, enabling our 10,000 tons of steel to slice through the water at 31 knots.

At full speed, standing high up on the signal bridge with the wind whipping my face to a deep scarlet, it seemed to me that the warship had taken off and was actually flying. My night-time watches in these northern waters of the Arctic Circle were particularly exhilarating, with a grandstand view of the *aurora borealis* and the feeling that one could reach up and pick a star from the galaxy above – there were so many it would hardly be missed. But I could not delude myself that I was on a free Cunard cruise to the Land of the Midnight Sun. There was no escaping the fact that we were at the gateway to war in a formidable fighting machine set on a course with a predictable landfall. In the war games in which we had just participated we had been successful. We had achieved surprise and pierced the defence.

Some four days later, still on patrol off Bergen, our peace was shattered by a bugle call on the loudspeakers and a voice summoning all crew to muster on the quarter deck. Arriving aft and standing in the space allotted to the signalmen I, and most of the crew of 900 men, faced the Captain, who stood on a small dais facing us. His message was brief and to the point: 'The balloon has gone up. Germany and Russia have signed a treaty of non-aggression. We are returning to Invergordon. Dismiss.'

Arriving at Invergordon, the naval base in the Cromarty Firth, the Second Cruiser Squadron anchored in line ahead. To starboard and parallel with us were the battleships *Repulse*, *Royal Sovereign*, *Royal Oak*, *Resolution* and *Rodney*, and on our port side a whole flotilla of destroyers. We were in good company and I felt safe. Catching forty winks in the mess deck, I was awakened by a loud and incessant hammering. On asking my opposite number to explain what was happening, he laconically replied, 'Oh, they are just screwing the warheads onto the torpedoes.' So this was it. We had now arrived at the point of no return.

My immediate thoughts were of my family. I was not going to be able to say even a brief goodbye to my father, my brothers and sisters. We would just sail off into the unknown. My self-pity was ended when the loudspeaker crackled with the announcement: 'All reservists wishing to leave the ship, muster at the port side gangplank, amidships, in half an hour.' I threw my few belongings into my kitbag, bade a sad farewell to my newly-made shipmates, collected a travel pass and was ferried ashore to take the first available train to London. Arriving at Perth station, I was amazed to see Rolls-Royce cars lined up on the platform, having just disgorged their passengers whose grouse shooting season had been so rudely interrupted by the threat of imminent war.

I locked myself in a carriage and drew the blinds, fearing that although I was in possession of a valid pass I would be intercepted and sent back. I was already feeling and acting like a deserter. I arrived home and the very next day the Fleet was mobilised, to be followed on Friday 1st September by General Mobilisation coupled with the news that Germany had invaded Poland, using provocation as the pretext.

7

Call to Arms

At home, the household was in turmoil. My sister Frances, a pupil at the Barratt School of Design, was packing to be evacuated with her fellow students to Luton. My oldest brother Harry, who had made a career as head wine steward on transatlantic liners, had planned to join our brother Joe in New Zealand and in fact had just left for Liverpool where he was to take passage in the Donaldson liner *SS Athenia*. I was like a cat on a hot tin roof, anxious, restless and waiting for the telegram that would summon me back to the Service. I travelled up to my office in the City. It was Saturday morning and the City streets seemed even more deserted than normal and I found that only three of our employees had come in to work.

No. 16 Coleman Street was a modern office block and one of the tenants on the same floor as Wilson Bigg & Co. was a firm of foreign-exchange dealers. From time to time in the past I would drift into their dealing room as I enjoyed the hubbub and excitement the dealers generated when buying, selling or just quoting foreign currencies. I was surprised to see that the room, which resembled a telephone exchange, was fully manned. Clerks faced a board and by placing a telephone plug in one of the holes, each of which bore the name of a foreign capital city, would transact his business. Today a forex dealer would sit in front of a battery of computer screens and digital telephones. I listened to the orders converting Swiss francs into sterling; United States dollars into Dutch guilders and Italian lire into Spanish pesetas, and then it was Warsaw on the line and I could hear a voice saying over and over again, 'We are being bombed.' Before I left their office I listened to the BBC news broadcast and heard that Chamberlain had served an ultimatum on Hitler that unless Germany ceased hostilities and returned to the *status quo ante* by 11 a.m. the following day, a state of war would exist between our two countries.

The next morning, Sunday 3rd September, as the notes of Big Ben striking eleven o'clock reverberated over the ether, the Prime Minister informed the country that we were now at war. Instead of the peal of church bells, within minutes the tranquillity of a sunny summer morning was shattered by the wailing of the first air raid siren. The final all-clear was not to sound for nearly six years.

Monday of the following week brought the expected telegram instructing me to report the next morning at 8 a.m. on board HMS *President* on the Embankment. This was a time of high drama for the family at home as we were still reeling from the shattering news that SS *Athenia* had been torpedoed in the Atlantic and we feared the worst. And so I left home for the last time. Shouldering my kitbag, accompanied by my sister Pauline who had insisted on seeing me off, I bade farewell to a father grieving over a son he thought he had already lost and another going off to a war still only a week old.

Arriving on board HMS *President* I found the ship heaving with reservists and was informed that we would be attached to the base at Portsmouth, appropriately named after Nelson's flagship HMS *Victory*. Naval bases never go to sea, but nevertheless are given the names of ships. Just as a soldier owes allegiance to his regiment so a sailor is proud of his home base and, in my case, it would henceforth and throughout my Service career be 'Pompey', as HMS *Victory* was affectionately known.

Before marching off we were served lunch. Haute cuisine it certainly was not and consisted of a slice of Argentinian corned beef with a large helping of pussers' peas. 'Pusser' is a word peculiar to the Navy and originates from the word 'Purser', the officer who is responsible for the issue of stores. The peas, of the variety known as marrowfat, had been dried and reconstituted and

69

now formed a grey-green mush surrounding the slab of brick-red beef edged with a border of grey fat. It had been newly rescued from a huge rectangular tin. Even had I entertained an appetite, the sight was decidedly off-putting and, had I realised it, was a portent of things yet to come. I was now in the employ of HM Government, being paid the princely wage of two shillings (10p) *per diem* in addition to board and lodging. Had I the right to expect any better?

Formed up on the Embankment in columns of four, we marched to Waterloo Station to embark on a special train for Portsmouth, where, as straight and erect as any squad of marines, we made our way to the main barracks. At the time I was upset and annoyed at the seeming indifference on the part of the many pedestrians we passed as we marched through the town. I should not have been. The burghers of Portsmouth had become inured to the sight of sailors. They had known the victors of Trafalgar and could be excused for ignoring a bunch of reservists, even if they were marching in step!

The next fortnight flew past whilst we awaited our first drafting. In the meantime wonderful news had reached me from home. My brother Harry had been rescued from the sea after the torpedoing of SS *Athenia*. It was several weeks before the family heard the full story of his escape from drowning, and then only after he had joined my other brother Joe in Auckland, New Zealand.

The war of 1914–1918 had brought home to the combatants that the days of chivalry, if they had ever existed outside the realm of the romantic historical novel, had gone for ever. It had been ended by new weapons of mass and indiscriminate destruction. By TNT. By mustard gas. By flame-throwers and landmines. When the madness of the Great War had run its course and fighting finally stopped, nations took stock of what had taken place in the name of a just cause and they resolved to set limits on the terms of engagement and the use of certain weapons. The use of gas was outlawed and the Hague Conventions embodied the new thinking. One of the rules covered submarine warfare and it was laid down that an unarmed merchant ship should not be sunk without prior warning, giving the crew an opportunity to save themselves by taking to the lifeboats. Germany had subscribed to the Conventions. In total violation of its undertakings, its submarine U30 had, within hours of the outbreak of war, sunk the SS *Athenia* without warning and without cause. My brother Harry was a passenger on the ill-fated ship and some months later sent the family a report from a New Zealand newspaper which gives his eyewitness account of the sinking. It reads:

TORPEDOED – SCRAMBLE FOR LIFE BY A SURVIVOR OF THE *ATHENIA*

A graphic story of the happening was told today by Mr Harry Janovitch of London who was one of the passengers.

'We cleared Liverpool on the afternoon of September 2, before war broke out and the following evening at 7.30 p.m, when we were about 300 miles out on our way to Montreal in Canada, an enemy submarine struck without warning. The sea was choppy, visibility good and we were not zigzagging. Some of the passengers saw a periscope show up a few hundred yards away. Then came a torpedo which struck the *Athenia* amidships. The submarine surfaced and fired two shells. They were evidently meant to cripple the ship's wireless, but they fell on deck, burst and caused loss of life.

'Acrid smoke rolled round the liner's decks and the ship listed about 40 degrees to port, so much so we thought she would go right over. Everyone was ordered to the boats. The crowded boats circled round all night and flares were fired at intervals. The boat I was in shipped water, and women took off their shoes and bailed. Then at 3.30 the next morning the first rescue ship came on the scene – the Swedish yacht *Southern Cross*. Soon came a second disaster. In getting alongside the yacht our boat was capsized by a wave and the occupants, about fifty, were thrown into the water. I could not swim and did not have a life belt. I remember sinking a couple of times and a sailor grabbing my arm and pulling me on to the upturned boat. Then a rope was lowered from the yacht and I was hauled aboard. By that time some of the other passengers had been swept away and drowned.

'Later in the day, the yacht which had picked up over 200 of the *Athenia*'s passengers met the steamer *City of Flint* which had also come up to give assistance. The passengers were transferred and on September 10 we landed in Halifax where we were met by officials of the company and Red Cross representatives. We were given clothing and arrangements were made to get us to our destinations.

'The *Athenia* after being struck floated until about 10 o'clock the following morning, gradually settled and eventually went down stern first. There would have been greater loss of life had the ship been sunk a day later as by then a storm was raging.

'The only souvenirs I have retained is [*sic*] a salt-water stained passport and a receipt for valuables lodged in the liner's safe. We had all taken to the boats in the clothes we stood in.'

An unprecedented expansion of auxiliary ships to support the Fleet was under way and their crews could only come from the volunteer reserve and the fishing fleet. The Navy needed to build or convert an armada of convoy escorts, submarine detection ships, patrol vessels and minesweepers, and the time had now arrived for the RNVR signalmen to go to war. The two weeks at Portsmouth improving my skills had been spent conjecturing on the type of ship to which I would be drafted. Would it be to another cruiser or perhaps a battleship? I was mentally prepared for either. The reality was that we were just numbers in a lottery which when drawn would have far reaching consequences for each one of us.

We queued in a long line outside a hut in which a chief petty officer sat with a sheet of names propped up in front of him which he paired off at random with a list of ships. I was apprehensive and nervous. I saw this man as a modern-day version of the Archangel Gabriel on the Day of Judgment, consulting his book and deciding who would live and who should die. He was poised ready to move pawns on a vast chessboard. I was one of those pawns.

In front of me, in the line, stood a former bank clerk whose experience of travel could well have been limited to commuting daily from his Surrey home near Woking to his branch office in nearby Guildford. The Archangel rasped out, 'Smithers, you're off to Montevideo to join an armed merchant cruiser as Commodore's signalman. Travel in civvies. Amongst these papers you will find a voucher for five pounds to buy yourself a suit. Next.'

I was next. 'Jackson, here's a railway ticket to get you to Lowestoft and the Royal Naval Patrol Service.' I asked him for the name of the ship. 'Ship?' he said with disdain. 'Most likely a trawler or a drifter. Next.'

The contrast in posting between me and my predecessor could not have been greater. I was crestfallen. Even more so when, after meeting with my two close friends before leaving the base, John told me he was to join the destroyer HMS *Anthony*, whilst Fred had been drafted to a large sea-going yacht requisitioned from Lord Harmsworth, the proprietor of the *Daily Mail*. So the three of us, for so many years as close as brothers, went off in different directions and to different oceans to experience the vicissitudes of war. What we had left in common was the desire to serve our country, to defeat the enemy and above all to survive.

I arrived in Lowestoft, a small fishing port on the Suffolk/ Norfolk border. A drafting naval base, which bore the unlikely name of *The Sparrow's Nest* had been hurriedly set up in a concert hall in the town. A more inappropriate title for a naval base could not have been devised and after a few weeks it had been changed officially to HMS *Europa*, probably more to confuse the enemy than to enlighten those sailors sent to join it.

The country was endowed with a vast fishing fleet. The larger ships were modern and had been built in the 1930s, quite a few of them in Germany. They had been designed to fish the deep cold waters well inside the Arctic Circle near Iceland and Murmansk and even as far away as the ocean that surrounds Greenland. They were robustly built and made excellent sea boats. They had to be, as they were called on to fish in all seasons and weather, with seas that could be whipped up without warning into green mountains. They would return from their trips with their holds full of the harvest of the sea: great catches of cod and haddock and prized hauls of halibut, often the size of a billiard table. Smaller boats fished closer to land and in good weather returned to harbour with their catch of herring and flat fish of seemingly infinite variety. Plaice, sole, skate, monkfish, even lobster and langoustine were scooped up from the predominantly sandy sea bed. The fishing fleets based on small ports and harbours strung along our coastline like a long necklace of pearls, were manned by skilled seamen, many of them third and fourth generation fishermen. Invariably they enrolled in the Royal Naval Reserve (RNR). It was predominantly these men, with a sprinkling of Volunteer Reservists like myself, who were now converging on Lowestoft to be drafted to the ships being hastily converted to war.

A night spent in a bed and breakfast boarding-house in Lowestoft whetted my appetite to try to avoid being drafted, and the rules on how to achieve this were spelled out to me by an old three-badge AB (an able bodied seaman with long service in the Navy). This would only be possible if I could manage to stave off the attentions of the chief petty officers whose job it was to make up the crews required to commission the newly converted ships in the numerous shipyards dotted around the coast. The trick was to lose oneself in the crowd of hundreds of sailors milling around the concert hall and never, but never, respond when one's name was called on the loud hailer. With a little luck one could avoid detection; the record achieved by one sailor was one whole week. What I did not reckon with was that there is some mechanism in one's psyche that makes an automatic response to one's name inevitable. I was aware, without concentrating on it, that somewhere in the background long lists of names were being rattled off. Hearing the Tannoy proclaim 'Signalman Leslie Jackson RNVR No. LD/3828', I forgot all the tips and instructions, raised my hand and shouted 'Here'. In doing this I had once again become part of the draw in the lottery and was about to find out whether my ticket bore a winning number. I drew His Majesty's Trawler *Cayton Wyke*.

The ship was in a dockyard in Blyth, Northumberland, on the River Tyne and was in the process of being converted from its traditional role of deep-sea fishing into an asdic trawler – a submarine hunter.

Armed with the requisite travel pass, I caught the train to Peterborough en-route to Newcastle-upon-Tyne. It was Sunday and the railway system was in chaos. Our train was frequently shunted into sidings, to the annoyance of the hundreds of passengers, all naval ratings. To make matters worse, we were confined to small third-class compartments devoid of toilet facilities and with no refreshments available at any of the numerous station halts. We were in the heart of sugar-beet country and whenever the train stopped, the fields were raided to quench our thirst and assuage our growing hunger. Arriving eventually at Peterborough a miracle took place which I can liken only to the manna which was showered on the Israelites of old in the wilderness of Sinai. There on the platform piled 2 feet high were hundreds of lunch boxes waiting for the imminent arrival of the *Flying Scotsman* on its way to Edinburgh. We fell on this godsend like vultures and within minutes nothing remained but empty cartons strewn along the whole platform. The *Flying Scotsman*, the pride of the London Midland & Scottish Railway, duly pulled into the station bellowing clouds of steam. Out jumped the restaurant car attendants, to be met with a scene of carnage that turned their faces scarlet with rage. When they took stock of their adversary – hundreds of unshaven and dishevelled matelots – discretion proved to be the better part of valour and they retreated to their dining cars muttering epithets that were only bettered by the cat-calls of the sailors. I thought back to the incident on the *Devon Belle* Pullman train some two years previously and of my humiliation at the hands of a dining car superintendent. I thought in my simplistic way that this was Divine providence and that God would be looking after me from now on.

Trains had always held a fascination for me and in my boyhood days I turned train spotting at the main railway terminii of King's Cross, St Pancras, Waterloo and Liverpool Street into one of my main recreational interests. The variety of ownership of the railway system, LMS, LNER, GWR and Southern, each with their own distinctive livery, made it easy for a normal curiosity to be turned into a fascinating hobby.

To arrive in Newcastle-upon-Tyne station at five o'clock on a Monday morning was quite an eye-opener. All through the night goods trains had been arriving with farm produce and parcels that were now strewn over the numerous platforms. There was no evidence of any passengers and very few porters but there were hundreds of sailors who, like the Assyrian in Byron's poem 'The Destruction of Sennacherib', *came down like the wolf on the fold*. In no time mayhem reigned and I was only too glad to leave Newcastle behind, catching the first workman's train of the morning to Blyth, just a few miles away. I approached the gates of the shipyard, which were guarded by a naval picket, and on enquiring where the *Cayton Wyke* was lying, was directed to an enormous dry dock. There lying on the stocks about 30 feet down in the middle of the basin was a ship looking very much like a toy boat in a bath emptied of water. The contrast with the 10,000-ton cruiser I had left only three weeks earlier could not have been greater – but an even greater shock awaited me. I still had to meet the crew, my fellow shipmates.

The complement for an anti-submarine trawler was 32 and until the ship was ready for commissioning our home would be a Nissen hut in the dockyard. I was the last member of the crew to join the ship and when I entered they looked up at me with incredulity. My involuntary reaction was to recite silently the opening verses of Samuel Taylor Coleridge's poem *The Rime of the Ancient Mariner*.

Even though not one of them had a long grey beard, each one had seen service in the First World War and I was their junior by at least 20 years. Had they been press-ganged in the alleyways of Hull or Greenock on the Clyde they could not have formed a more motley crew. They hailed from every fishing port in Britain from Stornaway in the Outer Hebrides to Falmouth on the south-western tip of Cornwall. Like the builders of the Tower of Babel they spoke in many tongues. Admittedly they enjoyed a common language but this was separated from my kind of English by 31 different dialects. After having spent 36 hours riding in third class railway compartments, I was ready to drift into a state of deep depression. That night I wrote my first letter home with the ink being smudged by the tears that involuntarily fell onto the page of my writing pad. I started the letter: 'Dear everyone ... I am about to join a ship in Blyth on the river Tyne. I think I have fallen amongst pirates ...'

Our ship was a typical coal-burning deep-sea fishing trawler of 373 gross registered tonnage. She was in her element in the icy and tumultuous seas around Bear Island in latitude 75 degrees north, well into the Arctic Circle. A first-class sea boat which, handled with skill, could survive the most violent storm that a capricious North Sea could produce at just a few hours' notice. But what of the crew? They seem to take to me and fostered me like a much younger brother. Perhaps it was because I was one of the very few aboard who could write as well as read. Even the captain, a 47-year-old native of Lossiemouth in northern Scotland, had difficulty in writing his reports. I was later told that he was known to sail to his favourite fishing grounds with his own unique navigational aids, which included the use of a knotted bootlace to measure his distance on the charts. He knew when he had arrived at the correct destination when, by heaving the lead, it was confirmed that the sea bed was sand and not pebbles or mud!

I assumed responsibility for checking and recording the arrival of stores, which ranged from bales of tarred hemp to a ton of cotton waste, from kitchen utensils to anchors, from pyrotechnics to blankets, from rifles and pistols to groceries, as well as shells for our 12-pounder gun and depth charges. The sheer variety of objects necessary to turn a harmless fishing vessel into a man-of-war was mind-boggling. I also discovered, to my dismay, that as fast as goods with an immediate street value came aboard they would be smuggled ashore and sold in the public houses that ringed the dockyard like wasps round a honeypot. Real chamois leathers, apparently, were very saleable as 12 dozen disappeared within hours of my checking them into store.

I started to keep a personal log which I wrote up daily. It commenced on Wednesday 4th October 1939 and concludes with a final entry on New Year's Eve of that year after having been informed that the keeping of a diary was forbidden under KR&AI (King's Regulations and Admiralty Instructions), the Navy's own holy script. I have this diary still and am surprised to see how little my handwriting has changed in 60 years.

Fishermen are notoriously superstitious. It was considered unlucky to start a voyage on a Friday. Consequently when our first sea trial was scheduled for Friday the 13th, there was nearly a mutiny. At our first meal on board no table knives could be found. There were spoons and forks in abundance, but no knives. I had checked in 12 dozen so I knew they had come aboard. I discovered that because they had ivory handles, considered to be very unlucky, they had been heaved overboard. I wondered how I could ever integrate with such a crew.

Finally, after sea trials, gunnery practice, asdic exercises and a visit on board by the Commander-in-Chief Rosyth, who was accompanied by Rear Admiral HRH The Duke of Kent, we were grudgingly given clearance for active service and received our sailing orders. Pandemonium then broke out below decks, particularly in the cramped seamen's mess which was situated in the former fish hold and still smelt of fish long past its sell-by date. It had been converted to accommodate 16 of the crew, myself included, in double-tiered bunks. The bad news was that we were to sail south and join the Dover Patrol. As veterans of 1914–18, my shipmates were able to recall that the expectation of life in this sector could be equated to that of an infantryman on the Somme – to be calculated in weeks rather than months. The war had found Britannia's Navy stretched to the limit in its endeavour to 'rule the waves'. Having already witnessed at first hand the discipline and efficiency of the professional sailor, I felt happy that in battle the Navy would be a very good match for the German Grand Fleet. But I had great doubts about what I had already seen of the reserves forming the patrol service. Just as in the army rookies were likened to a Fred Karno outfit, so the crew of the *Cayton Wyke* were cast in the mould of Harry Tate.

We sailed in accordance with our orders and encountered our first floating mine near Flamborough Head off the Yorkshire coast.

I couldn't repress my excitement on spotting it with my binoculars, but floating mines packed with 350 pounds of high explosive were soon to become so commonplace that they became an integral part of the seascape. As the signalman, my action station was on the signal bridge just above the wheelhouse. I was in charge of a Lewis machine gun and kept its magazines loaded with alternate rounds of armour-piercing and tracer bullets of .303 calibre. I was to get plenty of firing practice, although the horns of a mine bobbing up and down in a choppy sea made an elusive target which could only be detonated by accurate rifle fire.

Whilst I continued to have every confidence in the seamanship of the crew, I still entertained disquieting reservations about the navigational ability of the Skipper. It was very reassuring therefore when, almost by accident I thought, we 'discovered' Dover and proudly entered harbour after I hoisted our recognition flags at the yardarm.

We had joined the dreaded Dover Patrol.

8

The Dover Patrol

Indisputably the Straits of Dover is the most important strategic stretch of sea around our island. The English Channel at this point narrows down to a strip of water no more than 20 miles wide serving to separate Dover from continental Europe. Through the Straits passes the greater part of our sea-borne commerce, and command of this narrow waterway is vital to our very existence as a sovereign nation. Should control fall into enemy hands we would be starved quickly into submission. There would be no necessity to bomb the mainland and, in the process, destroy installations prohibitively expensive to replace. An enemy could achieve domination by blockading our ports, in particular the Thames estuary, gateway to the metropolis. His tactics would include the intensive mining of the shallow waters of the Straits, backed up by indiscriminate use of submarines – the U-boats that almost brought him victory in World War I. Our job was to frustrate his strategy. I confess that at the time, and as the signalman of His Majesty's Anti-Submarine Trawler *Cayton Wyke*, I did not feel any great sense of mission. It did not occur to me that I was engaged in a historic combat with an implacable enemy. I was nothing other than a pawn, to be moved around at will by the Board of Admiralty. There was no shortage of people like me. I was expendable. I only needed to focus my mind on how to survive.

A ship's complement would normally have included a wireless telegraphist but because of the acute shortage of these operators this role was added to my signalman's duties. All the secret code books were entrusted to my care, in addition to the task of keeping navigational charts up to date with the constant stream of signals from Admiralty. I had to map all the wreck buoys in our operational area and these grew in number day by day. On the declaration of war, as a defensive measure the Navy had begun to lay the Dover Barrage, a barrier of moored mines which, except for a narrow strip, would virtually close the English Channel right up to the Belgian coast. It was to prove effective against submarines and accounted for three U-boats in September alone. A further defence against submarines was a series of loops laid on the sea-bed which could detect underwater movements. The role assigned to *Cayton Wyke* was to patrol one of these loops off North Foreland.

By no stretch of the imagination could I describe our ship as a formidable or even an efficient fighting machine. On the other hand, we had managed in the short time since commissioning to 'shake down' and were working as a team. Considering all the disparate characters on board and living in such a confined space, it was vital to act in unison and spontaneously when in danger. I had every confidence in their seamanship and, despite the generation gap and my different background, the confidence was mutual. This was just as well as within days we were to be tested in action against the enemy.

It was the period before the invasion of France that became known as the '*phoney war*'. There was nothing *phoney* about it for *us*. Dover, part of the Nore command, had become the front line in an active and bitterly fought theatre of operations. True, we never caught sight of the enemy. It lurked unseen beneath the waves but its victims were very visible. Using submarines and seaplanes from bases on the Island of Sylt, the Germans laid thousands of mines at random. It was rumoured that they were also not beyond using coastal steamers flying the Dutch flag of neutrality for this purpose. Each day there was a new wreck. The sea was so shallow that at low tide the masts or the superstructure of a sunken vessel were only too apparent. To name but a few that fell victim to mines in our patrolling area: the passenger liner *Simon Bolivar*, the destroyer *Gypsy* and the French cargo steamer

Mahratta laden with a cargo of tea which on sinking littered the sea for miles around with floating tea chests; as it was flotsam, we were within our legal rights to salvage one. Before the end of October no less than 19 ships, accounting for more than 60,000 tons, had been sunk in the Straits of Dover – some *phoney war*! It seems incomprehensible that although Germany had embarked on unrestricted warfare at sea, the Cabinet had vetoed an Air Ministry proposal to bomb the enemy's submarine and seaplane bases, using as an excuse that this would be a breach of international law.

Looking at my personal log I see that the entry for Tuesday 24th October 1939 had been written in red ink, with the explanation that I had run out of blue/black. In fact that day was to develop into a real red letter day in the life of *Cayton Wyke*.

We had left Dover harbour at 0800 for a patrol that would take us to a position close to the Brake lightship, approximately 51 23N 2E. It was one of those perfect sunny days that seems to slide, as if by accident, into the otherwise drab month of October, a day when one was encouraged to believe in Robert Browning's poem that 'God's in his heaven – All's right with the world'. Through my binoculars and looking towards the shore, I could see Margate bathed in the morning sunshine and I wished that I was there walking on the promenade instead of keeping watch on the signal bridge of a warship.

The tiny radio office was adjacent and I darted in and out tuning the wireless receiver to our base for messages. The office was also close to the asdic equipment with which we were fitted, the metamorphosis that had turned us from a harmless fishing trawler into a submarine hunter. The word 'asdic' is derived from the initials of the Allied Submarine Detection Investigation Committee, which at the end of the Great War had pioneered the technique of detection of underwater obstacles, particularly submarines. Continuing experiments at the naval establishment at Portland had perfected the device which by the outbreak of World War II had become standard equipment on all destroyers, corvettes and anti-submarine ships.

The patrol had settled down to a monotonous beat up and down a 5 mile stretch of calm sea between two buoys. Going into the radio cabin, I tuned in to the BBC and through the loudspeaker listened to Geraldo and his orchestra playing some of my favourite tunes. After half an hour of music I had a prick of conscience and decided that this was no way to win a war, so I tuned back to Dover Port War Signal Station. In Morse, I recognised our call sign and was soon receiving a coded message of a loop crossing. Using my initiative, I called our leading asdic operator, who was below decks, and suggested he come up to the bridge. Then on the blowpipe I reported the signal to the captain, Skipper Noble, who was in his cabin 'getting his head down'. In his broad Scottish accent he replied, 'auch awa', laddie, that's miles awa' from us.' Nothing daunted, a full asdic watch was set with both operators crouched over the darkened screen. Suddenly, and apparently from nowhere, a destroyer appeared about 2 miles away, its bow wave indicating that it was travelling at full speed. The Skipper abandoned his after-lunch 'kip' and climbed up to the bridge. The senior asdic operator reported his first echo. The crew closed up to action stations. I hoisted a very large red flag from the main halyard, the very first time I had had to do this. It meant 'we are going into action and commencing firing'. The asdic 'ping' grew louder and more frequent and I felt that the submarine must be directly below us. Our engine room was producing a maximum speed of 12 knots and I was exchanging signals with the destroyer on my Aldis lamp. The Skipper began a heated argument with the First Mate about the depth at which the firing pistols of the depth charges should be set. We were only a few miles off-shore in shallow water. They finally agreed to take the risk and fire the pattern of depth charges to explode at a depth of 50 feet. At the stern we had a rack which held five depth charges and on either side of the stern we had a single depth-charge thrower. The command was given: 'Roll one', followed by 'Fire port and starboard charges'. To our consternation the stern depth charge failed to explode but the other two made up for it. In less than a minute huge spouts of water rose high from the sea as the charges detonated. Our stern was lifted clean out of the water, the propeller clear of the sea continuing to revolve at our maximum revolutions.

As the chief engineer was to say later, 'We were lucky not to blow our arse off.'

We cruised around in a wide circle whilst I flashed a report to the destroyer, which by this time was disappearing over the horizon. The sea around us was covered with an oil slick with shoals of dead fish floating belly-up. We remained closed-up at action stations with the gun crew ready to fire should the submarine surface. We had lost our asdic contact but continued to search until darkness fell, then broke off the engagement and resumed our patrol. We felt somewhat deflated and the Skipper confided in me that he feared a court martial for wasting three depth charges.

Returning to Dover the following morning and whilst stowing my identification flags away in their locker, I could see a deputation waiting on the quayside. I visualised the Skipper, who was in the wheelhouse bringing the ship alongside, and probably myself as well, being led away to the cells in leg-irons. One of the officers was the Commander A/S (anti-submarine), who shouted up to me as I pigeonholed my last flag and asked what had happened on our patrol. Looking down on to the quay I shouted back and told him that we had gone into action following an asdic contact. His reply was, 'Good show, Bunts, you have bagged a sub. It's lying on the Goodwin Sands with its conning tower smashed.' (Signalmen are known as 'Bunts', an abbreviation of Bunting tosser because of their flags.) By this time the Skipper had emerged from the wheelhouse; and told me to follow him to his cabin with a list of all the crew.

In all previous wars the Navy had been rewarded out of a prize fund and prize money was as old as the Navy itself. Its operation was regulated by an Act of Parliament passed in 1708. Sailors pressed into the Service had to rely on prize money for their pay. If cargoes or merchant ships were captured, they were sold and the proceeds shared between the Admiralty and the crew of the captor ship. Similarly there was 'blood money' when an enemy man-of-war was captured or sunk. Skipper Noble was of the old school and still had memories of the procedure in the war of 1914–18. He told me that the blood money for a submarine had

84

been £1,000. He expected to get £200 out of this for himself; my share might possibly be £5.

After the war I learnt that the German submarine was the U.16 and the following Admiralty description of the action is taken from the archives in the Public Record Office:

U.16 a type IIB boat of about 300 tons under the command of Kapitänleutnant Horst Wellner, left Kiel on 16 October 1939 on what was to be her last mission, to lay mines off Dover. The last signal received by U-boat headquarters from the submarine was timed 0430 on 25 October 1939 and this reported 'seriously damaged off Dover. Must scuttle'. From British sources the exact circumstances of her loss appears that, acting on the report from a shore station concerning a probable contact obtained about noon on 24 October 1939, H.M.S. *Puffin* and H.M. Trawler *Cayton Wyke* carried out depth charge attacks. On the morning of 25 October 1939 the U-boat was found aground with badly damaged bows on the Goodwin Sands. By the time the storm had abated (the following day) the wreck had been swallowed up in the Sands.

There were no survivors.

The next day it was business as usual. We went back on patrol but sank no more submarines! There was no shortage of mines, however, bobbing up and down on the waves which were now being whipped up into white sea horses by a strong south-easterly wind. The mines that we did not explode with rifle and machine-gunfire were sent to the bottom of *Davy Jones'* locker riddled with holes and rendered harmless to the warships and argosies on the surface.

That night at anchor, the wind having increased to gale force, the anchor cable snapped and we drifted towards one of our own defensive minefields. It was a case of all hands on deck in pitch darkness with the wind screeching through the rigging whilst a new anchor was fitted. By now I had become accustomed to the sudden changes in weather and at all times to expect the unexpected to happen. I had become used to working around the clock. This was no nine-to-five job, no five-day week. We slept whenever we could, and more often I chose the wheel house floor in preference to my bunk in the converted fish hold. Whilst on patrol I never changed out of oilskins or thick duffel coat complete with full length sea boots. An inflatable lifebelt shaped like a sausage was invariably fastened around my middle. I was glad when, later on in the war, the Mae West jacket became standard issue. I was a changed man – I had turned into a sailor.

The monotony, the danger, the hardships were all forgotten when on arriving back in harbour mail was distributed. Sometimes there would be the surprise of a parcel, playing cards, a novel, a balaclava helmet knitted by loving hands, and more often than not a box of candy. The routine was broken when a signal arrived for me to report to Dover Port War Signal Station for two weeks' further instruction and duty. Whilst I was sorry to leave the ship, I relished the opportunity of 'stretching my legs' ashore and I was anxious to sit the examination that would see me promoted to signalman from the lower rank of *ordinary* signalman. I moved into Dover Castle.

The signal station was dug into the cliff face and was more than 100 feet above sea level. It was an eyrie commanding the whole of the straits and the French coast was visible through our powerful telescopes. Nothing could move on the surface without being detected, recognised and logged. I was kept busy sending and receiving messages flashed from the destroyers and other naval vessels in the Downs and the approaches to Dover. I also shared responsibility for one of the teleprinters and a batch of telephones linking us to Chatham, Dungeness and other bases. At midnight on one of my watches, I received a teleprinter alarm which required an officer entrusted with the password applicable to that hour to operate the machine. It was the Admiralty in Whitehall. Within hours Winston Churchill arrived at the castle to embark on the destroyer HMS *Brilliant* to pay his first visit to the Expeditionary Force in France.

As an ordinary signalman, I was in the lowest rank of the Senior

My parents on their engagement in 1902

Family group - 1925 - My parents, three brothers and sister Pauline

As an ordinary signalman - 1938

On board H.M.S. Southampton - August 1939

Motor Minesweeper 250

Sub-lieutenant Jackson RNVR
June 1941

Wedding day - 18 August 1943

MMS 250 - Ship's company

Chicken Inn - Leicester Square

Service. I now found myself, in Dover Castle, standing just a few feet away from the First Lord of the Admiralty – the veritable Controller of the Navy. Churchill was no stranger to that office. One of the first acts which Chamberlain initiated after his declaration of war on Germany had been to appoint Winston to this position with a seat in the War Cabinet. Churchill had finally come out of the political wilderness and history, as it so often does, had repeated itself. The outbreak of war in 1914 had found him occupying this top job in the Admiralty, only resigning from it the following year after the disaster of Gallipoli which he had masterminded. He was now standing in front of me talking to the duty officer. I saw a pugnacious white haired man of 65, puffing away at the inevitable cigar. He was dressed somewhat nautically in a navy-blue donkey jacket with embossed buttons bearing an anchor and wore a cap with a Trinity House badge above the peak. Dover was the centre of the group of ancient ports (Deal, Rye, Hythe and Winchelsea) known as the Cinque Ports, of which Winston was later to enjoy the honorary title of Warden.

I have had several heroes in my life and they have all had naval backgrounds. Firstly there was Horatio Nelson and then Admiral Beatty. On my bookshelves in Oxford I have no less than four different editions of the substantive work of *The Life of Nelson* by Robert Southey, the first edition having been published in 1813. My prize trophy is a book entitled *The Life of the Late Most Noble Lord Horatio Nelson Viscount and Baron Nelson of the Nile*. It was written by Archibald Duncan Esq. What makes it so special is that it was published in December 1805, less than three months after the battle of Trafalgar.

I had found it by accident some 10 years ago, whilst delving through a box of old and damaged books placed in the doorway of Thornton's, the antiquarian booksellers in Oxford's Broad Street opposite Balliol College. It had no spine or covers and it was the frontispiece and the date that caught my eye. It had been printed and published by James Cundy of Ivy Lane, Paternoster Row London and contained not only 'Accounts of the Brilliant Victories over the combined forces of the Enemies of England' but 'an official account of the ceremonies of his funeral' with numerous pull-out engravings, of the battle of Copenhagen as well as Trafalgar. On enquiring the price I was informed that I could have it for £15. I was thrilled but, despite my obvious excitement, I had the temerity to offer £12 because of its condition, an offer that was accepted with alacrity. My wife Freda (my daughter's mother-in-law whom I had married in 1987, two years after Peggy's death) rushed me round to Maltby's the bookbinder in St Michael Street to have it restored and rebound. We chose handsome blue Morocco covers with the spine being blocked in gold leaf. As it was a present to me she did not negotiate on the price. It cost £75 to recover.

It is a fascinating book as it records with complete authenticity eye-witness accounts of the engagement and graphic description of the death of my hero. Contrary to popular belief, Nelson's last words were not 'Kiss me, Hardy.' The book records that, mortally wounded, he lay in the arms of the *Victory*'s surgeon, Mr Beatty, to whom he said, 'I could have wished to have enjoyed this but God's will be done.'

'My Lord,' exclaimed Hardy, 'you die in the midst of triumph.'

'Do I Hardy? then God be praised.'

That Nelson was a religious man there can be no doubt. On the eve of battle, having already revealed his battle plan to the captains of his fleet, he retired to his cabin and wrote this moving prayer:

May the great God whom I worship, grant to my Country, and for the benefit of Europe in general, a great and glorious victory; and may no misconduct in anyone tarnish it; and may humanity after victory be the predominant feature in the British fleet! For myself individually I commit my life to Him that made me; and may His blessing alight on my endeavours for serving my country faithfully! To Him I resign myself and the just cause which is entrusted to me to defend ... Amen ... Amen ... Amen.

The victor of Trafalgar had lived more than a century before I was born and the Industrial Revolution was still half as long away on the distant horizon. Although Nelson was my boyhood idol the gap between us of so many generations made it difficult for me to identify with him as an individual. With David Beatty it was different. He was a man of my time, the very epitome of British naval tradition that went back in history to the origin of Britain's maritime supremacy, pre-dating the Elizabethan stalwarts Raleigh and Drake. Handsome, intrepid almost to a degree of recklessness – so often the hallmark of a great commander – he had a total disregard for his personal safety. Like Nelson, when in battle he placed himself in an exposed position the better to conduct the operation. Nelson at Trafalgar scorned to change out of his full dress uniform with its glittering set of epaulettes and insignia. In doing so, he fell victim to a sharpshooter on the maintop of the 80-gun French ship-of-the-line *Bucentaure* flying the flag of Admiral Villeneuve, commander of the combined French and Spanish fleets. In like vein and when in action, the fearless Beatty would station himself on the compass platform, high above the bridge.

I counted myself very fortunate when I acquired a first edition of the *Life and Letters of David Beatty* written by Rear Admiral Chalmers and published in 1951. His nephew Charles Beatty had presented it as a gift and had inscribed it to the writer Dennis Wheatley whose *ex libris* bookmark it bears. With this volume came a three-page letter which Beatty had written to his sister-in-law Lu, Charlie's mother, on Christmas Eve 1915, a few months before the battle of Jutland. It is written in black ink, in a bold hand, on notepaper embossed with the words 'Second Battle Cruiser Fleet'. The letter-heading incorporates the pennant of a vice-admiral depicting the Cross of St George with a black ball in the top left hand corner. Headed in David Beatty's handwriting 'HMS Lion', it goes on to commiserate with the troops who will have to spend a second cheerless Christmas in the trenches and expresses the hope 'that this terrible war will soon be over'. The letter had been delivered in an envelope bearing a King George V penny-red stamp, and carries the initials of the censor. Not even the Admiral had dispensation.

My third hero with a naval connection was Winston Churchill, who, surprisingly, was linked with Beatty at an early age. As a 22-

year-old war correspondent covering the River War after the fall of Khartoum and the death of General Gordon in 1896, he wrote an eye-witness account of gunboat operations against the dervishes on the river Nile. He singled out 25-year-old Lieutenant Beatty commanding the shallow-draught boat *Abu Klea* who so distinguished himself in action that he was decorated with an immediate DSO, narrowly missing being awarded the Victoria Cross.

9

A Sweeper of Mines

Through the Chief Yeoman of Signals, I had put in a request for weekend leave, which had been approved by 'Flags', the Signal Lieutenant. I was preparing to leave the castle when I was summoned to the signals office and informed that my leave had been cancelled. I was to report forthwith to HMS *Almandine*, a minesweeping trawler moored at one of the jetties in the harbour. I was learning the hard way how the Navy works.

I was bitterly disappointed not to be rejoining *Cayton Wyke*, having integrated so well with the crew despite a shaky start. Little did I know then that in posting me to *Almandine*, the Chief Yeoman had probably saved my life. I later learned that at approximately 0110 hours on Monday 8th July 1940 she was sunk by an E boat off Dover. Of the crew of 32 who, as my shipmates, had commissioned the ship in Blyth in the early weeks of the war, there was only one survivor. It was not Skipper David Forbes Noble, RNR; he went down with his ship, leaving a widow and eight children to mourn him. The crew's foreboding on learning that they were sailing to join the Dover Patrol had been well founded.

Almandine, like *Cayton Wyke*, had been a deep-sea fishing trawler and with very little modification had been converted to sweep mines. Sea mines had been evolving over a long period, and in the American Civil War Confederate-laid mines were responsible for the sinking of about 30 Federal ships. Originally mines were primarily used as part of harbour defences but they soon became an important element in offensive strategy. By 1914 each of the main protagonists had developed the mine into 'an engine of destruction', as it was originally described, and had commissioned purpose-built mine-laying flotillas. Within hours of the declaration of hostilities in 1914, a converted German mail boat, the *Königin Luise*, had laid mines off the Suffolk coast and was intercepted and sunk by a British destroyer. The following morning one of her mines was hit by the cruiser *Amphion*, which sank with the loss of 151 of her crew. Aggressive and unrestricted mine-laying soon became a feature of the war at sea. The most intensive mine-laying was to take place in the North Sea and in the Straits of Dover and many hundreds of merchant ships and warships fell victim to the underwater menace. Mining was to become so widespread that flotillas of minesweepers by the hundreds were needed to ensure that every day there was a cleared channel around the coasts of Britain. The main burden fell on the former fishing fleet. They did an exemplary job but the price exacted was exhorbitant.

I quickly adapted to a new routine and found the crew well-disposed to their new Bunts. The task of the minesweepers, usually operating in pairs, is to maintain a strip of sea clear of mines. This is known as 'the swept war channel' and all shipping approaching or leaving a port or harbour must proceed along this channel; to stray is to court disaster. The mine, containing about 350 pounds of TNT or amatol, is anchored to the sea bed by a heavy sinker tethered by a steel wire which, subject to the state of the tide, permits the mine to float about 10 feet below the surface, waiting for its unsuspecting prey. The minesweeper tows a serrated wire cable which is maintained at the required depth, at an angle of about 45 degrees to the ship's stern, by the torpedo-shaped paravane. This float rides the waves and ensures that when the towing wire comes in contact with a mine-mooring, it cuts through it like a knife passing through butter. Ships fitted to sweep these moored mines were known as Oropesa trawlers, and not infrequently the minesweeper became the victim when a mine was entangled with the sweeping gear and exploded under the ship's stern. This then was my new profession which I was to pursue for the next six years. I was no longer a hunter of submarines but a sweeper of mines. In the words reputedly used by Queen Victoria 'I was not amused'.

We operated between Dover and Shoeburyness. It was tricky navigation in shallow water and strong tides, with the treacherous Goodwin Sands as one of our boundaries. Waiting in long lines in the Downs were the convoys, protected by the maids of all work, the Fleet destroyers. From time to time we would be detached from minesweeping duties and form part of the protective screen, finding ourselves posted at the tail-end of the convoy because of our lack of speed. This position was somewhat jocularly referred to as being the 'coffin ship'. It was our job to rescue survivors or pick up bodies.

We continued to sweep the war channel up and down the Straits with some success but every day there were new sinkings. Rumour swept the flotilla that we were facing a new breed of mine for which we were not equipped and incapable of sweeping. Admiral Raeder had boasted of Hitler's secret weapon. This was it – the magnetic mine. The Admiralty had no antidote and until one of these new mines could be recovered intact could only conjecture how it worked. It became obvious that the mines were not moored but had been discharged on to the sea-bed from the torpedo tubes of a U-boat or parachuted into the sea by a Junkers 52 bomber or a Heinkel 115. Losses of ships soared and, as we could see from the deck of *Almandine*, the Thames estuary was blocked with ships unable to get into or leave London docks. The outcome of the war was in the balance and defeat stared us in the face. The Admiralty was working on experimental counter-measures, which *Almandine* was selected to try out. We found them to be a seaman's nightmare and completely ineffective. The sinkings went on for several weeks and then a miracle took place.

On the night of 22nd November 1939 in the mud flats of Shoeburyness at low water mark, only a few miles from where we were operating, two complete mines were discovered still tethered to their parachute harnesses. For a first-hand and eye-witness account of the events that followed, I am indebted to my friend the late Captain Ashe Lincoln, QC, RNVR, who at the time was a lieutenant and had been a practising barrister until his mobilisation at the outbreak of war. He had been recruited by Admiral Wake-Walker, the Rear Admiral of Minelayers at the Admiralty, to work on the new species of mine which was creating such havoc with our shipping. His brief was to unlock the secrets of its mechanism, neutralise its anti-sweeping devices and perfect counter-measures.

Lieutenant Commander J.G.D. Ouvry of HMS *Vernon*, the Navy's mine and torpedo base, was summoned to a midnight briefing at the Admiralty at which Mr Churchill was to be present. His orders were explicit. The mines had to be recovered *intact* at any cost. Accompanied by another *Vernon* officer, he set off immediately for Shoeburyness and as the tide fell they saw in the light of their torches a 6-foot-long cylinder. They were joined by a mine recovery team and armed with a set of non-magnetic tools made specially for this operation, they crawled along the mud flats. Gently unscrewing the cap of the first mine, they dismantled not one but two detonators. The whole operation took three hours and for every second of this time they were in mortal danger. The mines, having been rendered harmless, were then transported to HMS *Vernon*, where the process of unlocking their secrets was accomplished. Counter-measures and minesweeping techniques were rapidly designed and a system to protect shipping from the new mines was perfected. This was called 'degaussing', a process of neutralising the magnetic field of a ship, giving it a significant degree of protection from the no-longer 'secret' weapon. Hitler had been assured that this mine was a war-winner and would bring Britain to its knees. He had good grounds for assuming this to be the case as the Germans themselves had tried for years, before launching their mining campaign, to work out sweeping techniques for their own magnetic mine and had failed. His Chiefs of Staff, however, had not reckoned on British ingenuity, resourcefulness and, above all, courage.

For *Almandine* and the flotillas of minesweeping trawlers there was no respite. Virtually the whole of the eastern coastal waters of Britain from Dover in the south to the Pentland Firth in the north of Scotland had become one vast minefield. As the year drew to a close we received sailing orders to proceed and set up a naval presence at Peterhead, about 30 miles north of Aberdeen.

New Year's Eve 1939, the last Saturday of the year, saw *Almandine* ploughing its way northward through a rough North Sea. We were due to pass Flamborough Head Lighthouse at midnight and the Skipper had asked me to 'first-foot' for him. He was a Scot from Wick in the County of Caithness at the very north-eastern point of Scotland, whilst I was a Sassenach, a London Cockney completely ignorant of the rites of Hogmanay. I turned to the Coxswain for guidance. He told me to go down to the bunkers (like all the trawlers we had steam engines), select a large glossy lump of coal and take it to the Captain's cabin at the stroke of twelve. With much trepidation I approached my initiation and at the witching hour knocked on the door of his cabin. At a bellowed 'Cummin' I stumbled out of the dark night into his brightly lit quarters filled with the ship's petty officers – Scotsmen all. 'A happy Hogmanay' rang out and I was soon grappling with a large tot of whisky whilst pocketing the half-crown he handed to me in exchange for the coal. I asked the Captain why he had chosen *me* to help him to greet in the New Year and to explain the significance of the lump of coal. He told me that it was considered lucky for a dark stranger bearing something black to be the first over the threshold. As my head was covered with a thick mane of black wavy hair and most of the remainder of the crew were showing differing shades of grey, I was the automatic choice to bring him and the ship good luck. I cannot claim that I brought the ship good luck, but she came to no harm during the time I served aboard.

My first glimpse of Scotland was of a prison. It appeared to dominate the small harbour of Peterhead as we steered towards the entrance and the Mole protecting the harbour from the cruel sea. Grey granite and menacing, the jail could share with Alcatraz the boast that no one ever escaped from it, but the inmates must have had the best sea-view of any jail in Britain. The only other prominent building on the skyline was a Crosse & Blackwell canning factory which processed the locally-caught herring and pilchards. As for the rest, Peterhead was the typical small Scottish fishing port with its cottages built from the silver granite hewn from the surrounding mountains within a stone's throw of the jetty. The war had not yet made any impact on this outpost of Britain. The inshore fishermen still went out in their small motor boats, trailed their lines hundreds of yards long, and returned with the prime haddock and cod that had impaled themselves on their myriad hooks. The drifters still followed the shoals of herring that from time immemorial had swum south from the Orkneys passing Peterhead and Aberdeen some 40 miles away. These boats became a constant and most generous source of the freshest fish any one of us had tasted.

Our orders were to patrol southward to Aberdeen, part of the time being spent in minesweeping and part in reporting any suspicious event – meaning a submarine sighting. Our main adversary did not speak German. It was the weather. The prevailing north-easterly wind, usually with gale force, blew down without hindrance from the Arctic Circle bringing sub-zero temperatures and whipping up mountainous seas. Every departure from harbour was hazardous and, on one occasion when the Skipper considered the weather too bad to continue with our patrol, it took us an hour to cautiously perform a 180-degree turn and, with a following sea, to finally find shelter behind the breakwater. The winter of 1940 is down in the record books as one of the coldest of the century and, for the three months that *Almandine* was based in Peterhead the snow lay unmelted in the streets; I was witness to the fact. It was the only time in my life that I found it necessary to wear two pairs of thick serge trousers.

Our patrols took us regularly to Aberdeen, Scotland's busiest and largest fishing port. Fifty years before its fortunes were so dramatically changed by the discovery of North Sea oil, its economy was based on fishing, particularly herring which was exported in huge quantities to Russia and the Scandinavian countries. The packing and salting in large oak barrels was the exclusive province of a special breed of women known as 'herring lassies'. Wearing leather aprons rendered as stiff as a board with the accumulation of salt, and thigh-length sea boots, they had the physique of Japanese *Sumo* wrestlers. Their arms bulging with biceps that left me quite envious, they would gut and pack herring with the speed of light. I would stand on the quay for hours watching them at work whilst reflecting on their fearsome sexual reputation. For the latter intelligence I relied on my shipmates who had served in deep-sea trawlers and who, as doughty and sexually active as any sailor, would not tackle an Aberdeen herring lassie no matter how desperate they were 'for a woman'.

The 'phoney war' ended on 8th April 1940 when German forces invaded Norway, landing troops at Trondheim and Narvik. Taken by surprise, the only assistance Britain could give initially was through bombing raids whilst units of the Fleet were detached to attack the German troopships. The two ships in which I had served before the war, the aircraft carrier *Furious* and the heavy cruiser *Southampton*, were soon in action in the North Sea. Meanwhile the German battlecruisers *Scharnhorst and Gneisenau*, covering the landings of their troops in Norway's fjords, had engaged the battleship *Renown*, and the short-lived Norwegian Campaign had begun. The effect on *Almandine* was immediate. We were ordered south to Grimsby to join the force assembling for a counter-attack. Because of the mountainous hinterland, roads were few and communications and traffic followed the sea lanes. Command of the sea was therefore essential if we were to help Norway, the first neutral country to be attacked since Hitler had overrun Poland.

I was now back in the Humber, where for me the war had started nine months – or was it nine years – earlier, so much had been crammed into such a short space of time. We entered the dockyard and emerged with our armament significantly enhanced! Now when at action stations I was to man a newly fitted twin Lewis machine gun instead of the single-barrel Lewis gun previously mounted. A wireless telegraphist ('Sparks') was added to the ship's complement, which gave me more time to keep charts and code books up to date.

A boiler-clean having been completed and with several dockyard 'maties' still on board finishing off various jobs, we left

Grimsby docks and ventured into the Humber to swing compasses, the term given to adjustments to the ship's magnetic compass housed in a binnacle in the wheel house. I was appalled to discover that the workmen were earning more per day than I was being paid for a whole week. To add insult to injury, they were entitled to a special 'danger allowance' for every hour they spent on board whilst we were in the Humber estuary. Job demarcation was another feature that raised my ire. On one occasion the ship was prevented for three days from sailing because a simple attachment to our degaussing gear, which encircled the ship and rendered it safer against magnetic mines, had to be fixed. Any carpenter or handyman could have done it but as it fell within the purlieu of an electrician, no other tradesman was allowed to touch it. The job took 45 minutes to complete. Such was the bargaining power of the trade unions even whilst a war was raging.

Almandine formed part of a small flotilla of four minesweeping trawlers all of similar tonnage. Our sister ships were *Goth*, *Elbury* and the flotilla leader *Sea King*, commanded by Lieutenant Robert Harvey RNVR. Looking back, I can recognise that this period was the most hazardous and most arduous of my whole wartime service. A shortage of ships, but not of mines, meant that we had to perform lengthy sweeps entailing four or five days at sea at a time, returning to harbour for a few hours solely to coal and provision. We would then sail and resume our job.

Life on board was hard and miserable. The forward mess deck where I had my bunk was frequently awash with sea water coming down the main hatch. Meals such as could be prepared in the tiny galley with the ship rolling and pitching were basic and we often ran out of provisions. On one occasion our signal requesting permission to return to base for re-provisioning was refused. An empty lifeboat, floating despite damage to its hull, was brought alongside and its store of emergency rations salvaged. Despite the fact that our own ship's biscuit infested with weevil was inedible, none of the crew would eat anything from the lifeboat exclaiming, 'What, eat dead man's food?'

* * *

The war was going badly. I recall going up to London on a short leave whilst our ship entered dry dock to be specially fumigated. We had been plagued by swarms of bugs emerging from the old wooden planks of the former fish hold, now the seaman's mess, and every one of us bore marks of their bites. On the train journey back to Grimsby the carriages were full of soldiers returning from Dunkirk. They were beaten men and the all-pervading air of despondency that they could not hide made me apprehensive that, despite Prime Minister Churchill's bluff speeches exhorting us to fight on the beaches, we could well lose the war.

I had a brief encounter in Liverpool Street Station with my friend John Hendeles. He told me that his destroyer, HMS *Anthony*, had done five round trips to Dunkirk, all the time under intense bombardment from the shore and from the Luftwaffe. He left the detail to my imagination but commiserated with me, saying that I had a worse job than he. I disagreed as I knew under what conditions the destroyers operated. Constantly in the front line, in the heart of the battle, they would be attacking the enemy head-on or escorting a convoy that had attracted a swarm of U-boats drawn to it like wasps to a pot of honey. I would not have changed places with him, even though by July 1941, one year after our meeting, no less than 362 mines had been blown up in the Humber alone and four of our minesweepers sunk.

From time to time it had been suggested that I should apply for a commission. I invariably refused to take the necessary steps, preferring to stay on the lower-deck and qualify for promotion as my expertise in signalling improved. Then came the episode that made me change my mind.

It was 9th October 1940; we were at sea, returning to Grimsby after a four-day routine sweep of the war channel with *Almandine* second in line astern of the flotilla leader *Sea King*. It had been blowing a full gale and we were glad when we entered the Humber estuary to find smoother water. Suddenly *Sea King*, only 2 cables (400 yards) ahead of us, was engulfed in a sheet of flame and a huge spout of water. She had struck a mine and was sinking fast.

I was on the bridge with the Skipper and the Coxswain and heard him give the order 'Full astern'. I turned to him and said, 'You must mean Full *ahead*.' 'Full *astern*,' he repeated to the engine room and wheel house. I could not believe my ears. I could see men clambering on to the main mast and hanging on to the 3-inch-high angle gun mounted on the fo'c'sle as *Sea King* with her stern blown off sank lower into the water. Their screams '*Almandine*, *Almandine*,' were to haunt me for months. I said to the Skipper, 'Go alongside or at least jettison our Carley Float upstream.' He did neither and within half an hour we had docked in Grimsby, dry and safe, but of the 26 crew of *Sea King* only four survivors were picked from the ice-cold estuary by a passing pilot cutter. In his report Skipper Alex Robb said that he believed that there were more mines in the vicinity and that *Sea King* had gone down so fast it ruled out any attempt at rescue. This statement was so economical with the truth, and I was so shocked, that I decided that I would get off *Almandine* as soon as I could organise a transfer. Within a week I had requested a 'white form', the application papers for a commission.

Thirty-eight years were to pass before, in a book of wartime minesweeping experiences entitled *Out Sweeps* by Paul Lund and Harry Ludlam, I read the account of Lieutenant Harvey, the flotilla captain and one of the four survivors of *Sea King*. Captain Minesweepers Grimsby had radioed his ship to the effect that six magnetic mines had been laid the previous night in the approaches to Grimsby. Five had been swept and it was the last of the six that *Sea King* had triggered off. The signal had not been repeated or passed on to the other ships of the flotilla. This still did not exonerate the Skipper of *Almandine*. I wrestled with my conscience as to whether I should make an independent report to a board of enquiry, which would inevitably be followed by a court martial. In the event I did nothing and failed my dead comrades of *Sea King*. By speaking out now, although nearly 60 years late, I feel I have exorcised a ghost.

The winter of 1940 drew on with no let-up in the enemy's mining campaign and our sweeps and patrols in fog and storm ranged southwards to E boat Alley and northwards to Bridlington, a happy hunting ground for the Luftwaffe. Exploding one magnetic mine often produced sympathetic explosions from others in the vicinity, producing a devastating chain reaction. The Germans had now introduced even more sophistication into their magnetic mines loaded with nearly a ton of a highly effective explosive; they were being set with highly sensitive mechanisms to counteract the degaussing effect. The casualties in the mine-sweeping flotillas operating out of the Humber grew week on week and crews were depleted by those sent ashore for psychiatric treatment.

Whilst waiting for the outcome of my application for a commission, I registered as a student at the Grimsby nautical school. For a modest fee paid out of my own pocket I enrolled for a course of lessons in navigation and pilotage which had been designed for fishermen aspiring to qualify for a Board of Trade's Second Mate's ticket. Whenever we came off patrol for a few days respite I attended the school, and managed to pass the examination.

One day *the* signal which I had been anxiously awaiting for months arrived. 'Signalman Leslie Jackson Official number L/D 3828 to present himself to Admiralty Selection Board at HMS Victory, Portsmouth'.

I said farewell to all my shipmates, except Skipper Robb, and left Grimsby and the Humber for good and without regret.

10

An Old Sea Dog

Of the three major naval dockyards on the south coast, Chatham, Plymouth and Portsmouth, I consider the last as being pre-eminent, despite my affection for Plymouth, the home of Sir Walter Raleigh and of Drake. When King Henry VIII laid the foundations of our maritime power it was Portsmouth that built our fighting ships. It was from Portsmouth on 19th July 1545 that the ill-fated *Mary Rose*, the 91-gun pride of the Navy, sailed to do battle with the French fleet anchored outside the harbour, only to capsize in full view of her Commander-in-Chief, King Henry, with the loss of most of her 415 crew. This ignominious event was further compounded when the French were able to withdraw to the Isle of Wight, land at Sandown and, as an act of bravado, set fire to some villages.

I was billeted in H Block in the naval barracks, ready to appear before their Lordships the following day at noon. In the early hours, an air-raid warning sounded and the block was evacuated into adjoining shelters. Inadequate early warning resulted in shrapnel and bombs already falling on the dockyard and barracks as we ran to a shelter. Given the all-clear, we returned to H block. As I re-entered the barrack room, originally built to accommodate 200 naval ratings but now crowded with 500, the foetid smell hit me like a blow to the face and I vomited. Sleep was out of the question; I was relieved when the trumpeter sounded Reveille and I could get out into the open air and help with shifting debris from bomb-damaged buildings. I was excused this fatigue after two hours to prepare myself for the interview.

With much trepidation I faced an array of gold lace in the persons of a Rear Admiral, a Commodore and two captains whose searching questions were aimed apparently at ascertaining whether I was officer-material and possessed leadership qualities. They came to the conclusion that I had a modicum of both and decided that I was a risk the Navy could afford to take. Given time and instruction I could be transformed from being just a rating to an officer and a gentleman so they despatched me as a cadet to HMS *King Alfred* in Hove.

Lancing College was to be 'my ship' for the next three months. Enjoying a commanding position overlooking the Sussex coastal town of Worthing, the school had evacuated its boys when war broke out and filled the vacuum with aspiring naval officers. The sudden transition from the danger and rigours of serving on a minesweeping trawler to the comparative luxury of the school is hard to describe. To sleep in a bed that did not move; to be waited on at meals by bright young waitresses; to be addressed as 'sir'; the simple luxury of successfully lathering a face not encrusted with sea salt; to have a choice of menu devoid of any hint of canned corned beef; all contributed to the illusion that I had arrived in Paradise, and on my first church parade to the school's impressive chapel, I offered up a silent prayer of thanksgiving.

Under the eagle eye and strict discipline of a band of hardened chief petty officers we were instructed in the martial arts of 'square bashing' and drill. Navigation, gunnery and seamanship formed the basis of the curriculum to be covered in three months instead of the customary three years at the naval academies of Dartmouth and Greenwich. The reward for success in the examinations was to be commissioned as a non-substantive/temporary/acting sub-lieutenant in the Royal Naval Volunteer Reserve. The penalty for failure was the option of being sent back to the lower deck or volunteering to be a mine-disposal officer. Neither of these two propositions held any attraction for me or for my fellow cadets so we all marched, drilled and navigated until we dropped exhausted into bed. Once a week there was a diversion from the usual routine as one of our duties was to defend the realm by patrolling the Worthing foreshore at night. Dressed in full marching order, armed with a short Lee-Enfield rifle with a long bayonet and sufficient ammunition to slaughter a whole platoon of Germans, I stood sentry on a 100-yard stretch of Albion's shore. On hearing any sound other than the waves lapping on the pebbles, my instructions were to thrust out my gun and challenge the darkness with the command 'Halt, who goes there?' Getting a reply, I was to say, 'Advance and be recognised.' No one had thought of giving me the German translation of this dialogue, so it was just as well that my hundred yards of beach was not the enemy's focal point for his threatened invasion.

The examination results came and I had scored 700 marks out of a possible 1,000. I was sent on leave with a bank draft for £50 to finance the purchase of uniforms and all the accoutrements of a naval officer. On 12th June 1941 I was commissioned as a sub-lieutenant (temporary). All wartime commissions were specified as being 'temporary', meaning that they were only for the duration of hostilities. In this way the regular peace-time naval officers were kept reasonably pacified against the intrusion of landlubbers into their exclusive domain. As a further sop to the regular Navy there was an embargo on promotion to the rank of Lieutenant Commander of an officer who had not yet attained his thirtieth birthday. I was destined to serve at sea in the rank of lieutenant for more than three years, ending my naval service in command of the 142nd Minesweeping Flotilla. Other officers of considerably less seniority were promoted to the higher rank with no qualification other than that they had passed the magical age threshold of 30.

I was no longer on the lower deck. I was now an officer and a gentleman. I was entitled to be saluted and called 'sir' by even the most hardened chief yeoman of signals in whose dread I had lived for so long. I now had to learn how to put a gap between myself and the ratings. I was now to experience the sweet taste of privilege.

The Navy could not turn me into a gentleman. They assumed it was in my genes and they could concentrate their efforts on turning me into an officer – a naval officer. To commence I needed to learn how to shoot; not pistols or rifles but real guns. My first posting was to Whale Island, the Navy gunnery school in Portsmouth. I was allocated a small cabin and came down to the mess on the first morning to behold an unexpected and wonderful sight. Officers were sitting at long refectory tables being served breakfast by stewards in white jackets. The remarkable aspect of this was that each officer was reading his chosen newspaper from a small music stand propped up in front of him. I not only approved but thought this must be the height of civilised conduct.

Gunnery instruction was soon to shatter any illusion I might have entertained that the Navy was just intent on giving me a five-star holiday. I became part of a gun team practising on a 6-inch monster. On one occasion I had been kneeling on my left knee, having handed a cordite charge to another member of the gun crew, when it slipped out of his hands and landed on the top of my head with such force that the cut needed several stitches to prevent any of my brain oozing out. Instruction went on for a week, seven intensive days spent on the firing ranges and in the classroom. I was taught about high explosives, armour-piercing shells and their trajectories, what to do when a shell got jammed in a gun barrel – without instruction my instinct would have been to get as far and as quickly away as possible. Armed with a Webley service revolver, I was taught how to fight in enclosed spaces, to crouch behind doors of a ruined building and burst into a room with my gun blazing. How to strip down and reassemble machine guns and pistols, place detonators in grenades and prepare demolition charges. All very useful stuff I kept assuring myself, without any real conviction.

There had to be compensations. Every night I dressed for dinner, revelling in my new uniform with its single wavy gold stripe on each sleeve. Dinner was served in the Mess with a Marine band in the background playing light popular classical music. If not actually forbidden, certain forgotten foods appeared as if by magic. Oranges and chocolate bars were available in abundance and not rationed. Was there no end to this state of bliss? Unfortunately there was, and my stay in the land of plenty came to an end with a draft to HMS *Lochinvar*, the Navy's Torpedo and Mining base outside Edinburgh on the Firth of Forth. Their

Lordships had decided that my previous experience should not be wasted and that I should serve as a minesweeping officer. I now needed to be taught how sea mines were laid and how to sweep magnetic, acoustic and pressure mines, all variants of the moored mine on which I had metaphorically cut my teeth. There were many devices built into its mechanism to render the new mines more difficult to sweep. I had to learn about the different kinds of explosive and detonators that were fitted in torpedoes as well as mines. Once again there were compensations.

I soon discovered that Edinburgh was not a faraway outpost of London, but a sophisticated city very attractive to a young officer despite competition from Polish officers prancing around and dressed up as if for some comic opera. Wearing cavalry breeches, their uniform jackets with nipped-in waists (I suspected they wore corsets), their faces made up with talcum and rouge we all felt uncomfortable in their company.

Several of my brother-officers and I were invited to be the guests of the hospitable Christian Salveson family in their fine mansion in Edinburgh. The Salvesens originated from Scandinavia and their fortune was founded on shipping and transport. Their home became an open house for us where we were always certain to find pretty Scottish socialites. One of them took my fancy and we became friends, enjoying the cinema and dancing when I was off duty and she could be spared from her voluntary work of serving refreshments to the armed forces passing through Edinburgh's Waverley Station. Whilst walking down Princes Street one day she pointed to the ramparts of the castle high up on the Mount, saying casually, 'I live up there and that's where Daddy works.' I thought no more of it, and the fact that her name was Hamilton had not meant any more than having to take a lot of banter from the other young officers, who taunted me with 'Nelson had a Hamilton, now Jackson's got one.'

One fine evening we were going out to dine in the city and she had asked me to pick her up from her home. Arriving at the door of a terraced Georgian house, I rang the bell which was answered by a maid who asked me to wait in the hallway. I idly looked at a silver salver on a fine Regency table and nearly fainted when I

106

noticed a visiting-card on top which read 'Sir Horace Hamilton – Under Secretary of State for Scotland'. It nearly spoilt my evening, before it had begun. When I asked her why she had not told me, or rather warned me, she passed it off, saying, 'It doesn't really matter, or does it?' I was surprised to find that not only did it not matter but it did not worry me and we continued to meet on every occasion that I was off duty until, having completed my course, I was ordered to Plymouth to join HMT *Sir John Lister*, a minesweeping trawler, as First Lieutenant. We said our farewells and never saw one another again.

On 10th September 1941 I arrived in Plymouth and proceeded to Devonport dockyard, which I had last viewed from the deck of the aircraft carrier HMS *Furious* some three years earlier. Then I was a callow youth with aspirations of becoming an accountant. Now I had been turned into an old sea-dog, 24 years of age, bloodied in war and about to become the First Lieutenant of a minesweeper. My instructions were to report to Captain of Minesweepers, whose office was in the former French battleship FS *Paris*, which had escaped from Cherbourg just before it was occupied by the Germans. I was about to meet a man for whom I was to develop the deepest respect, even affection. Captain G.L. Hodson, RN, had turned 60 years of age and on the outbreak of war had come out of retirement to do the job he knew best. He was an authority on mines and torpedoes. His brother, a well-known Appeal Judge in the Royal Courts of Justice, must have been very proud of his brother the sailor, twice decorated with the Distinguished Service Order. Captain Hodson, his white hair set off by a ruddy weather-beaten complexion, greeted me kindly and told me that I had been appointed to HMT *Sir John Lister*, whose commanding officer was Lieutenant David Pearson RNR.

I was intrigued by the name of my new ship as I had been with many of the colourful names given to former fishing trawlers and as a result had done some research as to their origins. There was a fleet of 17 minesweeping trawlers, all with the prefix 'Northern' such as *Northern Gem* and *Northern Pride*, and whilst operating out of Dover and Grimsby I got to know them well. The whole fleet had been purchased by the Admiralty from Lord Leverhulme, Chairman of the conglomerate Unilever Ltd, whose interests included the ownership of McFisheries, a chain of fishmonger's shops. Ironically the ships had been built in Bremerhaven at the mouth of the river Weser in northern Germany and had been acquired by Unilever in settlement of a debt or as part of a barter deal. My first thoughts were that the *Sir John Lister* had been named after the renowned pioneer in the field of surgical antiseptics, but as *his* name was Joseph and he had been ennobled, I am not so sure today that my attribution was correct.

Sir John Lister was to become my home for two years and Davy Pearson was not only to be my mentor in everything nautical but also a surrogate father. His home was a small croft in Vidlin, a remote village 20 miles north of Lerwick in the Shetland Islands – the most northern outpost of the British Isles. Bleak and forbidding, life there was as harsh and cruel as the weather. He had a wife, a son named after him and a daughter, a nurse in Lerwick Hospital who was the apple of his eye. The sea was in his blood as it had been in many generations of his family. As master of tramp ships before the war, he knew every major port in the world and whilst he was away at sea his wife looked after the smallholding of two cows and a few sheep which created a spartan self-sufficiency. His time between trips would be spent cutting peat, the only fuel the homestead would have for cooking and heating during their cruel winters.

Davy Pearson taught me all the fine points of seamanship: how to splice ropes and wire, how to navigate using a sextant and by dead reckoning, to forecast the weather by interpreting cloud formations, what to do when blanketed in thick fog with nil visibility when, sailing in total silence, one was deluded into thinking that the sea was made of cotton wool. He was an inveterate pipe smoker and he taught me how to make a plug of tobacco from tobacco leaves moistened with a solution of molasses and rum and rolled so tight in a square foot of ship's canvas that a blow from a pound of leaf could kill. For his pipe he would slice the plug very fine, but it served a dual use as chewing tobacco. On the bridge at night the act of lighting up a pipe might have resulted in our being blown out of the water. For fun we spoke to one another in pidgin English, in the same way that he used to converse with Chinese dockers and coolies on the wharves of Shanghai or Hong Kong.

'Number One,' he would say, 'you savvy the rat?'

I would answer, 'Yes, me savvy the rat.'

To which profound remark he would then say, 'No have cheese, rat him savvy the cheese.'

He was fond of quoting Robert Burns. One of his favourite mutterings when we were in a tight and dangerous spot or when heading into a gale with the bow of the ship completely engulfed, and he had draped himself around the binnacle compass to steady himself, was to scream into the wind, 'Ye hoor o' hell, I ken ye well.' For the two years we served together he never once addressed me by my first name or even as Lieutenant Jackson. It was always 'Number One'.

The capitulation of France in the summer of 1940 had made Normandy and Brittany virtually provinces of Germany, placing enemy airfields within 30 minutes' flying time from the south-west coast of England. My arrival in Plymouth shortly after a heavy air raid left me in no doubt that the dockyards had become a prime target, and the advent of a full moon was invariably accompanied by a resumption of the Blitz that had already devastated the town centre. All the main utilities had been disrupted by the bombing to the extent that fresh water now had to be supplied through canvas fire hoses laid in the street gutters. Homes were without their supply of gas and domestic cooking was carried out on small Calor gas stoves. Every night half the population, packed into open lorries and overcrowded buses, would migrate to Dartmoor, induced to leave either through fear of renewed bombing or because they had been rendered homeless.

The minesweeping flotillas were based in Millbay Docks, which, in happier times had been the point of departure for the tenders that ferried passengers and their luggage to the transatlantic liners anchored in Plymouth Sound. The task of *Sir John Lister* was to sweep the war channel, starting at the Eddystone lighthouse and ending in Plymouth Sound, overlooked by the Hoe on which, legend has it, Drake delayed his sailing to confront the Spanish Armada in order to complete a game of bowls. To the east we were responsible for the channel as far as Dartmouth and to the west to the Cornish port of Falmouth. It was less arduous than minesweeping in the North Sea and the weather very much kinder; furthermore, the Devon and Cornish harbours were much more attractive than those on the east coast where I had spent the first two years of the war. Hit-and-run raids on shipping by Fokker Wolf aircraft had now become quite commonplace and on one of them I had a grandstand view. One sunny day in the early afternoon whilst anchored in the estuary in Falmouth, I had occasion to attend to some defect high up on the mast. Hearing the roar of engines, I looked down to see two German fighter planes below me coming in at almost sea level, firing their cannons before dropping a stick of bombs. I shinned down the mast so fast that I left most of the skin of my hands on the wire stays.

From time to time we would patrol westwards up to the Bristol Channel, but the approaches to Falmouth, a great natural harbour and used by vital oil tankers, was the western limit of our minesweeping responsibility. I enjoyed coming into Falmouth and tying up to the quayside, always mindful of the strong tides that gave rise to a fall of 35 foot in the sea level between high and low tide. The importance of Falmouth to our war effort was greatly increased after the fall of France which, in addition to the Channel ports, had given the Germans control of the great French harbours of Brest and Cherbourg where they had established vast submarine pens whose U-boats had open access to the Atlantic and the convoys sailing in from the United States.

Going ashore in Falmouth I would walk along the quays studying the shipbuilding activities that were going on. An ex-American destroyer was obviously being fitted out for special duties and I went on board, cautiously making my way across a deck criss-crossed with hosepipes and shipyard tools, to find a very spacious ship that made my own minesweeper appear tiny by contrast. Her name was *Campbeltown*.

Shortly before the war the blue ribbon of the Atlantic had been won by the great luxury French liner *Normandie* and an exceptionally large dry dock had been constructed especially for her at St Nazaire. Following the sinking of the *Bismarck*, the even more powerful German battleship *Tirpitz* had become operational. A nightmare scenario for the Admiralty was a *Tirpitz* let loose on our Atlantic convoys from a safe haven on the west coast of France that commanded the approaches to the English Channel. A hazardous and daring plan was drawn up by the naval staff and passed to Admiral Mountbatten, the Chief of Combined Operations. To forestall the use of St Nazaire by the *Tirpitz*, the lock gates of this dry dock would need to be destroyed and the facilities of the harbour denied to other major units of the German Navy. To my mind it was reminiscent of the Navy's heroic action against the port facilities of Zeebrugge during the First World War.

For months I had walked along the quay to see *Campbeltown* and then one day she had gone. Many months passed before I learned that she had been the centrepiece of this suicidal mission. The work I had watched with such interest was the preparation for her to ram the lock gates of St Nazaire. The fore-part of the ship had been reinforced and then packed with three tons of high explosive. Delayed fuses had been fitted, timed to blow up two and half hours after impact. Sailing from Falmouth in the late afternoon of 26th March 1942 on her last and epic voyage of 400 miles, together with 16 motor launches armed with torpedoes, and carrying troops and commandos she achieved total surprise. The enemy's defences were penetrated and at 0134, *Campbeltown* rammed the lock gates and embedded her stem firmly into them. The troops and commandos landed and, whilst facing intense fire at point-blank range from German troops, went about their task of demolishing the dock facilities. As luck would have it, the charges on the *Campbeltown* failed to go off until noon, about eight hours late, very soon after a large number of German officers had gone on board to examine the ship. The operation was a complete

111

success although it cost the lives of 140 brave men, nearly a quarter of the task force. The Navy likened the operation to that of Sir Francis Drake who, 350 years previously, had penetrated the stronghold of Cadiz harbour and 'singed the King of Spain's beard'.

The war at sea had been going badly. The Battle of the Atlantic, as crucial to our survival as the Battle of Britain had been, looked as if it was being lost to the U-boats, which like wolves were hunting in packs. On 24th May 1941 the German battleship *Bismarck*, before being destroyed herself, had sunk the battle-cruiser *Hood*, the pride of the Royal Navy and considered by all to be invincible. Out of a crew of 1,324 men and 95 officers, only one midshipman and two sailors were rescued. The shock ran through the whole Fleet and everyone felt bereaved. Then a month later probably the most dramatic and decisive event of the whole war took place: the German invasion of Russia, code-named 'Barbarossa'.

The sense of imminent danger had passed and feeling that we had been sidetracked into a backwater, I began to develop a guilt complex. Our minesweeping patrols had become routine and were far less hazardous than those I had been involved in on the east coast. There, in addition to the high concentration of mines being laid every day by submarine or aircraft, we had been under constant threat from E boats at night and dive-bombers by day. One morning a Dornier 'flying pencil' had approached the ship as dawn was breaking. I mistook it for the morning star, only to be brought back to reality by a stick of bombs falling too close for comfort. At night we had navigated in a sea filled with flashing green buoys marking the graves of ships, fully expecting at any moment to run into a marauding pack of E boats, the very effective fast German motor gunboats. When things got really bad I took comfort from repeating silently to myself a conviction I had forged, entirely fictional and without foundation of course, that whatever happened around me, I was immune. It would not be *me* who would get killed – *I* was a survivor.

The intensification of the war at sea was being brought home to me through letters from my two closest friends. Fred, who had survived the sinking of his patrol yacht, was now serving on the destroyer HMS *Fury* and wrote to me with graphic details of his exploits among some of the most hazardous convoys of the war, those from Reykjavik in Iceland to Murmansk in northern Russia. It was mid-winter in the Arctic Circle, with very few hours of daylight and atrocious conditions at sea. Spray immediately froze on the ship's rigging, adding the danger of capsizing to those posed by the enemy, and their guns were constantly iced up as the destroyer ploughed through mountainous seas. He described the ten-day running battle fought by convoy PQ13 sailing from Reykjavik on 20th March 1942, which has gone down in naval lore as during its voyage the German battleship *Tirpitz* was lured from its shelter in a Norwegian fjord to join the German attacking force of warships, aircraft and submarines. It was miraculous that only a quarter of the convoy was sunk and in the running engagement, his ship *Fury* destroyed U585. He went on to recount that having fought their way through, against incredible odds, the crews of the Allied ships were made to feel like prisoners, confined to the harbour perimeter and not permitted to go ashore in Murmansk. Short of food and before facing an equally hazardous return trip to Iceland, *Fury*'s reward for their bravery was to be grudgingly given a few sacks of potatoes by the ever suspicious Russians.

I also got to hear of John's exploits on HMS *Anthony*, which was now part of Force H in the Mediterranean. The Japanese had swept through South-East Asia and the Allies were apprehensive of their continuing to advance westward, threatening India. The island of Madagascar, fortified and defended by Vichy-controlled French troops, was strategically placed to command the southern Indian Ocean. An invasion force under Admiral Syfret had been successful in taking control of the southern section of the island but was then held up by a superior and entrenched enemy. An attack behind the enemy lines through Diego Suarez to the north was planned to break the deadlock and HMS *Anthony* was chosen to undertake this daring mission. The ship's captain, Lieutenant Commander Hodges, briefed the crew over the loud hailers and explained the plan. He did not mince his words and told them that there was every likelihood that they would be sunk and that in effect they would be embarking on a suicide mission. To achieve surprise they would need to attack under cover of darkness. *Anthony* would, at full speed, enter the harbour, which was mined and heavily fortified, and land a force of 50 Royal Marines. As they steamed through the pass without accurate charts, they were at first undetected, but when the shore batteries opened up, *Anthony* went in with all its guns blazing. The Marines were landed and forced the surrender of the French defenders. Madagascar had been saved for the Allies.

It was whilst serving on the aircraft carrier HMS *Furious* that I first became aware of the privilege enjoyed by the Navy of buying goods, particularly tobacco, free of excise duty. This applied only whilst the ship was at sea. I had never smoked cigarettes before but was now tempted to try out the duty-free system by going to the NAAFI shop on board and asking for a packet of Woodbines and a box of matches. I put sixpence down on the counter and waited. I was then asked for a further halfpenny, which I tendered, and was handed a packet of 20 cigarettes and a wrapped parcel which, on being opened, I found contained not one but ten boxes of Bryant and May matches.

Despite their cheapness, I did not become addicted to cigarette smoking and can recall the very few times that I succumbed to the habit. The most memorable occasion was whilst on patrol off Harwich when a stick of bombs dropped by a Stuka dive-bomber scored a near-miss whilst I was on the bridge manning the twin Lewis gun. When you know that the aircraft is aiming at you specifically, it has the effect of concentrating the mind wonderfully well. The attack completed, the only adverse effect being a good drenching, I turned to the Coxswain, saying, 'For God's sake give me a fag.' I did, however, take up smoking a pipe and after being commissioned found pleasure in smoking Scott's No. 1 Burmah cheroots – 4½ inches of jet-black tobacco leaf. The cheroots, packed in a cedar box and tied into a bundle of 100 by a yellow ribbon, cost the munificent sum of 30 shillings, equivalent to 1.5p for each cheroot. After the war, and as an even greater indulgence I substituted Monte Cristo No. 2, the torpedo-shaped Havana cigar which I consider to be the finest cigar on the market. I smoked in moderation, and then only on those occasions when I could be joined by a friend. It would never occur to me to 'light up' when I was alone.

On a ship with a crew of only 25, the First Lieutenant becomes involved in many diverse activities that in a bigger ship would be dealt with by a paymaster – the clerical branch of the Navy. One of these was victualling – or ordering food for the ship's company. On board *Sir John Lister*, a steward, in conjunction with the cook, would do the ordering from naval stores whenever we were in harbour. It fell to me to purchase duty-free cigarettes and tobacco for the crew, and alcohol for the wardroom for the use of the Captain and myself. Our requirements would be purchased from a ship's chandler who would supply us direct from his bonded warehouse, located on the quay and within sight of the Customs House, where a vigilant watch was kept for any attempts to bring duty-free goods ashore. I felt that customs officers placed petty smuggling on a par with spying for the enemy, so rigorous were their physical inspections when sailors went ashore.

The only alcoholic beverage that a sailor was permitted to imbibe on board was his daily tot of rum, which in *Sir John Lister* was taken by all members of the crew. They disdained to be categorised as teetotal even though the inducement was to receive an additional three pence per day in lieu. On small ships and in flagrant disregard of Admiralty regulations, the rum was served neat and not diluted with the prescribed two parts of water. It was, however, even in the small ships, an offence for the rum to be saved up from day-to-day. It was meant to be consumed as soon as it was dispensed. Those sailors who were not partial to drinking rum would endeavour to save up a pint bottle of the neat spirit. Ashore it was a very tradeable commodity. Stripped of excise duty, the cost price of cigarettes was 3p for a packet of 20 Players, whilst a 75cl bottle of gin cost 20p.

I purchased our allocation of cigarettes and liquor from Dunstan & Co., prominent ship chandlers, whose bonded warehouse was situated in the Barbican just off Plymouth Hoe. I was surprised when meeting American naval officers to learn that liquor was not allowed on any of their ships. This embargo probably originated from the time that Prohibition was introduced in the United States early in 1920, a law that remained in force until rescinded some 13 years later, completely discredited. My American colleagues envied our privilege and took every possible opportunity of enjoying my offered hospitality based on pink gins and whisky sours. I would send them a signal which commenced 'R.P.Y.C. (request the pleasure of your company) on board at — hours'. They would arrive laden with frozen chickens and delectable canned fruits.

Alcohol featured in several of my enduring memories. When my ship was tied up to the jetty in Millbay docks, I was awakened early one morning by a loud hammering on my cabin door. Still in pyjamas, I opened the door to be confronted by a giant bearded blond Viking, a skipper of one of the whalers that had been operating with our minesweeping flotilla. These very sturdy ships had been adapted from their pre-war role of whale-catching in the Antarctic to the even more arduous task of cutting mines in the English Channel. He was unshaven and dishevelled, his eyes red and bloodshot, but he wore his Norwegian naval cap at a jaunty angle. I asked him what I could do for him. He replied with a monosyllable: 'Yin', which I interpreted as 'Gin'. I was soon to find that this was the only word the giant could utter, so I led him into the wardroom, eased him into a chair and placed in his clenched hands a large tumbler into which I had poured nearly half a pint of neat Gordon's gin. Gin was supplied to us with a proof strength of 86% alcohol compared with the normal 40% available now in supermarkets and off-licences. His hands and fingers were rigid and it was as much as he could do to grip the glass and slowly lift it to his lips. As the spirit trickled down his throat I was amazed to see his whole body relaxing. He finally placed the glass, emptied of its life-restoring elixir, on to the wardroom table and exclaimed, 'Now I go to sea', and with these five words departed as swiftly out of my life as he had entered it.

On another occasion I was summoned by my Coxswain to the Petty Officers' mess, where I was confronted by a macabre sight. One of the engineer petty officers, together with a leading seaman, was slumped over a wicker-covered demijohn which had originally contained about half a gallon of neat navy rum and was now empty. They had been fighting one another and blood was running from deep scratches on their faces. Neither was capable of speech and they were obviously in an advanced state of *delirium tremens*. I ordered the Coxswain to wrap them from head to toe in blankets and have them put in bunks. They remained unconscious for 48 hours and when they were capable of understanding the charge, I gave them the option of a court martial or a summary sentence from me, whilst leaving them in no doubt that they had narrowly missed dying from hypothermia. They declared a preference for judgment from me, consisting of a loss of 14 days' leave and pay. In reality a very modest price to pay for such an offence when on active service.

11

Naval Engagements

Without realising it at the time, I was now approaching the most important milestone of my life and, despite the passage of time, these events remain evergreen in my memory.

I had heard on the grapevine that the Plymouth Hebrew Congregation operated a small social club for members of the armed forces who were billeted in the city, where the daughters of congregants spent their weekends providing light refreshments. The highlight was afternoon tea on Sundays served in the vestry of the beautiful small synagogue just off the Hoe which had been built in the mid-eighteenth century. It was Sunday 14th February 1943 and I found myself being offered a cup of tea by a slim blonde with the true Devonshire complexion, all peaches and cream and no make-up. The father of one of the girls had called to take his daughter home and arranged to give a lift to my tea-server, whom he addressed as Peggy. At the same time he extended an invitation to me to visit his club for a drink, so I accepted. Together with Peggy I sat on the back seat of his car and on arrival at her house I too jumped out, making a feeble excuse to the driver that I would like to join him for a drink on some future occasion. Invited in, I met her parents and asked permission to take their daughter out for dinner. I could see the apprehension on their faces and I was quick to assure them that we would not be late, attributing their concern to the fact that it was full moon and an air raid was a strong possibility.

All the major decisions I have made in my life have been of an impromptu nature, having relied on 'gut' feeling to quickly assess the pros and cons. I had already made the decision that this was the girl I wanted to marry; the moment of truth, in fact, having come in the synagogue vestry when she had asked me whether I would like sugar in my tea!

On returning to her home, on the doorstep of the house I said, 'Have you got a kiss for a lonely sailor?'

'No,' she replied.

'Go on,' said I, 'it's Valentine's day.' So, pursing her lips, she let me kiss her once and we made arrangements to meet again ten days later after my return from patrol.

Those ten days seemed to drag on interminably until we were back in harbour and she accepted my invitation to come on board, which gave me the perfect opportunity, in our tiny wardroom, to propose. I did not do it on one knee, but so as not to appear to be over-hasty I hedged it with a *caveat* 'let's get married when the war is over'.

Her reply was, 'It's OK with me right now.'

The only problem that remained, or so I thought, was how to break the news to her parents. We mutually decided to keep it secret for a whole fortnight. They duly gave their blessing, we formally became engaged and the wedding was fixed for Wednesday 18th August. Wednesday was the preferred day for weddings in a community dominated by retailers, as it was Plymouth's half-day closing.

As the day approached I became increasingly worried.

Stalin had been placing Churchill under increasing pressure during the whole of 1942 to open a second front. The German armies were storming relentlessly eastwards towards Moscow, whilst our own land battles raged in North Africa. The Prime Minister knew that we were, as yet, ill-prepared to undertake a frontal assault on a powerfully entrenched enemy across the English Channel but had to appease Stalin and at least go through the motions of preparing an invasion armada. The threat of invasion had to be seen to be real if it was to have the desired effect of tying down divisions of the Wehrmacht that otherwise would be employed on the Eastern Front.

Sir John Lister was taken off minesweeping duties and given a role of towing Thames barges up and down the Channel from Plymouth to London Docks. The strongly built barges were long and capable of carrying several hundred tons of cargo. They had to be towed in pairs on a bridle of very thick wire hawsers. They were cumbersome; being empty, they rode high in the water and made slow progress in the strong tides we encountered. Each barge was manned by two soldiers of the Royal Army Service Corps. They had a lonely job, even a hazardous one when, on one trip made in a howling gale, the tows parted and we were extremely lucky to find our way in pitch darkness into the port of Newhaven at midnight. When I think of those RASC soldiers I hope they made it.

As 18th August, my own personal D Day, drew close, I asked Peggy if her mother had invited many guests to the wedding reception. She replied, 'About fifty,' and then asked me why I wished to know the number.

I said, 'I want to know how many cancellation letters she might need to send out because I'm not so sure I'll be there.' A normally quiet, placid and reserved girl became hysterical and it took all my tact to pacify her.

For some weeks, whenever we were in harbour, we had been under 48 hours' notice for steam. This meant that the fires in the engine room could not be doused and the boilers had to be ready in just a few hours to enable us to sail. We had to be in constant readiness for action and shore-leave was out of the question. Every evening a messenger would arrive from the Commander of Minesweepers, bringing with him the sailing orders for the following day. The duty officer on board would have to sign for them. Invariably they would be headed 'in all respects being prepared for sea and ready to meet the enemy you will, at first light...' followed by detailed orders for the channels to be swept, giving their latitude and longitude.

Late one night I was aroused from my bunk by Davy Pearson asking for the sailing orders for the morning. I told him that there were none, and was he not pleased that we were having the day in harbour? He then produced the signal which he told me he had pieced together from fragments thrown into the wastepaper basket in the wardroom. Apparently I had no sooner signed for them than I had absentmindedly torn them up and thrown the pieces away. It brought home to me that not only was love blind but it could be the most powerful of forces.

The Captain had condoned my stupidity over the sailing orders but not long after, tragedy struck. He received a telegram from his wife asking him to get compassionate leave and return home immediately. This was granted but it took 48 hours to get to the Shetlands, by which time his beloved and only daughter, stricken with influenza, had died. He returned to *Sir John Lister* a changed man. I became aware of this most forcibly on the following patrol when he did not come onto the bridge for two days. I felt confident in my ability to handle the ship and at first was not over-concerned, but on the third day I forced my way into his cabin to find him slumped over a table littered with empty whisky bottles, unshaven and gaunt, reading a large family Bible. The smell of singeing was all-pervasive as a result of his having set fire to the hair on his chest. It was a situation I did not know how to handle and thought that only the passage of time could act as a healing balm. The day before the wedding I left the ship with a heavy heart, fearful for this wonderful and brave man who had seen me through two horrendous years.

The 18th of August dawned and I had been granted two weeks' leave, my first for more than a year. My brother Cyril, who at the age of 37 had joined the Army the previous year, was to be my best man. By a stroke of good fortune, HMS *Anthony* with leading signalman John Hendeles on board had called in to Devonport the previous day and he was able to join me on the happiest and proudest day of my life. Peggy had written to 15 seaside hotels in Devon and Cornwall to reserve our honeymoon suite. Of these, only one had not closed for the duration of the war or been requisitioned by the Forces. The Imperial Hotel in Exmouth confirmed that they would welcome us for two weeks, ending their letter with a reminder to bring our ration books. But there was a problem. Local train services had been curtailed and the last direct train to Exmouth via Exeter left Plymouth at 6 p.m. There was, however, a train that would take us to Totnes, tantamount to a half-way house, enabling us to complete the journey to Exmouth the following morning.

Following a tea-dance at the Continental Hotel in Millbay, my mother-in-law, Phoebe, had planned a wedding reception for close friends and members of the family to be held in her home. For the main course of her menu she had decided to offer ox-tongue braised in Madeira wine, an unusual choice, but offal, although in short supply, was not rationed. A friendly butcher promised to take care of this and two days beforehand had delivered the tongues to her sister's house, where she was to store them until required in a very large refrigerator she had in her kitchen. That night there was a devastating air raid with an unexploded bomb sealing off the road where our precious ox-tongues were languishing in the cold. It took all of Phoebe's undoubted charm and cajoling to get the ARP wardens manning the barricade to allow her a fast run into the house and an even faster one back, clutching the bag of tongues.

Escaping from our wedding guests, after making our abject apologies, we caught the train to Totnes and duly arrived at the reception desk of the Seven Stars Hotel. I signed the hotel register with a flourish, and for the very first time wrote 'Lieutenant and Mrs Jackson'. 'Sorry,' said the receptionist, 'we are fully booked and we have no reservation for you.' We were nonplussed until Peggy produced the hotel's confirmatory letter, when she realised she had booked the room for the night in her maiden name.

When the honeymoon was over, we returned to Plymouth. Reporting to base, I found that *Sir John Lister* had gone off to the Bristol Channel and I had been temporarily replaced as First Lieutenant. Captain Hodson greeted me back and asked after Peggy. Then with a puckish look on his face asked me how a month ashore, acting as Minesweeping Officer of Dartmouth, would appeal to me. I would be relieving a Lieutenant Commander of the Royal Navy who had not had any leave since being called back from retirement at the outbreak of war. I responded with such enthusiasm that within an hour we were on our way.

Even in wartime, Dartmouth had not lost its charm as one of

Devon's most attractive harbours. Sited at the mouth of the river Dart, which meanders from the sea for 7 miles until it reaches the market town of Totnes, it nestles in its estuary surrounded by lush Devon hills and cliffside farms. It is also remarkable in a further respect; it has a railway booking office but no trains. One has to cross over the Dart by ferry to Kingswear to catch a train. To the Navy, Dartmouth is synonymous with the Royal Naval College – the *alma mater* of so many generations of naval officers. I had got to know the approaches to the harbour and the channel as well as any Devon fisherman. Many were the times when, approaching the harbour in thick fog with visibility down to just a few yards, we would clear the entrance and having crossed the bar find the town bathed in glorious sunshine.

The month passed only too quickly. Returning to Plymouth, I was greeted with a signal requesting me to report to the Commander at Millbay Docks who informed me that I had been appointed to my first command – a motor minesweeper. I was not prepared for the news and started to remonstrate with him. I told him that my ship-handling experience had been with triple-expansion coal-burning trawlers and I had no knowledge of the wooden-built diesel-driven motor minesweepers. Furthermore, my *forte* was cutting moored mines and not sweeping magnetic mines lying on the sea bed. The Commander was curt in his dismissal, saying, 'You cannot refuse the King's Commission. Motor Minesweeper 250 is lying in the basin and you will relieve Lieutenant Chambers in command. You sail at first light tomorrow morning.'

MMS 250, which was to be my home for two and a half years, had been in service for no more than two months. Built entirely of Canadian timber in a shipyard on the St Lawrence river, she was powered by two parallel Fairbanks Morse diesel engines and fitted out to sweep acoustic as well as magnetic mines, the latter by streaming from the stern, at a safe distance of about 400 yards, a massive copper wire cable encapsulated by protective rubber sheathing through which intermittently passed an electric current generated by a hundred car batteries. The electric current was converted into a powerful magnetic field mirroring that which a very large ship would create on the sea bed. Relying on the low signature created by our own wooden hull and the efficiency of our degaussing, we would be able to pass over the magnetic mine and explode it at a safe distance. That was the theory and most of the time it worked. In addition to creating a magnetic field, a ship's propellers leave an audio signature on the sea bed and it was for this characteristic that the acoustic mine had been designed, to add to the already awesome range of underwater weapons. To sweep this latest type we had a rather Heath Robinson contraption of a very large steel bucket which, set in a triangular frame, would be lowered from the ship's bow. Inside the bucket was a Kango hammer which beat against a diaphragm at the rate of 3,000 times a minute. The resultant vibration simulated, well ahead of the minesweeper, the propeller noise of a ship the size of an ocean liner. Thanks to the ingenuity of the scientific boffins at the Admiralty, these contraptions proved to be the answer to Hitler's vaunted secret weapons.

For protection against hostile aircraft we carried twin Oerlikon guns manufactured in Switzerland, a country not averse to doing business with both sides of the conflict. This is called neutrality!

My crew, numbering 21 including several volunteers from Newfoundland, were considerably younger than those I had previously sailed with. They referred to me as 'the old man', the colloquial, and often affectionate, name given to the captain of a ship. I was 25 years old, in a happy ship and I revelled in my command.

By Christmas 1943 one could sense a turning of the tide. There was a perceptible feeling that the fortunes of war were at long last beginning to go in our favour. In the east, the Germans were inexorably being pushed back from the vast Russian territory that they had conquered and occupied. Victory had been achieved in North Africa, and although the Allies were bogged down in their offensive in Italy, Mussolini had paid the ultimate price for having backed the wrong side. The Americans had geared up their vast industrial capacity to meet the logistics of a war being fought out on a global scale, and whilst in the midst of a take-no-prisoners campaign in the Pacific to avenge the treacherous attack on Pearl Harbor, they had been building up a formidable invasion army for Europe. However, Operation Overlord, the code name given to the second front which a vociferous Stalin was demanding almost daily, was still in the planning stage. The Russian bear had sought specific undertakings when the Allied commanders met in Teheran in November but Churchill and Roosevelt knew, but did not disclose, that we were still six operational months away from being in a position to launch Operation Overlord.

I became adept at the new minesweeping techniques and MMS 250 continued to maintain swept channels into Plymouth and Falmouth with opportunities for Peggy and me to meet in-between patrols. At sea a quickening in the tempo became very discernible in the early spring. This was particularly noticeable in the area of Dartmouth, where American troops in gathering strength, together with hundreds of landing craft, had begun to concentrate. At the end of May it was obvious that D Day was not far off. Dartmouth was ringed by a tight cordon of security. Telephones were tapped and monitored and outgoing mail, always subject to censorship, became delayed. Ships' crews were confined on board and when the necessity arose for me to report personally to base, having been rowed ashore, I was invariably met on the quay by a shore-based officer who escorted me wherever I went – even to the toilet – until I returned to my own ship.

The first landings had been planned to take place on 5th June but a gale had sprung up in the Channel and raged throughout the previous night, threatening to disrupt the finely-tuned and precise timetable. I recall Dartmouth being lashed by rain and hail and knew that the plan to land on the Normandy beaches would have to be aborted. In all the Channel ports an immense Allied armada had been concentrated and many units were already at sea. Now it had become impossible for the tank and infantry landing craft to make the crossing and discharge troops in combat readiness on to the beaches. Hundreds of minesweepers (but not MMS 250) were standing by to spearhead the invasion and sweep safe channels for the battleships, cruisers and destroyers that had to provide fire-cover for the troops as they landed.

Next morning, as if by a miracle, the skies cleared and as dawn was breaking the landing craft, jammed with GIs or Jeeps, had started on their journey to the sea in an unending stream down the 7 miles of the river Dart. As I watched this procession of armed strength flowing down the narrow river, not unlike a stream of lava down the side of a volcano, I was filled with feelings of awe mingled with foreboding for the troops packed shoulder to shoulder in their open and vulnerable boats. The following day, 7th June, 23 hours after the first beach-head in Normandy had been secured, my ship was heading back to Plymouth.

Within hours of tying up in Millbay Docks we received a signal to return immediately to the Dartmouth area; a German aircraft had been detected dropping mines in Torbay by parachute. Two American troop carriers, each with a Division of men and their equipment, were held up unable to move out of their anchorage in what had now become a danger zone, but still only 5 miles off the Devon coast. We went back to clear a safe channel for these ships. Markers, in the form of dan buoys, were laid in a line from Brixham to Torquay. We swept this channel and signalled the freighters to follow whilst we led them into deep and cleared water. They proceeded on their way to the hotly contested Sword beach, where the Americans were suffering heavy casualties.

For the week that followed, MMS 250 conducted an intensive magnetic and acoustic search and exploded three magnetic mines. Despite our success, I still felt guilty on finding myself off the Devon and not the Normandy coast, knowing that other minesweeping flotillas were not only facing the hazard of mines but were being subjected to constant attack from shore batteries as well as from the Luftwaffe. We were not destined to participate in the great mine clearances of the French and Belgian ports as they were being recaptured by our troops, and we continued to sweep off the Devon and Cornish coast.

Brooklyn is a long way from Normandy. I was on leave in London when I heard that my cousin Marvin Greenberg, who had been born in New York, was lying wounded in an United States military hospital in Oswestry, just on the Welsh border. I went to visit him. His bed was in a long Nissen hut with a score of cots on either side, all occupied by post-surgical cases, many of them amputees. Marvin, a captain in the US Army, had been a tank commander fighting in Normandy with General Patton's armoured division. They had been edging their way towards St Lo', fighting for every yard of a road screened by high hedgerows, when his tank received a direct hit from a shell fired from the dreaded German 88-mm gun which had already proved devastating against Allied armour. Marvin was wounded and had been evacuated to England with a hole in his thigh into which, he told me, one could put a fist. I was astonished to see not only how cheerful he was, but the high morale of his fellow officers in the ward. All he wanted was to return to his unit and continue to serve under 'two-pistol-packing' Patton; his leadership was magical. But for Marvin Greenberg the war was over and he was eventually invalided back home to Brooklyn. In his honour I named my son David Marvin when he was born the following year.

12

The Last Days of the War

The battle of the Ardennes during Christmas 1944, the last German offensive in the west, took the Allies by complete surprise and nearly succeeded in rolling them back from the banks of the Rhine to Antwerp in Belgium. I was told by an English girl attached to the medical section of the American army and working in Paris at the time, that the position was regarded as being so serious at SHAEF (Supreme Headquarters American Expeditionary Force) that the American command started burning documents in preparation for a possible withdrawal. Air superiority was re-established when the weather dramatically improved, and the German advance was reversed. The Allied offensive resumed early in the New Year, establishing several bridgeheads across the Rhine, and rolled into Germany's heartland despite having to fight, often hand to hand, for every town and village.

April witnessed the last inglorious days of the Third Reich as it passed ignominiously into history amidst scenes of unparalleled destruction. Germany had been marginalised in the air, and its surface fleet and U-boats had become bottled up in ruined harbours and bombed-out submarine pens.

The best hope that the German soldier had was to be captured by the English or Americans rather than to fall into the hands of the avenging Russians, who had adopted a 'take-no-prisoners' policy.

Isolated German naval units at sea began converging on our coast with the intention of surrendering, their Commander-in-

Chief Adolf Hitler having committed suicide at 3.30 p.m. on Monday 30th April in his Berlin bunker.

I received a signal to sail to a point some 60 miles to the south west of the Eddystone lighthouse and intercept a large German minesweeper heading towards Plymouth. Embarking a boarding party of ten armed marines, I was to prevent the German crew from scuttling their ship and escort it into Devonport. I was excited at the prospect of seeing the enemy I had been fighting for six years, face to face for the first time.

I spent half an hour looking up in an English/German dictionary certain nautical phrases to supplement my rudimentary knowledge of the language. Having reached the rendezvous and boarded, I posted a detachment to the engine room and around the decks and climbed up to the bridge with my coxswain. I saw a fair-headed bearded officer of my own age and equivalent rank at the top of the ladder, his cap worn at a jaunty angle and a pair of Zeiss binoculars around his neck. I then made a tactical error which I later regretted. Addressing him in German I said, '*Sprachen Sie Englisch?*' (Do you speak English?), to which he replied, '*Nein, kein Englisch*' (No, no English). From then onwards I gave all my orders in German until we berthed in Devonport. Going down to his cabin, and with the same arrogant attitude he had adopted all day, he now addressed me in perfect unaccented English with the words 'Well, and what do we do now?' I was furious and decided that I would continue speaking to him in my ungrammatical German. I rounded on him saying, '*Sie sind ein verfluchter Hund*' (You are a dirty dog) – I was using the same expression I remembered hearing Hitler use on the radio before the war at one of his infamous rallies, whilst screaming a torrent of abuse and invective against '*die Juden*' (the Jews). He took a packet of cigarettes from his desk and offered me one. I declined, but noted with amazement that he was holding a packet of Senior Service manufactured by Gallaghers and each cigarette was rolled in paper printed with the words '*H.M. ships only*'. I was left to conjecture how he had come into possession of cigarettes that we could only buy through a NAAFI.

News was only now beginning to filter through describing the

Nazi concentration and extermination camps that were being overrun in Germany and occupied Poland. I had but one question to ask him and said, '*Sie Sind Nazis, Was haben Sie mit den Juden in den Konzentrakonslagern gemacht?*' (What have you Nazis done to the Jews in your concentration camps?). He was taken aback and reverting to speaking in German he replied, '*Ganz* (all) *Propaganda.*' Then pointing to a framed photograph standing on the cabin table of a young woman with two children, he enquired, in English, when did I think he would be reunited with them? Continuing to speak to him in German, I asked where they lived and on receiving the reply 'in Hamburg', I got my revenge. My German must have been good enough for he got the message when I replied, 'Hamburg? Well, *if* they are still alive, then perhaps in seven years' time.' Only then did the supercilious mask fall from his face. He sat in his wardroom a dejected figure until, together with his officers and crew, he was marched off into captivity – but not before I had relieved him of his pistol and the pair of magnificent Zeiss binoculars, which I appropriated as my spoils of war.

The following day I had the opportunity to board a U-boat that had surrendered. I went aboard as the German crew were being taken ashore. Going down the cockpit ladder into the heart of the submarine, I was hit by the most obnoxious stench. The Germans had invented, during the war, a tube to which they had given the name of Schnorkel. Just as a submarine's periscope enabled the crew to reconnoitre the surface whilst remaining submerged, so the schnorkel allowed the submarine to draw fresh air into the boat whilst it cruised well below the waves. Air and oxygen are vital not only to sustain life on board but to recharge the boat's batteries. The submarine, according to its log, had schnorkelled for 45 days, during which time it had remained submerged and its rubbish had accumulated. To have discharged it would have given its position away to any scouting RAF Catalina or Sunderland flying boat.

Victory in Europe (VE Day) was proclaimed on Tuesday 8th May. A Deed of Unconditional Surrender had been signed by the

Germans the previous day, with the provision that the cessation of all hostilities would come into effect at midnight. The war against Germany was over throughout the world with the exception of a tiny part of the British Empire, in fact the only part of the British Isles to be occupied – the Channel Islands. Here, ever since 1st July 1940, a powerful enemy force of 30,000 troops, dug in and protected by massive reinforced concrete bunkers, their heavy guns covering the sea approaches to the islands, had every reason to feel themselves impregnable and they were ready to die for their Führer. We had heard of the privations which the islanders had suffered, their only link with the outside world being through the International Red Cross, on whose occasional food parcels they had become almost entirely dependent. In those heady early days of May 1945 we did not realise how near they were to famine.

VE Day brought orders for MMS 250 to join Task Force 135, which had been assembled in Plymouth for the liberation of the islands. Our role was to sweep a cleared channel for the armada of ships that was to follow. Accompanied by three of my flotilla (I had now become senior officer of the 142nd Minesweeping Flotilla) I was ordered to rendezvous with the advance force, consisting of the destroyers *Beagle* and *Bulldog*, off Les Hanois lighthouse on the Guernsey coast, which we reached under a full moon at 0300 the following day. I was told to anchor and await further orders. As dawn broke I could clearly see through my binoculars a German gun crew closed-up at an 8-inch naval battery sited on the headland. We were sitting ducks. We waited and waited. At 0715 the German commander of Guernsey, Admiral Hoffmeier, reluctantly signed a deed of unconditional surrender, using a rum barrel on the quarterdeck of HMS *Bulldog* as a desk. A signal was flashed to me to proceed and enter St Helier harbour in Jersey on the flood tide. The harbour entrance had been filled with concrete blocks that would have ripped out our ship's bottom had we tried to go in on the ebb – the tide had a range of nearly 40 feet.

I shall never forget the next 24 hours. MMS 250 was the first ship flying the white ensign of the Royal Navy to have entered St Helier since the occupation had begun five years earlier. We

tied up at the pier next to the Customs House, where hundreds
of islanders had gathered. They all wanted to come on board
at the same time, with the result that we took on an alarming
list to starboard. The jubilation and the emotion of the moment
were tremendous. I recall giving the young children wrapped
sweets whilst reassuring them that they were edible – they had
never seen a sweet before. On going ashore we were followed,
like the Pied Piper of Hamelin, by a long line of youngsters.
My fellow officers and I had filled our gas mask cases with
cigarettes, tobacco and chocolate, and as we walked into town
we handed these out to passers-by. It was a strange sensation to
move through the streets and be saluted by German soldiers, still
armed, many of them on motorbikes and going about their daily
routine.

The shops in St Helier were empty. Out of town I recall lines
of Polish and Russian slave labourers trudging along the country
lanes. Looking gaunt and pathetic, their feet bound in rags, on
seeing me they pointed to their open mouths repeating over and
over again the word '*Niet*' (the Russian for 'nothing'). Meanwhile
horsedrawn farm carts loaded with hessian sacks were being
driven into town filled, I was told, with German occupation money
which the farmers would be allowed, within a certain limited
period, to exchange into sterling.

Sweeping a mine-free channel proved to be a difficult
navigational exercise. I found that the fast-flowing tides frequently
ran faster than my ship could speed through the water whilst
towing our minesweeping cable. When, at low tide, large outcrops
of rock were uncovered in the approaches to the harbour, it served
to concentrate the mind on the dangers of a navigational error,
particularly in periods of poor visibility. Using the swept channel,
the transports arrived and commenced the embarkation of the
German occupation troops, taking them back to prisoner-of-war
camps in England.

As a 'Liberator' of the Channel Islands I have had the pleasure
of being the guest of the Jersey States when they celebrate their
Liberation Day on 9th May. Their grandest one yet was the fiftieth
anniversary in 1995 when Prince Charles attended and was fêted

in St Helier by the entire population of Jersey. The opportunity was taken to get HRH to inaugurate the newly created Liberation Square, in the centre of which had been erected a striking sculpture commemorating the occupation and deliverance. In brilliant sunshine, the unveiling ceremony was attended by many survivors of Task Force 135 proudly wearing their decorations. My attention was drawn to a small group of ex-servicemen in whose midst stood a most attractive lady wearing two medals pinned to her jacket lapel, neither of which I could identify. I strolled across the square and with temerity asked if she could tell me about the medals as I had not seen them before. With great modesty she explained that one was the George Cross and the other the Croix de Guerre avec Palme. I was speaking to Tania Szabó, the daughter of Violette, who, as one of our secret service agents (Special Operations Executive – SOE) was captured by the Germans, tortured in the notorious prison at Ravensbruck and then shot by firing squad in January 1945. She was only 23 years old. The story of her short life has been recorded for posterity in the 1958 film *Carve Her Name with Pride*.

I told Tania that I was about to go to a reception and *Vin d'honneur* to be held in the open air with Prince Charles as the honoured guest and I would very much like her to accompany me as I felt sure he would like to meet and talk to her. With true modesty she said, 'But I haven't been invited', to which I replied, 'But *I* have, and that's good enough'.

Forcing our way through the throng, we positioned ourselves so that as he passed down the line of guests we could not be missed. I made the introduction and, as I had forecast, the Prince was obviously happy to talk to Tania. He, of course, immediately recognised the medals and asked Tania whether she attended the annual dinner given to the holders of the Victoria Cross and of the George Cross. Without waiting for her to reply, he then added, 'No, of course you would not as my grandfather invested you with the decoration as a posthumous award.' I have for long been an admirer of Prince Charles for his undoubted ability, his wide range of interests and the genuine enthusiasm with which he embraces causes which he considers are good for the public weal.

We do enjoy *something* in common – we have both commanded a minesweeper.

Tania accepted an invitation to join me and some friends for dinner that evening at my hotel, L'Horizon in St Brelades Bay. I felt privileged to hear from her an account of her mother's bravery and understood her anguish at having been left an orphan at the age of two. Her father, Étienne Szabó, an adjudant-chef in the French Foreign Legion, was killed in action in the North African campaign at Bir Hakeim near Tobruk.

Very recently I was the proud recipient of a photograph of Violette inscribed to me by Tania. At the top of the photograph was a poem which was written as a secret code and given to Violette by Leo Marks, cryptographer-in-chief of the SOE, for her last and tragic drop into occupied France. I found it so moving that I was given permission to repeat it here.

> The life that I have
> is all that I have
> and the life that I have
> is yours.
>
> The love that I have
> of the life that I have
> is yours and yours
> and yours.
>
> A sleep I shall have
> a rest I shall have
> yet death will be
> but a pause.
>
> For the peace of my years
> in the long green grass
> shall be yours and yours
> and yours.

Advancing into Germany, our troops had uncovered huge caches of forged five-pound notes. These had been printed by the Nazis with the intention of destabilising our economy. As soon as the forgery was discovered, the Bank of England withdrew the genuine notes from circulation, thus ending the longest period that a banknote had lasted; in its unchanged form it had been in circulation since 1793. From 1st March 1946 the old and much-loved large white 'fiver' ceased to be legal tender; but was given a short reprieve and reissued later as a similar note, slightly larger than the previous one, but with a metal thread incorporated in the crisp white paper which literally rustled as it was counted. Like its predecessor it was printed in monochrome on one side only, the reverse being left blank.

I have always been interested in money – I can think of no other reason for my having chosen to become an accountant. The acquisition of money *per se*, however, was never my goal – it never became an obsession. Unlike many of the 'captains of industry' I was to meet in later life, I refused to make Mammon my god.

One of my hobbies has been numismatics, coin collecting. My first purchase shortly after the war was a silver half-crown of Elizabeth I. Its cost was only five shillings (double its face value when minted more than four centuries earlier, but enjoying a vastly greater purchasing power) and for its age it was a fine specimen. In 1973 I had built a villa overlooking the Roman aqueduct in Caesarea in Israel, a city founded by King Herod and named after his royal master, Augustus Caesar. I had visited Spinks in Duke Street, St James's, famous for medals and ancient coins, and purchased a silver denarius, a coin which was the pay for one day of a Roman legionnaire. With this coin he would have to keep himself in food and maintain his arms and accoutrements. The state of the coin was '*fleur de coin*', meaning that it was in mint condition and had never been in circulation since it was struck in Lyons, France in the year 11 BC. On one side was a magnificent portrait relief of a young and handsome Augustus and on the obverse was the date 'Act XX'. To my surprise, the salesman was able to give the coin a precise date, explaining that it referred to the twentieth year after the battle of Actium, which, fought in 31 BC, had decided the fate of Mark Antony and Cleopatra. I discovered that for a mere £90 I had bought 2,000 years of history.

13

A Fishy Business

I was demobilised on 24th December 1945 and a week later was back at my desk in the offices of Wilson Bigg & Company trying to bridge an absence of six and half years. I was now 29, rather late to be starting out to build my first career. On the credit side, I had matured, gained in confidence and developed what my peers at the Admiralty called 'leadership qualities', all of which were to stand me in good stead. It was in the City, later on, that I discovered that although there was no shooting, a war was constantly being waged – there was never any shortage of adversaries! Today, it is given an innocuous name and is known as a 'challenge', and as so often happens in waging war, the 'take-no-prisoners' philosophy frequently prevails.

A grateful nation awarded me a demobilisation gratuity of £105, which was topped up by a further £350 from the Ministry of Labour to enable me to study for my finals. I needed a home and a base in London and I was most fortunate and very grateful to my newly married sister Pauline when she offered me a room in her small house in Kingsbury, a north-west London suburb. Leaving Peggy and our son David Marvin in Plymouth, I returned to a London devastated by bombing and still in the grips of wartime restrictions which affected every facet of life. The prospect of an early resumption of residential development to rebuild the housing stock, decimated in every major city by the Blitz, was still very remote. The City as I had known it before going off to war had been almost obliterated and such office accommodation as was available carried an unaffordable premium. After so many years of regulation I yearned for freedom of choice and action and decided that after qualification I would set up in private practice. The normal two and half years of study for the final was squeezed into nine months and I qualified at the November examinations. Having no prospect of renting an office, I answered an advertisement in the *Daily Telegraph* which read: 'Office accommodation offered in return for assistance with a sole-practitioner's accountancy practice.' I came to terms with John Theobald, who had qualified as a chartered accountant in 1926 and who occupied a small suite of offices in Bedford Street, a road which ran from the big fruit market in Covent Garden down to the Strand.

A small portfolio of clients was transferred and as a *quid pro quo* Theobald allowed me to use an office, which I can best describe as a cubby hole, the size of a walk-in larder. It was 'furnished' with a tiny desk just big enough to accommodate my portable Underwood typewriter and a telephone. I also had a stool and a small filing cabinet. The Navy had taught me how to make the best of a bad job and despite the sparseness of my surroundings I was grateful for the opportunity.

Amongst the clients for whom I now took responsibility was the vicar of a country parish. I was soon to become *au fait* with ecclesiastical matters. I was intrigued to discover a quaint asset known as an advowson, which gave the owner the right to appoint a clergyman to a 'living'. It has a capital value which, on the death of the owner, forms part of his estate and is subject to Inheritance Tax. Queen Anne's Bounty and tithes to the Church Commissioners (now relegated to the rubbish heap of history) as well as the tax levied on a parson's meagre Easter offerings, came within my domain. Preparing my vicar's income tax return, I claimed a depreciation allowance which for many years had been granted on his motorised invalid chair. I entered into an acrimonious correspondence with a new Inspector of Taxes who, when he took over the vicar's file from his predecessor, disallowed the claim. The inspector, although being made aware that my vicar could not, otherwise, get around his parish, maintained that a wheelchair was not 'wholly, exclusively, and *necessarily*' required by a clergyman and therefore there would be no allowance. I telephoned the inspector, appealing to his better nature and asked him to use his discretion in favour of my client, but it was all to no avail. I knew that the inspector's ruling on the *necessity* for every clergyman to have a wheelchair was correct in law and I finally had to admit defeat and accept his deletion of my claim for an allowance of £8 in the vicar's computation. This was my first lesson in the field of taxation, that there is no room for discretion or flexibility, or for that matter sympathy. It was the letter of the law that prevailed and not necessarily its spirit.

Another client was Oxford Restaurants (London) Ltd., operating a very busy restaurant at 299 Oxford Street very close to Oxford Circus. The company had an issued capital of only £100, Mr Theobald held one share and a Mr Leopold Müller the other 99. Under the wartime defence regulations Mr Müller, as an alien, was debarred from being a director despite his being engaged full-time in the business, and for a small fee had arranged for an ex-Army officer to 'front' for him. This was my first experience of that class of company director colloquially called a 'guinea pig'. I was introduced to Müller and agreed to maintain the accounts whilst Theobald acted nominally as the company's auditor. Little did I realise that Müller was destined to play a major role in my life – in fact for the next 40 years – and that through this early introduction I would develop skills not only as an accountant, but also as a restaurateur and hotelier. From the very start I enjoyed his confidence, but throughout the years, and although we developed a close business relationship and became partners, we maintained an unusual formality, an expression of his personality that I soon found to be strange and complex. He always addressed me by my surname and I responded by invariably calling him *Mister* Müller.

Leopold Müller was born in Vienna in 1901. When he was eight his family moved to Brno, an industrial city in Moravia, then part of the Austro-Hungarian Empire of which Vienna was the capital. He left school early and, to the amazement and despair of his parents, trained as a butcher and later on established a factory canning the internationally acclaimed Czech hams. His family had hoped that he would become a lawyer.

139

Having lost the war, the Austrian Empire was dismembered at the Peace Conference held in Versailles in 1919 and the Federal Republic of Czechoslovakia headed by Thomas Masaryk was born. It was due to Masaryk's genius that this new country became a model democracy – a beacon of justice in a riven Europe. It was not easy, as he had to unite four ethnic groups, Slovaks, Bohemians, Moravians and Czechs, the latter considering themselves a cut above the others, particularly the Slovaks, whom they looked down-upon as boorish peasants. The new republic shared a common frontier with five countries – Germany to the north, Poland and Russia to the east, Hungary to the south and Austria to the west. The country developed into a highly industrialised society and through its Skoda works became a major arms manufacturer well able to equip its highly trained army and modern air force. This was the country against which at the end of 1938 Adolf Hitler created a *casus belli* (a justification to go to war) on the pretext that he was protecting the German-speaking Czechs living in the Sudetenland. When on 16th March 1939 he annexed Bohemia and Moravia, war had become inevitable. It was only a matter of time.

Earlier in these memoirs I have described the tensions created by Hitler's insatiable appetite for expansion and how it came to dominate my life, and millions like me, in the late 1930s. It was no wonder, therefore, that despite Leopold Müller having a successful business in a liberal-minded country, he should contemplate leaving it all behind and forging a new future. The persecution of the Jews by the Nazis in neighbouring Germany also weighed heavily on him and he made plans to move his family to any country that would grant them asylum providing it was far removed from Europe. He chose New Zealand. To make the necessary arrangements he travelled alone to London at the end of 1938, having previously deposited the sum of £30,000 in Lloyds Bank. Early on in our relationship he showed me the paying-in counterfoil, no doubt to impress me that he had not come to England as a penniless refugee. I was indeed suitably impressed. This sum in 1938 would today have had the purchasing power of £3 million.

The Czech authorities had imposed stringent currency controls with dire penalties for anyone breaking them. Many of his relatives and friends must have been desperate to get some of their money out of the country and placed in a safe haven. Leopold might well have acted as their courier and part of the Lloyds Bank deposit could well have represented funds belonging to third parties. The official rate of exchange at the time was approximately 140 Czech crowns to £1 sterling but in the black market £1 would buy 700 crowns, five times the official rate. No further testimony is needed to illustrate the foreboding and desperation of many of the Czech Jews.

But there was an enigma attached to the man who had just become my client that began to unravel as we became better acquainted. He lived on his own and I wondered why, but could not pluck up the courage to ask. Having told me of the plans he had laid just before war had begun, I was left to speculate on the reasons why, having managed to get to London and purchased four steamship tickets for his family to take passage to Christchurch, New Zealand, he had been unable to extricate his wife and two young daughters. The annexation was still three months away. What insurmountable problems stood in their way to prevent their escape to safety? One would have thought that with the intimacy that grew up between us over the years he would have given me the answer to the question which at the time I dared not ask. At one of our first meetings he reported the bare facts of the tragedy that had befallen his family and, realising how painful and traumatic the subject was I did not question him further, but there is little doubt that it had deeply affected and probably changed his personality. At a very early stage in our relationship he told me that 'he would never forgive the whole of mankind (sic) for the fate that had befallen his family'. I think that the rest of his long life was a personal rebuke and he had to live with the realisation that whilst he had saved himself, his family had perished. He bore the mark of Cain. I am sure that many of his actions and decisions, which at times I would find frustrating and even incomprehensible, were influenced by his personal tragedy and it is in this light that I have had to judge them.

141

It is only in the course of writing these memoirs that I have been able to fill in some of the gaps of the tragic Müller story which was enacted some 50 years ago; and then only after contacting the *Magistratu Mesta Brna* – the authorities in his home town of Brno. The correspondence gives only the barest of hints of the terror his wife and children must have experienced, their degradation and their horrible end. Recorded in the Czechoslovak archives are the stark details that on 2nd December 1941, Leopold's wife Elsa, with her two daughters Lisolette and Eva, were taken from the house they owned at No. 6 Francouzska in Brno and transported to the dreaded Czech concentration camp of Terezin. There they remained until 28th October 1944, when they were taken to the hell of Auschwitz in Poland and brutally murdered.

Lisolette was 12 and her sister Eva 8 years of age.

I was living with my newly married sister Pauline and her husband in their house in Valley Drive, Kingsbury. At the end of the road where it joined with the main thoroughfare, Fryent Way, was a large wooden sign, which had survived six years of war, on which was written 'Houses for Sale £950. No legal costs no road charges'. Pauline's house was a pleasant semi-detached three bedroom home of the type popular with pre-war developers who had been responsible for extending London's boundaries into green pastures. Where the houses went, the London Underground followed. Her back garden looked out over fields that formed part of the Metropolitan green belt. Facing her front door, on the opposite side of the street, was a pair of houses that the builder had not been able to wholly complete by the outbreak of war. Boarded up for the duration, they were only now being made ready for sale.

Seeing the builder visiting the site, I walked across and, above the din of a small cement mixer chugging away in the front garden, I introduced myself and enquired whether there was any possibility I might be able to purchase one of them. He told me that over the war years he had accumulated a long list of potential buyers to whom he ought to give preference and he thought it very unlikely that he would be in a position to sell one to me. Nevertheless I continued to chat to him whilst he told me of his experiences in the First World War in which he had served in the Royal Navy. We started to compare notes, with my telling him what it had been like in the Senior Service in the war that had just ended. We parted with my insisting that he took my address in Plymouth, just in case it was my turn to become lucky. To my incredulity and delight, two weeks later he wrote offering to sell me one of the units for £2,250 freehold with 'decorations to my choice'. I dashed back to London, hastened to the offices of the Abbey National Building Society in Baker Street and secured a 20-year mortgage of £1,750 at a *fixed* rate of interest of 4%. We now had a home and my tentative plans to emigrate to Australia on a £10 assisted passage were abandoned.

Living next door was a Major Neil Matthews, whom I learnt was an executive with Associated Fisheries Ltd in the City. He approached me one day and enquired whether I had a *post-restante* address that he could use in connection with a forwarding agency representing a group of departmental stores in Vancouver owned by McLellan, McPheeley & Prior. When I replied that he was welcome to use my small office off the Strand, he offered me a 50% interest in his company, Matthews Pett & Co Ltd., saying that a post-restante with an address in the Strand would be a distinct improvement on his current arrangement, which was based on a public telephone box close to his office in Billingsgate market.

The work for the Canadian group was not demanding or time-consuming. Unfortunately it was not long before our principals discovered this too, and terminated the arrangement, but not before my having enjoyed a much needed boost to the meagre earnings from my accountancy practice.

I was soon to learn that as one door closed another one opened, and Matthews approached me once again with quite a different proposition. Would I be prepared to become a wholesale fish-monger with a stand in Billingsgate market? The opportunity had arisen to acquire for a mere £100 the shares of W. Buckley & Co. Ltd., whose sole asset was the right to trade in Billingsgate. As

Matthews' service agreement with Associated Fisheries could lead to a conflict of interest he thought that I, as a self-employed chartered accountant, would be under no such restraint. To soften the shock he was quick to point out that I would *only* need to work 'on the pitch' for four hours a day, namely from 6 a.m. to 10 a.m., when I would be free to carry on my professional practice. I agreed as I was prepared to undertake anything that was legitimate that would help support my wife and son. Strangely enough, I could see the humorous side of the proposal. In fact it was so preposterous that it appealed to my sense of fun and we agreed that we would share profits on a fifty-fifty basis. I had no previous experience of buying and selling and I just hoped that we would earn profits.

The central markets of London comprise Smithfield for meat, Covent Garden for fruit and vegetables and Billingsgate for fish, and came under the jurisdiction of the Corporation of the City of London. The right to trade in a market was a jealously guarded privilege. Employees within the markets were highly organised and the trade unions operated a 'closed shop' policy. I was ill-prepared for the hostility from other traders with which I was confronted as soon as I took my place on the stand, but the Corporation, although unhappy about the position, could not prevent the company from trading.

Every weekday morning at about 5.15, Matthews and I would push his small Ford 8 motor car to the end of the road. We were determined not to awaken our immediate neighbours when, furiously turning the starting handle, we finally were able to get the engine to fire on all of its four cylinders; not an easy task on a cold winter morning and hours before any self-respecting accountant was even awake. Dressed in a full length white cotton coat with deep pockets and wearing my old naval rig of sea-boots and white roll-collar sweater, I sold boxes of fish from samples displayed on the stand. Our customers were fishmongers and the owners of fried fish and chip shops. I think my knowledge of the different varieties of fish was at least as good as theirs and they never suspected that I was only masquerading as one of their ilk. I could not, however, fool the fish porters, or *bummarees* as they were known, who, wearing yellow oilskin aprons and hard flat hats on which they could balance nearly a hundredweight of fish boxes, dominated the market. I also had problems with the odd client calling at my accountancy office after a morning in the market, who would sniff and say, 'There's rather a funny smell here.' It was really a 'fishy' business, as Matthews left all the trading for me to carry out as he was apprehensive of being seen within a hundred yards of our pitch.

The fish business took me to Denmark, where we developed a close association with a Mr Djekear, a leading merchant in the fishing port of Esbjerg who specialised in exporting plaice. I believe we were the first to introduce into England a consumer-pack for the housewife of two rather magnificent frozen plaice fillets in an attractive carton. Registering the tradename of 'Jacmat' they found a ready sale, in the days before supermarkets, in the freezer cabinets of grocery stores. I was particularly pleased when one Saturday morning I received a telephone call from the Pullman Cars division of Great Western Railways asking whether we could deliver two boxes of Dover soles on Monday morning for the royal train as they had been let down by their traditional suppliers. This was the beginning of a profitable association with them, but business generally was not without its anxieties. Stealing from fish boxes en-route to the market was rife. It hardly seemed possible for a wooden box that had been tightly sealed with metal bands to be broken into and some of the contents pilfered without any suspicious marks showing. The first indication would be a telephone call from an irate customer complaining that the 2-stone (28-pound) box of soles or turbot was several pounds light. In the event I was not sorry when my fishmongering career came to a close and we submitted to the *fiat* of the Corporation of London. I was about to become an industrial chemist and an authority on selective weedkillers!

14

The Sweet Smell of Success

My accountancy practice and other commercial interests now justified my employing a secretary as well as having an office where I could meet my clients. I was fortunate in finding both. Eleanor Adair was the first, and only, applicant sent for interview by an employment agency and I had no hesitation in engaging her. Facially and in stature she bore a close resemblance to Queen Mary, her identical coiffure never out of place. Although she was to stay with me for 25 years until she retired, I never knew her precise age until two years ago, when I received a letter from a solicitor informing me that she had left me some silver in her will. I asked him how old she had been when she died and he told me that she was in her ninety-second year; so when she began her employment she was nearly 20 years older than me. No one could accuse me of employing a young chick!

My new office was on the mezzanine floor at 6 Duke Street, St James's, above Duits, the specialist gallery dealing in Dutch old master paintings. Next to my office was a room occupied by a picture restorer and whenever I had time to spare I would call in and watch him painstakingly remove layers of grime and varnish from a painting, seeing the glowing colours that had been hidden for years, sometimes for centuries, emerge from the canvas. He regularly attended auctions and would bid for paintings which had not been positively identified by the auction house but in which he could discern a certain style; he would then make an attribution, which more often than not was correct. I respected his judgment and expertise and bought several paintings from him which my family and I have retained to this day. My favourite is a Pre-Raphaelite painting of a girl seated in a meadow, making a daisy posy-chain. The brushwork is exquisite and the colours so vibrant that it contrives to illuminate the wall in my daughter's house in Oxford where it now hangs.

I had lost contact with my boyhood friend George Revonetz until he contacted me using the name Dr George G. Richardson. He came to my new office and quickly filled in the gap years. Earlier in these memoirs I have written about George as my youthful mentor whose scholarship I had envied. Like me, he too had encountered prejudice when seeking employment, solely on account of his foreign sounding name, so he had anglicised it to Richardson. He had taken his doctorate in chemistry and had chosen to write his thesis on rubber technology. He was working as a chemist for British Celanese, by whom he had been employed throughout the war, but now wished to prepare the ground for going into business on his own account in the near future. 'Would you form a small limited company for me?' he asked. 'Certainly,' I replied, 'just give me the details.'

He then told me that he had chosen the name Aralkyl Chemicals for the embryo company, which should initially have the smallest nominal capital possible, as he needed to do everything on a shoe-string. My hopes of being at the cutting edge of a chemical company that would rival ICI were immediately dashed to the ground. I asked, 'Why Aralkyl?' – a question which he answered by explaining that the name was a combination of the chemistry terms 'aliphatic' and 'aromatic', the former describing certain organic components. I assumed that 'aromatic' referred to some sweet-smelling product. On my further questioning him for the names of the proposed directors, he pointed to me and said, 'Only you.' He then went on to explain that his contract of employment with British Celanese precluded him from taking up any other employment and acting as a director, and the same restriction applied to his two colleagues who would be joining him in the new venture. They had acquired basement premises in Islington but needed a 'posh' address for correspondence and the occasional visit. I then asked him what they intended to manufacture in the basement in Islington. He replied, 'A selective weedkiller – two-four D.' I then asked him if this was 'aromatic' and he replied enigmatically, 'Of course, just wait and see.' He gave me the chemical name, which was two-four (2:4) dichlorphenoxy acetic acid. My chemistry studies had ended at school with my acquiring very little knowledge other than how to make stink bombs which I later let off in the school playground. I said, 'Now look here, George, for old times' sake there is nothing I would like more than to help you and your friends, but I am an accountant not an organic chemist.' George told me not to worry and promised to provide me with a vocabulary of chemical terms that would see me through. I caved in and went ahead and formed the company appointing myself as the sole director, and George and his friends started to manufacture.

My first test came unexpectedly when I received a visit from a sales representative of Albright and Wilson, a leading manufacturer of basic chemicals, who called to check on our creditworthiness before they would open an account for the new company. I was taken by surprise and on looking at his business card and seeing a whole string of degrees after his name, I regretted having allowed George to take advantage of my easy-going nature. The conversation started with his asking me about our manufacturing process using his product. I decided to ride out his questions by employing the technique which one of my minesweeping colleagues invariably used when being quizzed by higher authority. He called it the three Bs – which stood for *'bullshit baffles brains'*. Somehow I got through the interview and they opened a credit account.

My knowledge of weedkillers was limited to the product I bought for my lawn from a garden centre. I had never come across the agricultural variety, but this was now to change. I had occasion to call George and his fellow shareholders to a meeting and they arrived, coming directly from their basement factory. Even before they came into the office I could smell them. I could smell them as soon as they came out of the lift. Their clothes were saturated with the most vile odour I had ever encountered. I opened all the windows and cautioned them not to come within 10 feet of me. I

148

was now being exposed to the 'aromatic' side of the company – no sweet-smelling aromas here, but the whiff of a mobile cesspit. I brought the meeting to an early close and made a conscious decision to extricate myself from Aralkyl Chemicals Ltd as soon as I possibly could without damaging George's fragile finances.

The rationing of food was introduced very early on in the war and was not lifted for several years after its end. Basic foodstuffs, such as meat, fats, sugar and flour were controlled by the Ministry of Food. Wielding wide-ranging powers, it ensured enforcement of a framework of regulations aimed at establishing a fair distribution of the limited supplies available. Every man, woman and child had a ration book containing coupons which could be used to purchase the meagre weekly ration from a shop with whom they had previously registered. Restaurants were obliged to make a monthly return to the ministry of the number of meals sold, on the basis of which they were allotted coupons entitling them to purchase their requirements of rationed commodities. Prohibited from serving a meal of more that three courses, restaurants were further restricted to charging a maximum of five shillings (25p) to any one customer. At one critical stage, a bread roll was considered as constituting an individual course! The regulations were complex, sometimes ambiguous, often contradictory and invariably onerous, particularly to a small caterer.

I recall an incident at the Oxford Restaurant, four years after the end of the war, when a customer who had just had afternoon tea and was in the process of paying his bill at the cash desk, commented to the cashier that he had much enjoyed the slice of cream gateau. He asked if he could purchase a whole one for a tea party he was planning. The cashier in refusing pointed out that the cake was only available for consumption on the premises and that food regulations restricted the quantity to a single slice. The customer was insistent, so much so that the cashier seeing a queue beginning to form at her desk, finally agreed to sell a whole cake and handed it over in a carton. The customer paid and immediately produced a card which identified him as an inspector employed by the Ministry of Food. He then proceeded to tell a frightened cashier that the restaurant would be reported for breaking the food regulations. A prosecution followed at Bow Street Magistrate's Court which I attended and at which the *agent provocateur* from the ministry gave evidence. The company was found guilty of a contravention of the wartime food regulations and fined £50.

Mr Müller, who was hoping to apply for British nationality, was extremely concerned that this conviction might prejudice his naturalisation application. I pointed out that it was the company that had been fined and not him personally, but he was far from being reassured.

I received a call from him one day asking me to respond to a London *Evening Standard* advertisement for the sale of a West End restaurant and to negotiate its purchase. The restaurant in question was the Chicken Inn, an imposing double-fronted shop in a busy passer-by location at the top end of the Haymarket, close to Piccadilly Circus. The vendor was Mr McKenzie, the owner of the Green Park Hotel in Half Moon Street in Mayfair. I struck a deal for the business at a price of £25,000. The restaurant was held on a wartime lease, of which 30 years still remained unexpired, at a fixed annual rental of £5,000. I was elated at my first successful negotiation, little realising at the time what a momentous purchase it was to prove and how it would open up an entirely new career, laying the foundation of my subsequent fortune.

Having exchanged contracts to purchase the business, Müller asked whether I could operate it for him as his time was fully taken up in his restaurant in Oxford Street. I assured him I could run it profitably as not only did I have the time but also the expertise! He responded by offering to sell me a 25% interest in Chicken Inns (London) Ltd., the company I was in the process of forming. I now felt this was a golden opportunity of rewarding Neil Matthews for the support he had given me in the early days, and with Müller's agreement each of us took up 125 shares out of the issued capital of 1,000 shares of £1 each. Matthews was able to pay for his allotment in full, and Müller agreed that I could have two years' grace to pay the required consideration of £3,125 for my 12½% stake in the business.

I continued with my accountancy practice, at Duke Street, St James's, being no more than a five minutes' walk away from the new restaurant which I was able to administer from a suite of offices on the first floor – literally living above the shop.

Business, nationwide, boomed as the public, after years of danger and austerity, celebrated peaceful times. Every opportunity was taken to indulge and to enjoy, and where better than in the West End of London with its innumerable cinemas, theatres and restaurants? American soldiers (GIs), on their way home after postings in Europe, thronged the streets and with their billfolds stuffed with dollars came to the Chicken Inn, often twice a day, where our menu and style of cooking was very familiar and reminded them of home.

Oxford Restaurants (London) Ltd had remained the personal property of Müller. He had purchased the company from George Rose who had, a few years before the War, been deposed as Chairman of Great Universal Stores by Isaac Wolfson, at that time his Sales Director. In addition to the main restaurant in Oxford Street, the company owned a small snack bar called Pam Pam on the south side of Leicester Square adjoining the old Dental Hospital. It seemed to me that the snack bar was being carried on primarily so that its allocation of rationed foods could be utilised in the Oxford Street branch. I formed this conclusion because there were only *two* items on the menu; Cod and chips and Cornish pasty and chips, the latter containing some mystery filling which had escaped the rationing regulations. All the same the 20 seat snack bar was full all day long, mainly with American servicemen probably sheltering from the prostitutes pestering them in Leicester Square. I called there one lunchtime to collect some invoices and on asking to see the Manageress I was told that she was out to lunch.

'Out to *lunch*?' I queried. 'Yes sir, Miss Brown always goes out for *her* lunch.' Müller took my advice and closed the snack bar.

Having spent the war years 'cosseted' by the Navy, I had not been exposed to food rationing and shortages. I now found it surprising that, although price-controlled and in short supply, poultry, game and fish had not been subjected to the restrictions placed upon meat, a situation that was to work to our advantage in operating the restaurant. Our menu was based on the efficient utilisation of the entire chicken – as with the pig, we used 'everything except the whistle'. Purchasing poultry with a standard weight of three and a half pounds provided two breast and two leg portions, the former selling for 4s 6d (26p) and the latter for 3s 6d (20p), each being generously garnished with fried potatoes and minted garden peas. The sale of a large puff-pastry vol-au-vent filled with pieces of chicken in a cream sauce, and a chicken 'cutlet' made from wings and giblets and served with a mushroom sauce, was sufficient to cover the cost of the entire bird. The proceeds of selling the prime portions was profit.

We had not been operating long before I realised that the Chicken Inn concept could be developed into a brand and that we could establish a chain of similar restaurants in the West End without adding greatly to our central costs. Designing a logo which was a chicken wearing a chef's hat, I arranged for our resident electrician to build a revolving spit that would barbecue 48 chickens at a time. I then went shopping for shops. With Mr Charles Forte doing likewise, it was far from easy. In later years Lord Forte and I were to become friends, and I have a great affection for the grand old man of catering whose achievements in the hotel industry have earned him a unique place in its annals, but in the late fifties and sixties we were rivals with no quarter given.

Each year three or four units were added to our chain, and a centralised production kitchen was established in the extensive basement of our main restaurant in Leicester Square, close to the Empire cinema. Chickens were prepared for the spit on a conveyor-belt principle, with sauces and soups being made in vast cauldrons. An air-conditioned pastry kitchen was kept busy all day long manufacturing lemon meringue and apple pies as well as the puff-pastry vol-au-vents, all these products being delivered to the restaurants in refrigerated vans. I believe that our concept was ahead of its time and long before the fast-food revolution had crossed the Atlantic. I did, however, borrow one idea from America, and that was to introduce the popular fried chicken

Maryland to our menus. Hesitantly, I launched a trial run at the Leicester Square branch and gave precise instructions as to how the dish was to be cooked and presented. Calling for a report the day following its introduction, I was delighted that we had sold 98 portions. The Manageress expressed her amazement when one customer, not knowing why the finger bowl was provided, drank the water it contained, thinking it was part of the ritual, whilst several took away the wicker baskets in which we served the chicken.

To his credit, Müller gave me every encouragement to expand the business and happily remained on the sidelines and took no active part. Had he not done so, I am sure that our different styles of management would have brought us into conflict, making inevitable my departure from the business which I was building up and enjoying so much. He was content to continue working in his personally owned restaurant in Oxford Street, relying on my daily reports whilst expecting major business decisions to be referred to him for approval. He was by nature speculatively minded and a born wheeler-dealer, whilst I regarded myself as an empire builder. Like all speculators, he was always ready to take a quick profit and had become spectacularly successful in his dealings on the Stock Exchange. One share he was particularly keen on was the Anglo Persian Oil Company.

The history of this company makes fascinating reading, as it represents the best of British enterprise. It commenced in May 1901 when William Knox D'Arcy obtained a concession from the Shah of Persia to explore virtually the whole of the country for oil. It took seven years before oil was struck in commercial quantities and in 1909 a company was formed to capitalise on the discovery of what was to become known as liquid gold. The Anglo Persian Oil Company was born. In 1914, shortly before the outbreak of war, with Winston Churchill as First Sea Lord anxious to secure vital supplies of fuel oil for the Navy, the company sold a controlling stake to the British Government in return for an investment of £2 million.

The subsequent success of companies engaged in the oil industry is mirrored in the sale by the government in 1987 of its remaining shareholding in BP for billions of pounds. Ironically, the name British Petroleum Company originated when, in 1917, the Anglo Persian Oil Company purchased from the Custodian of Enemy Property the British marketing subsidiary of the German-owned *Europaische Petroleum Union*, although the final change of name to British Petroleum did not take place until 1954. On the outbreak of World War II, the company trading as Anglo-Iranian Oil, played a major and crucial role, in the course of which it lost almost half of its tanker fleet, together with more than 600 of its brave crews. The D Day landings – Operation Overlord – could not have been mounted without Pluto, the undersea pipeline by which the company fed petrol right into the Normandy beach heads.

I became interested in BP when, in 1951, Mossadaq, Iran's Prime Minister, nationalised the company's Persian assets and their shares dropped like a stone. Müller was keeping a keen eye on the share price and when after three years Mossadaq was toppled and oil production had been resumed, he recommended the shares to me. It was my first investment on the stock exchange – £250 in all. Shortly after, the company split its shares by issuing four new shares for every one held and Leopold Müller made a small fortune.

I am indebted to the Secretary of BP for providing me with the history of his company, at the same time informing me that £100 invested in 1948 in his shares and retained for 50 years would today be worth more than £10,500. One could make out a very good case for locking a share certificate in a tin box and forgetting about it.

15

Inns and Hotels

My post-Navy days saw me leading a Jekyll and Hyde existence: differing roles jostling for a greater share of my life at the expense of the time I could devote to being an accountant in private practice. I would, from time to time, step back and take a detached view of my varied activities and, realising the incongruity of it all, have a good laugh at myself. I enjoyed being my own master and the intellectual challenge of having to project myself as an authority in several unrelated industries but I was never able completely to reconcile my strict professional ethics with those I found in common usage in the commercial world. Building up the restaurant chain was making increasing demands on my energy and I felt that I now had to change direction and become more focused. It was not a difficult choice to make as I had become convinced that the catering industry offered me the greatest opportunity. Today one would attribute this feeling to my genes, a throwback to my father's role as a tavern-keeper at the turn of the century. I had never forgotten the quotation from Shakespeare's *Julius Caesar*: 'There is a tide in the affairs of men which taken at the flood leads on to fortune'. Until the present day, I have always found myself swimming *with* the tide.

Contacting my friend Eric Ellis, with whom as a 17-year-old I had worked in the accountancy offices of Scott Mitchell Boswell-Phillips, I revealed my plans for the future and transferred to him my accountancy practice as a gift. All my clients had given their consent and wished me well, but before I draw the final curtain on my accountancy career I have to record a bizarre episode which occurred in the early days.

Late one Friday afternoon, I received a telephone call from Arthur Dolland, a solicitor and friend, asking me to see a Mr Arthur LaBerne who was in his office and needed an accountant to prepare a Statement of Affairs in connection with his bankruptcy proceedings. I was feeling very tired, having spent the early morning in Billingsgate market, so I told Arthur that I would be pleased to see his client on the following Monday morning at eleven o'clock. Arthur responded with a garbled statement, of which I only caught the phrase 'I am putting him in a taxi now and he will be with you in ten minutes.' I was certainly not prepared for what was to follow.

Responding to a knock on my office door, I opened it to see a slightly built man clutching a brown paper parcel. As he did not say anything, I said, 'You must be Mr LaBerne. Do take a seat.' There was no reply so I started again. 'Mr Dolland tells me that you need to prepare a statement of affairs.' Still no reply; he just sat looking at me. Drawing on my naval experience I thought, this man is so drunk that he can't speak, and pushing a pencil and notebook in front of him I said, 'Write it down.' After a laborious interview lasting two hours his story emerged from our dialogue, which took the form of my asking the questions, and he scribbling the answers, of a kind, on to a notepad. It transpired that he was an author and had written a book called *It Always Rains on Sundays*. The book had been made into a film, for which he had written the screenplay and he had made a great deal of money from both.

On checking through his brown paper parcel I found cheque book stubs, his bank statements and several letters, all of a threatening nature, demanding payment. I was intrigued by a series of cheques made out to the Savoy Hotel, on occasion six or more on the same day and each one for £5. Subsequently, I discovered that he frequented the Savoy. Sitting up at the bar and calling for a drink, he would make out a cheque for £5 and repeat this each time the barman signalled that he needed to replenish his credit. Amongst the papers was a summons to appear in the

Bankruptcy Court in Carey Street on the following Monday – only two days away. I told him to leave his parcel with me and I would meet him in court on Monday morning half an hour before the hearing.

On Monday he was sufficiently sober to be able to give me an advance on fees of £100 in *cash* – I would not accept a cheque – and I was able to secure an adjournment of one month to enable me to prepare a Statement of Affairs. I then arranged an appointment for him to meet me in my office a week later. He did not keep the appointment and I did not hear from him again until some months later when I received a letter written on the notepaper of Brixton Prison. It was terse and to the point and read 'Mr Jackson ... get me out of here ... LaBerne'. I managed to do this by giving assurances that he would make his appearance in court and that I would be in a position to present to the Registrar the required account. This having been accomplished, I terminated our professional relationship and told Arthur Dolland, if that was the best he could do, not to send me any more clients.

Fishing around for suitable sites netted us a very good haul of units in busy locations. The first, and as it turned out the most profitable one, was a corner site in Leicester Square the upper floors of which were occupied by the National Society for the Prevention of Cruelty to Children. This acquisition was followed rapidly by two shops in Oxford Street, another opposite the Palladium theatre in Argyll Street and a very large branch in a prominent position facing Victoria Station in a former ABC restaurant.

ABC was the abbreviated name of the Aerated Bread Company, a subsidiary of Associated British Foods, the vast Canadian bakery company founded and controlled by Garfield Weston. For very many years they had operated a bread shop and cafeteria on the ground floor and in the extensive basement of a block of offices in Victoria, named Abford House. Finding that the entire building was on the market, with vacant possession of the cafeteria, and had the benefit of an attractive rent roll from the lettings on the upper floor offices, we instituted negotiations with the Managing

157

Director of ABC and agreed to purchase the freehold for the sum of £525,000. On their conclusion Müller and I were invited to lunch in their head office in Camden Town where, in the presence of most of their board of directors, contracts were exchanged, with completion to take place six weeks later. By arrangement with their company secretary I duly arrived for the completion ceremony with the requisite banker's draft. The secretary was alone and this time there was no lunch, and no board of directors. I understood that they had all been dismissed by Mr Weston when he got to hear of the disposal of this landmark building.

The expansion of the Chicken Inns was being financed from cash flow through the reinvestment in the business of the profits that were being earned. Meanwhile Müller had started to speculate in the shares of an almost moribund hotel company called Spiers & Pond. He had very little knowledge of the company and had been attracted to it by the low price at which the shares were being traded. I was asked to monitor the price daily and to keep a register of our dealings in the shares which, to safeguard our anonymity, we arranged to have registered in the name of our broker's nominee company, the beneficial ownership being vested in Chicken Inns (London) Ltd. I soon became interested in the company *per se* and made it my business to find out more about its activities.

The hotel industry had developed from a long tradition of English inn-keeping and anyone familiar with Charles Dickens's books will have gained an insight into the workings of the coaching inns which in the bustling nineteenth century were the main providers of food and lodging to travellers throughout the country. The Victorian and Edwardian years witnessed the golden age of hotel development as the railways extended their network and an increasingly affluent society began to move around, firstly by train, and then by motor car. Hotels were built in all the seaside resorts and spas and every major town and city boasted a station hotel developed by whichever railway company operated its line. Local investors financed other projects, very often losing their initial investment in what soon became apparent as a high-risk enterprise, and consequently the hotel industry grew up in a very fragmented fashion. Hotel chains as we know them today hardly existed, but Spiers & Pond having started to trade in England in 1864, had amassed an impressive portfolio of hotels. My research into the antecedents of the company revealed a fascinating history.

Mr Felix Spiers and Christopher Pond first met in Melbourne in the 1850s and found catering in that city during the early gold rush days a very lucrative business. They are credited with having initiated the Test matches by financing a cricket team from England to play in Melbourne, the first match taking place on New Year's Day 1862. Out of this venture was born the battle for the Ashes, the most prestigious cricket challenge of our times. Leaving behind their lucrative catering businesses in Melbourne, these two enterprising characters sailed for England to repeat their success in London, initially catering for the expanding railways in their buffet bars and dining cars and finally graduating to hotelkeeping which included the Grand Hotels in Brighton and Scarborough.

As a result of my research I was able to tell Müller that the company appeared to be stuffed with under-utilised assets and advised that we should stop speculating in their shares every time they rose to show a profit of sixpence or so a share and should concentrate on building a significant holding which would become the launch-pad for a takeover of the company. Our initial stream of purchases was made at an average price of six shillings per share (30p) and intensive buying on some days could raise the price by three farthings (.003p) a share – hardly a volatile stock by today's standards! We were concerned not to alert the Board prematurely, nor did we wish to push the price up against ourselves, so we took our time until, after a period of nearly two years with the shares at a peak of 11 shillings (55p), the market dried up.

We sought advice from our stockbrokers, A. Miller & Co. Edward Miller recommended that we should now proceed to make an open offer to the shareholders, but as it was our intention to retain Spiers & Pond as an active quoted company we should limit the offer to the number of shares that would raise our existing holding to 51%. He advised us to use the services of a small merchant bank and recommended Investment Registry owned by

159

Mr Charles Clore. Mr Clore, rarely out of the headlines, was known to us as a formidable takeover specialist. He had created Sears Holdings, a conglomerate owning many prominent businesses including Selfridges, and with Harry Levison at the helm had built up the British Shoe Corporation, a subsidiary company which was the biggest shoe retailer in the world. He was also prominent in property investment and development having, in partnership with Jack Cotton, built the Hilton Hotel in Park Lane and the skyscraper office block known as 40 Wall Street in New York.

Investment Registry's offices were in a fine Georgian building in Grafton Street, a stone's throw from New Bond Street. A Mr Toby Waddington received us and introduced himself as the Managing Director. I outlined our plans, informing him that we had accumulated a stake of 17% in Spiers & Pond Ltd and now wished to acquire sufficient shares to enable us to control the company. Would his firm act for us? He said they would. 'How much will you charge us?' I asked. After some thought he replied, '£5,000'. Müller told him it was too much and in true European fashion said 'Will you take £4,000?' Waddington replied, 'No, but remember that the fee will include all expenses including legal costs – the only extra will be stamp duty on the shares acquired.' As a last attempt to negotiate a lower price Müller offered £4,500, whereupon Waddington replied, 'I will ask Mr Clore.' Without leaving the room he telephoned his chairman and told him of our proposals. We could hear a muffled response with an angry voice saying, 'Not a penny less ... tell them to push off if they won't pay £5,000.'

We agreed to pay and made an appointment to see Titmuss Sainer & Webb, the solicitors who would be acting for the merchant bank on our behalf; their offices were at 61 Carey Street, close to the Law Courts. Müller entrusted me with the conduct of the discussions leading up to our making the offer so I went to see them, climbing up three flights of stone stairs of an unmodernised early Georgian building. I was introduced to Herbert Bart-Smith, the partner who would be handling the offer, and we discovered a mutual empathy. We worked extremely well together and laid the foundation of a friendship which has endured for nearly 50 years.

We made the offer and bid £1 for each of the shares needed to secure control, against a market price of 12s 6d on the day prior to our announcement. The bid (the last occasion the Stock Exchange permitted a limited offer to be made) was successful and at the end of the summer of 1954, Müller and I, accompanied by Bart-Smith, found ourselves sitting in the board room of Spiers & Pond facing a hostile board of directors. The meeting was very brief and the atmosphere icy. Bart came quickly to the point and, addressing Mr Venables the Chairman, said, 'My clients have gained control of the company and now wish to have control of the Board. Please let me have your resignation and that of your colleagues.' Without further ado, he slid the resignation letters across the table to the Chairman, asking for his signature first. The whole proceedings had taken up no more than ten minutes and as the old directors filed out of the boardroom with their cheques for £1,000 as compensation for loss of office, I could not help but feel sorry for them and regret the rather brutal way in which we had deposed them. I eased my conscience with the thought that they had done little, if anything, for their shareholders for many years.

Müller was appointed Chairman; I was elected Deputy Chairman and Managing Director, Cyril Upton Mather was retained as Company Secretary and Reginald Cyrus Constable, who had been with the company for several years as General Manager, was promoted to the Board. Constable, who had served with the Eighth Army in the Western Desert, had been captured at Tobruk and incarcerated in a succession of prisoner-of-war camps for three years; the experience left him with a pathological hatred of Germans and anything made in Germany. Unlike me, he was a professional hotelier, having worked his way up through the kitchen, and at the young age of 21 he had quit as banqueting head waiter at the Great Eastern Hotel to volunteer for the Army at the outbreak of war. He had a prodigious memory and an encyclopaedic knowledge of wines which was to prove invaluable over the years. I could not have wished for a more formidable and capable lieutenant.

The acquisition of Spiers & Pond was a quantum leap for Müller and me. I felt that the chicken concept still had a long way to go before reaching its optimum level and that it would be premature at this moment in time to incorporate the restaurants into the hotel group. There was little doubt, however, that the new acquisition needed a kick-start by a hands-on operator, which it had sadly lacked since the war. Neil Matthews decided to give up his job with Associated Fisheries and take on the administration of the hotels from the offices in Gloucester Road. This freed me to concentrate on expanding the Chicken Inns chain and to devise an overall financial strategy for the group.

My first test came quickly. Within 24 hours of our press announcement of the successful conclusion of our bid for Spiers & Pond, I received a telephone call. I had no switchboard operator; no one to give the hackneyed phrase, 'I'm sorry he's at a meeting … who shall I say called?' I heard the voice at the other end say, 'Mr Jackson, you won't know who I am but I have just bought the Green Park Hotel from Mr McKenzie who sold you the Chicken Inn some years ago. Can I come and see you?' My curiosity was aroused and I invited him to come that afternoon.

My office was over the restaurant in the Haymarket. There was a knock on my door and the short, slim, dapper man who entered introduced himself as Maxwell Joseph. I asked him to take a seat and he came quickly to the point. His opening remark was, 'I see you have bought Spiers & Pond – you have paid too much for it. You could have got it cheaper.'

This riled me and I had to control myself to keep calm. I replied, 'You are entitled to your opinion but we think that £1 was a fair price and, in any case, the average price for our holding is somewhat less than that.'

Then by way of presenting his credentials he said, 'I own the Washington, the Green Park and the Mandeville hotels.' I knew the first two as minor hotels in Mayfair and the Mandeville close to Wigmore Street, a road that runs parallel to Oxford Street. The hotels were old and desperately in need of modernisation and I was not over-impressed; the look on my face showed this. He then said, 'I would like to join you and Müller. I can bring some very good ideas and … (he paused, to play what he considered to be his trump card) I can invest £10,000.'

162

It was probably this last remark that influenced my decision. It was not that I had become so blasé that I now considered £10,000 to be merely petty cash, but I could not help comparing it with the million pounds we had just invested in our new acquisition. I said, 'Mr Joseph, we are not looking for a partner, but it was nice to meet you.'

With the benefit of hindsight I greatly regretted my decision. I could have worked extremely well with Joseph but I knew instinctively that Müller and he were incompatible. I was unaware that despite our abrupt meeting we would, over the years, establish a friendship founded on mutual respect for each other's achievements even though our respective interests frequently clashed and we found ourselves competing fiercely for the same businesses or properties. In the majority of instances Maxwell Joseph was the victor, usually overbidding us. It is now history how, from modest beginnings, he grew the Grand Metropolitan Hotels group (which he had acquired as a shell company and given a new identity) into one of the largest companies in the country, with international interests in brewing, hotels and wines and spirits. Now the company which he founded, having merged with Guinness Plc and been renamed Diageo, is capitalised in the stock market at more than 25 *billion* pounds.

I feel sure that Max had spotted what I had missed, namely the unique advantage that a quoted public company had over one that was private. Spiers & Pond, with its quotation on the London Stock Exchange, not only had access to the vast capital resources of the City of London, denied to a company without a quotation, but acquired a licence to print money – its own currency. To finance expansion it could always call on its shareholders or the public at large to invest, but to grow really big it did not need cash. It could use its own 'paper'. Admittedly a Spiers & Pond share certificate would not carry the comforting signature of the Chief Cashier of the Bank of England and instead would be signed by me; but it would be up to *me* to see that it did not turn out to be 'funny money'.

I now began a search for Spiers & Ponds' under-utilised assets. The first one I found was a chain of tobacconist shops which had contributed little to the 'bottom line profit'. As they were all in good main road positions they were quickly sold. I then discovered The Southampton, which had ceased trading as a hotel after the war and now lay derelict, occupying a site of nearly half an acre on the forecourt of Surbiton railway station. I had been introduced to a Mr Samuel Messer of Jack Cotton & Partners, estate agents in Dorland House Lower Regent Street, and I asked him to advise the company on its property potential. Guided by the builders Taylor Woodrow, he estimated that we could build a 30,000-square-foot office block on the site. When he told me that the offices would not let for more than ten shillings (50p) per square foot even I, ignorant as I was of the financial mathematics of development, could see that the figures would not add up so I instructed him to find a buyer for the site. He found the property subsidiary of the Pearl Assurance Company, who agreed to buy for £90,000. A contract was drawn up and I attended to sign and exchange it at the offices of their builders, Holland, Hannan & Cubitts, who 200 years earlier had built those architectural gems, the Regency Nash terraces in Regents Park. With increasing anxiety I waited for the Pearl's solicitors to arrive. After two hours of nail-biting I placed a call through to their head office, only to be informed that they had changed their mind and that they were withdrawing from the transaction. I was left high and dry with an acute sense of grievance and disappointment.

Going back to Sam Messer, he started to market the site in earnest. Two serious potential buyers were found and invited to come and see me in my office. The first to arrive was a man some ten years younger than myself. He introduced himself by reeling off the names of several prominent central London office buildings, proclaiming that he had promoted or developed them all. I was impressed. He then said, 'Look here, Mr Jackson, I am the only person in London who can pay you in cash.' With that remark he flicked open the two locks of a small leather attaché case and said, 'You can count it – there is £100,000 in there. That's what I am bidding you for your site.' His action had the opposite effect to what he hoped to achieve.

I was nonplussed and could only blurt out to the man who

became one of the most successful and richest of the post-war property developers, 'Thank you for your offer, I will let you know, as we have other interested parties.' To the other potential buyer who offered the identical price, I intimated that we would hold a sealed bid auction in the offices of our solicitors, who had by now moved from their ancient offices in Carey Street to prestigious headquarters in the newly rebuilt Sergeant's Inn, adjoining the Middle Temple.

Mister *Attaché Case* stuck to his offer of £100,000. Mr Edwards, in contention, raised his to £105,000 and so secured the deal. I had made the sale conditional on the ground floor and part of the basement of any new building, approximately 3,000 square feet, being let to Spiers & Pond for a pub, the terms to be a lease of 99 years at a fixed peppercorn ground rent of £1 per annum. I was beginning to learn how to create value. Mr Edwards, using another firm of builders, was able to double the size of the building and secure a Swiss pharmaceutical company paying a rental of £1 per square foot as a tenant for all the office space. I was not only satisfied with our deal but had a little fun when we fitted up the ground floor pub. Because of its location virtually on the railway station, I decided to have a railway theme and I turned to the talented illustrator Roland Emett, whose zany train drawings I enjoyed so much. I located him and went to see him in his home in West Sussex and placed a commission (at not so zany a price) for a mural that would stretch around a wall of nearly 60 feet. He filled it with his crazy characters and fanciful steam trains. The commuters of Surbiton loved it and packed the bars.

16

A Bonus from the Great Train Robbers

The prosperity of the Edwardian era had spawned numerous emporiums – London departmental stores that catered not only for the landed gentry and the 'carriage trade' but for cosmopolitan London with the 'man in the street' enjoying an increasing purchasing power. Between the wars, these large properties sited in the main shopping streets of the West End of London continued to flourish but were badly affected by the stock market crashes of Wall Street in 1929 and London two years later and the Depression that followed. The aftermath of the Second World War saw the demise of several household names that originally had started as partnerships between two drapers. There was Swan and Edgar in Piccadilly Circus, Bourne & Hollingsworth in Regent Street, Marshall and Snelgrove and Robinson & Cleaver, but few are now likely to recall a name that I shall never forget ... Stagg & Russell.

Stagg & Russell enjoyed a commanding position in Leicester Square but their building had taken on a neglected look and the owners had failed to modernise the interior. Its lease was coming to an end and the decision had been taken to discontinue trading. It came to my knowledge that the freeholders, the Automobile Association (AA), with their headquarters in Fanum House immediately opposite the store were offering a building lease for 999 years for a premium of £500,000. I put a proposition to the AA that we would, subject to getting the necessary planning consents, buy the lease on offer and erect an office building with the upper floors being used as a 100 bedroom hotel. Our architects estimated that the hotel bedrooms would cost approximately

£2,000 per room to build and furnish. The easy part of the negotiations was to secure local authority agreement in principle for the proposed scheme. The difficult part was to get Treasury consent for a new investment. The country was going through a very difficult economic cycle and any project involving more than £50,000 required the approval of the Bank of England. Application was made on our behalf by Barclays Bank and rejected by the authorities. However, I continued my negotiations both with the AA and Westminster City Council in the hope that a window of opportunity would open for us before the site was snatched up by a property predator.

Some two months later Barclays reapplied and this time the answer from the Treasury was in the affirmative. Our bank agreed to fund the initial purchase of the lease, leaving us to raise the building finance from either the City or our shareholders. Meanwhile Müller had gone on holiday and I kept him informed of progress. I pressed Westminster Council for a formal outline planning consent, which they promised they would issue after the next monthly meeting of their planning committee. The AA was now insisting on an early exchange of contracts and gave us a seven day deadline. I called Müller on the telephone and informed him of the position, that we had received Treasury consent and could now proceed to contract stage. He concurred. I told our solicitor Bart-Smith and arranged to meet him and the AA at the Strand offices of Amery Parkes, their solicitors, at midday on the following Monday morning to exchange contracts.

On Friday I called at the Marble Arch branch of Barclays Bank and picked up a banker's draft for £50,000, the required deposit. I went to bed that night in a state of euphoria. I had pulled it off. Very early on Saturday morning I was awakened by Müller speaking from his hotel bedroom in the South of France. 'Have you got the piece of paper?' he asked. I knew what he meant.

'No,' I replied, 'but I have been assured by the chief planning officer of Westminster Council that it will be forthcoming.'

He was brusque almost to a degree of viciousness. 'No planning consent ... no contract' he almost screamed on the telephone. I got the message and replaced the receiver. To reinforce his statement he sent me a telegram that I received later that afternoon … it was even briefer.

On Monday morning I arrived in the waiting room of Amery Parkes to find Bart already there. He was very affable and congratulated me on the successful conclusion of a very promising deal. He asked for the banker's draft. I took it slowly out of my wallet and with a sense of theatre tore it across. He was aghast when I told him of the drama played out in the previous 48 hours. He expressed his sympathy; we made our excuses to the AA representative and left. Twenty-four hours later Leonard Sainer, senior partner of Titmuss Sainer & Webb acting on behalf of their clients, Charles Clore's City and Central Properties, exchanged the identical contract with the AA. When Müller returned from holiday and learnt of the outcome he was furious. The fact that he alone was responsible for aborting the deal and diverting it into other hands was shrugged off. He accused our solicitors of double-dealing and even threatened to report them to the Law Society but we all knew that *he* had to bear complete responsibility for the fiasco. Leicester Square did not get a new hotel, instead it got the Swiss Centre, one of the prize commercial properties in the whole of London.

Business in the West End was booming and the Chicken Inn chain was not only profitable but beginning to overtake the earnings from the hotels. Kemp Chatteris, the auditors of Spiers & Pond, were consulted on the best way in which we could reverse the restaurant business into the hotel company without straining the liquidity of Spiers & Pond. Our two objectives were for the directors of Chicken Inns (London) Ltd to increase their personal shareholdings in the quoted company, at the same time boosting the earnings per share of S & P. As the directors of Chicken Inns would be 'wearing two hats' in this transaction, we secured an independent valuation of the restaurant business and a formula that would satisfy the outside shareholders of S & P. The proposal for S & P to acquire the Chicken Inn business was put to an extraordinary general meeting of the quoted company and approved. Chicken Inns became a subsidiary company of S & P and I was left with a significant holding of shares which were now quoted. Investors perceiving the dramatic changes that were taking place in the management of the old hotel company put the shares on a rising curve as new developments and acquisitions were announced. Meanwhile Neil Matthews, after a furious row with Müller, tendered his resignation on the telephone, which Müller accepted with alacrity leaving me as chief executive, a position which I had been occupying, *de facto*, ever since we had taken control of S & P.

Our portfolio of hotels had been built up haphazardly by our predecessors over nearly a century, without any evident plan or strategy. As an example, the Grand Hotel, Brighton had nothing in common with our small hotel, the Calverly in Tunbridge Wells. The hotel had formerly been the home of the Duchess of Kent, the mother of Queen Victoria, and of Victoria herself as a very young girl. The walls of one bedroom, reputedly the Queen's nursery, had preserved its original wallpaper. Entering the hotel was to slip back a century, with nearly one third of the rooms occupied by 'permanent residents' ... mostly single ladies of a certain age or the widows of retired Army officers who had made the hotel their home. Permanent residents were a significant feature of all the small hotels in London and the provinces, a trend which had grown considerably between the wars as domestic staff became increasingly expensive and difficult to find. Their presence acted as a deterrent to normal hotel patronage and the attitude they would adopt, particularly in the dining room, was resented by the other guests. For the very modest weekly sum that they paid for their room and full board they would assume a proprietorial air and act as though they had bought a share in the hotel's freehold. In the restaurant 'their' table was sacrosanct and woe betide a casual guest who innocently tried to occupy it. At the Calverly, I soon got to know that the favourite dish was roast guinea fowl, as it appeared without fail on the table d'hote menu every day of the week. The manager had become so accustomed to his specialised clientele that he had become integrated into the scene I have described. I could not help but be reminded every time I had to visit the hotel, of Noel Coward's play *Separate Tables*. My first

169

objective was to replace the manager and then ease the old ladies out with as little inconvenience to them as possible.

The Calverly was, however, a modern *parvenu* when compared with some of the other hotels in S & P's portfolio. The 'daddy' of them all was the Royal Clarence in Exeter – an old inn with credentials that took it back to the fifteenth century. It enjoyed a magnificent location facing Exeter's beautiful cathedral. I really loved that hotel but spent many sleepless nights there – but not because I whiled away the nocturnal hours carousing in its cosy oak-timbered bar, which had changed very little over the centuries. The cause of my insomnia was the cathedral, or more precisely the cathedral's clock which insisted on celebrating the passing of time by chiming every quarter of an hour. The decibels, I would have sworn, progressively increased as the night wore on. When midnight struck, the chimes seem to rise to a crescendo and despite my counting whole flocks of sheep, away went my slumber. All the supplications from the manager to the clergy to reduce the number of chimes fell on deaf ears. They obviously had their homes far removed from Cathedral Square. Lucky clerics!

In the antiquity stakes the Bull's Head Hotel in Aylesbury ran the Royal Clarence a very close second. With its entrance on to Market Square and the rear facing the High Street, we believed that it dated back to the time of Henry VIII. One wall had been preserved by sheets of thick perspex to reveal the original wattle and daub construction and there was a wealth of oak beams and panelling which over the centuries had acquired a patina the colour of a bar of dark plain chocolate. The narrowest of oak staircases wound its way from the reception to the low-ceilinged bedrooms above, furnished in Jacobean style with many authentic period wardrobes and tables; American tourists just swooned over the four-poster beds.

The year 1963 was noted for many notable historic events worldwide as well as parochial. On the international front, the world froze with horror at the assassination of President Kennedy and nearer home and receiving an equal amount of local news coverage was the Great Train Robbery. On 8th August a daring and complex plan to rob a mail train culminated in mailbags containing £2.8 million being stolen from a Royal Mail express train which an armed gang had forced to stop at Linslade, 10 miles from Aylesbury. Most of the gang were caught and their trials duly opened at the Buckinghamshire Assizes in the county town of Aylesbury. The Bull's Head had never known such business in all its four centuries – it was booked solid for a whole year by newspaper reporters and lawyers engaged on the case, and when not in Court they kept the bar-tills ringing away merrily into the early hours. It was glorious trading whilst it lasted but, sad to say, a few years later the hotel came to an ignominious end. It fell down.

Of much later vintage was the Berners Hotel, built in 1906, seemingly taking its name from Berners Street, a road that starts at Oxford Street and ends at the Middlesex Hospital. A typical Edwardian property of some 200 rooms, it was popular with provincial visitors to the capital on account of its central location and proximity to the great shops of the West End. It was placed on the market by Hotel York Ltd. – a small company owned by Mrs Amy Rose, a very enterprising lady who owned The Rose Court, another but very much smaller hotel near Marble Arch. Our negotiations to purchase the Berners Hotel for £530,000 were tough but were conducted in a friendly spirit and were quickly concluded. It was very rare then for a hotel to have a complete and up-to-date inventory of its furniture, fixtures and fittings. When ownership changed, it was implied that the purchaser would be buying 'lock stock and barrel', with only the stock of food and liquor to be paid for separately, usually on a valuation made by an independent licensed stocktaker. Once contracts had been exchanged the vendor was trusted not to remove any items except with the knowledge and prior approval of the buyer. Imagine my surprise, therefore, when, on handing Mrs Rose a banker's draft for the balance due of £477,000 to complete the deal, she picked up a battered Royal portable typewriter from her desk and said, 'You know, Mr Jackson, this is not included in the sale ... it is my personal property.' I was flabbergasted but kept my counsel, at the same time thinking, this lady will go far. Little did I realise at that moment how far the lady *would* go.

Amy was not the type to celebrate her very advantageous sale by buying a luxury yacht and having it sailed down for her, to be moored in Villefranche on the *Côte d'Azur*, where she would spend the rest of her days sipping a kir on deck and watching the world go by. Neither did she, at the age of 60, go into retirement regretting having sold the one object that had absorbed all her energy for the past few years. Instead she went out shopping and came home having bought a whole town – Letchworth Garden City in Hertfordshire. Her purchase of the controlling interest in the shares of Letchworth First Garden City Limited provoked a violent reaction from the city fathers of Letchworth and this fascinating story has been told in a book which makes compulsive reading. Entitled *A Tale of One City*, it was written by the man at the heart of this unique and controversial takeover – Horace Plinston, Clerk to the Letchworth Urban District Council. Amy, true to form, was a redoubtable adversary and fought the council through the High Courts. It needed a special Parliamentary Bill to be passed before control could be prised from her grip, but not before she had pocketed several million pounds' profit on her deal.

With that kind of money; you can buy a whole load of *new* portable typewriters.

Staying in a hotel today one assumes that it will have central heating, more often than not air-conditioning and, of course, bathrooms-en-suite. One is apt to forget that these amenities now considered essentials are comparatively recent innovations and before the war were to be found only in luxury hotels in major cities. My initiation into the hotel industry in the early 1950s brought home to me the enormity of the task and the investment involved in modernising the infrastructure of the three and four star hotels which made up Spiers & Pond's portfolio. Boilers that provided domestic hot water and central heating were fired by solid fuel, requiring mountains of coal, coke or anthracite to be stored in cellars close to the furnaces. The first phase of modernisation was invariably to convert the central heating boilers to use oil, and finally these were replaced completely by gas boilers when an assured, consistent and economical supply of natural gas became available from the North Sea. It was rare to find a hotel with more than a third of its bedrooms with their own private bathrooms en-suite; electricity was usually DC (direct current) and had to be converted to AC (alternating current) and the whole hotel rewired. Lifts frequently were hydraulic, that is to say they were powered by water pressure and had to be replaced by new and more reliable automatic electric lifts that were programmed to stop selectively at different floors. There was a vast backlog of replacement of out-moded furniture. Out went the Lloyd loom chairs and settees, to be replaced by upholstered armchairs, and fitted bedroom furniture was substituted for free-standing wardrobes and dressing tables. The high degree of attrition on soft furnishings, necessitated complete recarpeting, usually wall-to-wall, now very much in vogue. The magnitude of such reinvestment programmes impacted on hotel values so that freehold hotels were selling for as little as £1,000 to £2,500 per bedroom – a sum that today would be barely sufficient to buy a set of twin divan beds. To cite just one example, in 1953 the 165-bedroom Grand Hotel in Brighton had been on the market for £180,000 fully furnished and freehold.

The hotel sector in the stock market was for many years out of favour and when bankers were approached to finance hotel acquisitions they would withdraw into their walk-in safes and close the steel door. Too many fingers had been burnt in the years between the wars from too many bankruptcies and it took nearly 20 years of peace before the hotel industry was to regain the confidence of the financial markets. Meanwhile, we did as much modernisation as our cash flow permitted, whilst continuing to knock on City doors just in case one was to spring open and a beneficent banker be found ready to lend money for expansion. Occasionally I was lucky and there would be an addition to our group of Empire Hotels but, despite numerous bomb sites going for a song, wartime building restrictions still in force deterred the building of hotels to replace those lost in the Blitz. The boom in tourism which followed on the heels of the expansion of air travel was still somewhere over the horizon and the conference trade had yet to be invented.

17

The Days of Milk and Sausages

I was now to find out in earnest that Müller's main interest in the business lay in the price that our company's shares were quoted. He remained in blissful ignorance of the day-to-day problems of running the group and the immense task involved in resurrecting a formerly moribund hotel company – that was not his concern. He enjoyed visiting the hotels providing they were on the south coast and then did so incognito and would stay only for lunch. He knew none of the hotel's employees by name and they knew him solely from a photograph that one year he allowed to appear in the company's annual report and accounts. From time to time he would inspect a hotel but usually from the opposite side of the street. I never knew him to go into a kitchen and talk to the chef – to listen to his problems (and which chef has no problems he wants to air?) or to give him encouragement. I found this surprising, because his knowledge and mastery of meat and butchery were quite exceptional and he would have discovered many admirers amongst our chefs.

The speculative element in his psyche was soon to come to the fore.

I have referred earlier to Sam Messer, a partner of the redoubtable property developer Jack Cotton, in an estate agency they ran in London. Sam's success in the property market enabled him to indulge his hobby of building a collection of English furniture of supreme quality which was considered to be the best in the country. He lived as a country squire in the village of Peasmarsh in Sussex, his manor house exquisitely furnished with

Georgian and Regency furniture, Tompion clocks and antique barometers. It was all in very good taste and Sam confided in me that he had been promised a peerage if he would agree to leave the collection to the nation on his death. He never did, and many years later Christies sold the major part of it for more than £7 million.

Leopold was not interested in Sam's aesthetics. The attraction was Sam's position as a non-executive director of Express Dairies and the son-in-law of its chairman, Walter Nell. Express was a major supplier of milk and dairy products and ranked third in size in the industry. Although not as large as Unigate, its immediate competitor, it had over nearly a century of trading built up a formidable business. The price of milk was still regulated through the government's Milk Marketing Board, which exercised a restraint on profits, but these were still in the respectable range of £3–4 million a year on a turnover of £70 million. The feature that set them apart from their major competitors in the industry was their operation of no less than 50 tea-shops. Most of them were in London, and operated on a limited and reasonably priced menu. The years between the wars had been the golden age of the tea-shop, with those operated by J. Lyons & Co. being the public's favourite and the market leader.

Müller was not content to wait for the share price of his S & P shares to reflect the improvement in the company's trading figures; he was impatient and wanted to see a big boost. Approaching Messer with the suggestion that Express Dairies might take over Spiers & Pond, he found Sam willing to listen and to talk. Both men were deal-makers by nature, but there was little that a hotel company like S & P had in common with a milk giant. Diversification for its own sake rarely succeeds but I suspect that Express was apprehensive of being left further behind by the more aggressive and acquisitive Unigate.

Negotiations were opened and progressed rapidly, with the terms being agreed that Express would make an all-paper offer using their non-voting 'A' shares that would price our shares about 50% higher than the market quotation.

Müller was a good negotiator and I was more than happy to

leave the bargaining process to him. Walter Nell, a trained engineer, had spent his lifetime working in Express Dairies and was a redoubtable adversary when it came to looking after his company's interests. He was not prepared to dilute his share-holders' equity, even though the 'A' shares held by the general public carried no vote and company control was firmly in his family's hands. Nell and Müller knew that whatever terms they mutually agreed on would be passed by the shareholders of both companies.

Our final meeting took place on a Friday at the Express head office in Tavistock Square. It went on until 8 p.m., when the basic terms of the merger were settled. A letter setting out the heads of agreement was drawn up and signed by Walter Nell and his cousin William Bell, respectively Chairman and Managing Director of Express Dairies and by Müller and myself for Spiers & Pond.

I went home and told my wife Peggy of the deal and spent a sleepless night worrying whether I had done the right thing. My concern was that after only five years working up S & P and enjoying complete autonomy to grow the company, I would now become subservient to a large board of directors completely ignorant of the hotel and leisure industry and who our own company secretary described in a derogatory fashion as being 'only milkmen'.

Early next morning I telephoned Müller and we arranged to meet at Kahn's, a small continental-style restaurant that he personally owned. I expressed my apprehension of linking up with a dairy company and my concern at our having disposed of our company and lost our independence. To my surprise I found that he was entertaining the same doubts and over endless cups of coffee we discussed how we could extricate ourselves from the deal. I suggested that on Monday morning we should seek the advice of Leonard Sainer, the senior partner of our solicitors Titmuss Sainer & Webb. Sainer had a well-earned reputation as one of the most astute corporate lawyers in the City, his deep knowledge of the law being heightened by an acute business sense. As Charles Clore's right-hand man, he had been instrumental in building up Sears Holdings as well as City and Central Properties.

I felt that he was our man. At first Müller was totally against this step as he still entertained the delusion that Sainer had robbed him of the Stagg & Russell deal some years previously. However, he could not come up with an alternative suggestion and finally agreed to pocket his pride and see Leonard Sainer.

We met at Sergeant's Inn and I gave Sainer a resumé of our negotiations and the final meeting of the previous Friday. We told him that we were unhappy with the deal in principle and would like to find a way in which we could extricate ourselves with some semblance of honour. He started by chiding us for conducting negotiations to a final stage and attending the fateful meeting without having legal advice available to us. He then studied the document that we had all signed on Friday and a smile spread across his face. He said, 'Mr Müller, you have nothing to worry about. What you have signed is not a *binding* agreement. It is an agreement to enter into an agreement.' We then discussed a face-saving formula that would enable us to walk away from Express Dairies. We decided that we should ask them to add a significant cash element to the 'paper' consideration which we had already agreed on. I insisted that the plan would only work if we asked for such a large 'sweetener' for our shareholders that Express would consider it exorbitant and break off negotiations. We fixed on 12s 6d (62$\frac{1}{2}$p) a share as the contract-breaker, thanked Mr Sainer for his advice and left for an afternoon meeting with the Express Dairy board which I had requested their secretary, Mr Redman, a Scottish chartered accountant, to convene.

Müller and I were very nervous when we entered the boardroom and told Walter Nell and his colleagues that we felt that we could not sell the deal to our shareholders unless there was a significant cash element added to the paper consideration. Nell was blunt. 'How much?' he said.

'Twelve shillings and sixpence,' Müller replied.

Pandemonium broke out and when some semblance of order had been restored, Nell said, 'But that is outrageous, we have an agreement.'

We then told him that we had been advised that it was not enforceable, a view which with reluctance his directors eventually

177

accepted. I had no idea what was going through Müller's mind whilst the altercation was going on, but his resolve to walk away from the deal seemed to ebb away.

'Mr Nell,' he said, 'the very least I can expect our shareholders to accept would be an extra 2s 6d in cash.' I was dumbfounded and knew in my heart that Nell was sufficiently pragmatic not to let this sum spoil his deal. 'I must give my shareholders a bone,' concluded Müller.

'A bone, Mr Müller?' retorted Nell. 'All right then, but you must give me your undertaking that that will be the end of the meal.'

And so it was that Spiers & Pond after a hundred years as an independent hotel company passed into the ownership of Express Dairies and Müller and I joined their board.

It had been agreed that we would continue to develop and expand the hotel division and initially we were made very welcome by an enthusiastic Express Dairies board. We were particularly keen to start on the task of modernising the 50 tea-shops and to integrate them into the Chicken Inns chain. At the first meeting on joining the board, one of the dairy directors told me, 'Thank God you have joined us. As for the tea-shops and our restaurants, we couldn't run a whelk stall!'

When I repeated this to Müller his only comment was, 'What *is* a whelk stall?'

We soon discovered that the board was split down party lines – 'family' lines would be a more apt description. In the family camp was Walter Nell the Chairman, two sons-in-law Sam Messer and Patrick Galvani, together with two cousins of the Chairman William Bell and his brother. Collectively they controlled the company through their shareholdings, their ordinary and preference shares being the only ones carrying votes. The remainder of the board formed a vocal but toothless opposition. Sam Messer was a non-executive director, his advice being sought purely on property matters. Patrick Galvani, on the other hand, despite his youth, had overall responsibility for the burgeoning group of supermarkets trading under the banner Premier Supermarkets, pioneers in this new field of grocery retailing. Within Galvani's fiefdom came the tea-shops and obviously he was the one we had to cultivate.

Central to our success with the Chicken Inns group was the centralisation of the purchasing and preparation of the 10,000 chickens we were using every week. Continuing this policy, as soon as wartime restrictions were lifted, we had established a state-of-the-art butchery in Smithfield market. Not only were we able to supply our hotels and restaurants with the choicest sides of beef, veal, lamb and pork in an oven-ready form, but we could now make our own brand of succulent pork sausages. Müller was a past-master in blending choice spices with the off-cuts of pork taken from the pigs we personally selected from the abattoir in Caledonian market, a privilege I had been able to secure through my acquaintance with the chairman of the Fatstock Marketing Corporation. I was fascinated with the whole process of sausage making: seeing how the powerful bowl cutter with its blade revolving at thousands of revolutions a minute could reduce meat and even small bones to the consistency of toothpaste, and the action of the automatic filling machine which also twisted the sausages to the required size and weight. I became personally involved in buying the sausage skins, known as 'casings', and found that the top grade were sheep casings imported from China. Although I never ate one (there is no such thing as a *kosher* pork sausage), I relied on my panel of tasters – thousands of satisfied customers every week. I felt certain that we could quite easily expand our production tenfold if Premier Supermarkets would stock them.

Galvani expressed curiosity, which I misguidedly interpreted as enthusiasm, and I arranged for a pork sausage-tasting in our Haymarket kitchens. I put a lot of effort into the arrangements, briefing the cooks on the importance of the trials. Six varieties were cooked and laid out on separate plates, each one with a different combination of spice and texture. My eyes were glued on Galvani as he cut the first one and popped a third of it into his mouth and chewed. Then there was a scream as he spat out what he had just eaten and there on the plate was a small copper clip.

I had seen hundreds of them before but then each one had been impaled in an ear of a newly slaughtered pig and fastened to a label on which was written the weight of the animal. It had no right whatsoever to turn up at this crucial moment. It was a thousand to one chance that it had escaped our inspections during processing and odds of a million to one that it should have surfaced at this vital demonstration.

I turned white. Galvani turned red and stormed out of the kitchen. Premier Supermarkets lost the opportunity of selling the best pork sausages in London.

Attending the regular board meetings, I was able to gain an insight into how the business of Express was conducted, a complete contrast from my own hands-on approach. One of the board meetings that remains fresh in my memory took place early in 1960, when the main item on the agenda was 'yoghurt'. This was a new venture and a new product and consequently there was animated discussion on its manufacture, packaging and marketing, followed by a tasting of samples laid out on the boardroom table. Little did any of us realise that Express was about to create a market that would grow to more than £1 billion a year.

Müller and I were always treated by Walter Nell with great courtesy but he was progressively letting go the reins of power, having accepted the appointment of life President and promoted his cousin William Bell to Chairman. We were left to deal directly with Patrick Galvani over the modernisation of the tea-shops. Galvani, whose only qualification for board membership appeared to be his relationship as Nell's son-in-law, was resentful of our intrusion into his domain and increasingly laid obstacles to the implementation of our plans for the tea-shops. His procrastination became a source of frustration, and board meetings for us became fraught, relieved only partially by invitations to stay on for lunch which was served by the President's butler. These eventually became a source of embarrassment to me when, after the meal, Müller would with a flourish take his wallet from his breast pocket, extract a new £5 note and in front of the other directors

180

hand it to the butler as a tip. This may have gone down well in Vienna in the days of the Austro-Hungarian Empire, but I felt it very much out of place in London's Tavistock Square.

The Mirabelle restaurant was a legend. It deservedly enjoyed the reputation of being one of the best restaurants in Europe. Consequently, when we were approached early in 1961 by business agents Ackroyds & Sons of St James's Street with the news that it might come onto the market, we were very excited and brought it up for discussion at the very next meeting of the Express board. We asked to be authorised to enter into negotiations for S & P to purchase the business. The reaction of the board came as a bombshell. They were vehemently opposed to the purchase, with Walter Nell expressing the view that it was a very risky business prone to bad debts!

Our relations with the board steadily deteriorated as each proposition we brought was, for one reason or another, turned down. Amongst them was the purchase of the Castle Hotel in Norwich, a main road freehold property facing Castle Mount in the prosperous capital of East Anglia. When they refused to support the acquisition of the De Vere hotel, an elegant Edwardian property facing Kensington Gardens, we knew that we had to make a break with these myopic milkmen. We had also become disillusioned with the performance of the Express Dairy 'A' shares. Express had paid £2 10s (£2.50) for each Spiers & Pond share, using their own shares priced at 12s 6d (62½p) each, plus of course the 2s 6d (12½p) '*Danegeld*'. At the time of the takeover, Walter Nell had assured us that the Express shares would rise to £1 within a year, but instead they had now sunk to a low of 9s 6d (48p). The Express board were jubilant when we tendered our resignations and we departed, each with a 'silver' handshake of £25,000. The days of golden handshakes for 'fat cats' was still some two decades away.

18

And Pulled out a Plum

Müller, who had just turned 60, and I, at 44, now had to assess the future; whether we should stay together or go our separate ways. He had, during our 13 years of partnership, commencing with the purchase of the first Chicken Inn, accumulated a considerable fortune. In financial terms I too was well satisfied with my achievements. He turned to me, and taking it for granted that we would not be splitting up, asked whether I saw our future to be in a small company or whether I wanted the 'big time', adding that he was able to finance whichever we decided on. Faced with the choice, there was no hesitation on my part. I felt that having grown up in the culture of a large business I needed to have the stimulus and intellectual challenge that creating an important new group from scratch would give me. My reply was, 'The bigger the better.' I think he was hoping for just such an answer and in no time we started to plan.

Our first purchase was the De Vere hotel in Kensington, which I negotiated with Edward Langton, the senior partner of Stoy Hayward, the accountants to the owner, Mr Michael Lewis. We agreed a price, subject to my seeing the most recent balance sheet. When this was produced, a trading loss was revealed which I felt called for a reduction in the purchase price. Langton's answer to this claim was, 'Not a penny. I am not selling you a hotel, I'm selling a valuable piece of London real estate.' He had a valid point and it was up to us to make the hotel profitable. On Monday 1st January 1962 we completed the purchase and started to turn the business around. Taking my cue from the up-market name of the hotel, situated as it was in the Royal Borough of Kensington and Chelsea, I formed a company which I called De Vere Hotels Ltd. We mutually agreed that whilst building the business we would subscribe for shares in the proportion of 75:25 until the issued share capital had reached £1 million. Additional finance would thereafter be lent by us to the company as required, as near to the same ratio as my personal finances would stretch.

We purchased the Castle Hotel, a property that Express Dairies had declined, and I started to make enquiries about the Mirabelle.

No. 56 Curzon Street in Mayfair, close to Shepherd Market, was built in 1936 as a seven-storey block of service flats. Primarily to cater for the residents on the upper floors, the Mirabelle Restaurant, taking its name from a small golden plum grown extensively in France, was established on the garden level. The origins of Mayfair go back to 1280, when King Edward I granted a royal licence for a week-long fair during the month of May to be held each year on farmland on the western outskirts of London. Known as May Fayre and in close proximity to St James's Palace, its cattle market eventually gave way to small shops and stalls frequented by the *haut monde* and those close to the royal court. Some of the farmland had been acquired during the time of Queen Anne by Sir Richard Sutton, and it was on this land, now worth many millions of pounds an acre, that No. 56 was subsequently built. Many years later, I was to deal with the Sutton Settled Estates in an effort to purchase the freehold interest of the building, and we were not talking agricultural land prices!

The restaurant, which had introduced dinner dances, was under the direction of the Marchese Sartori, the founder of Quaglinos restaurant and later of the Coq d'Or. It had survived the war undamaged, both physically and in reputation. It had come on to the market in 1951 and had been bought for £20,000 by Danny Brock, the multi-millionaire industrialist who had founded Automotive Products, the makers of Lockheed brakes. His lineage was the Brock fireworks family and he was intent on putting a rocket under the restaurant that would blast it into the gastronomic stratosphere.

The immediate post-war years saw numerous new clubs and

restaurants opening in the West End, responding to the pent-up feelings of elation at having escaped from the dangers and tribulations of the war. At the heart of this movement were several talented Polish ex-servicemen who, in their native country, had been young waiters. To name just two, there was John Mills, who opened the highly successful Les Ambassadeurs in Park Lane, and Erwin Schleyn, brought in by Brock to run a refurbished Mirabelle. With Schleyn as host and Brock as financier, their joint aim was to create a restaurant to rival the best in Paris, then the gastronomic capital of Europe. These Poles were not chefs but were able to locate and recruit outstanding culinary expertise to complement their own talents as 'mine host'. Chefs were expected to stay unseen in the kitchen and cook and check every dish before it was presented to the customer. It would be many years before they were to achieve their present-day celebrity status. The *prima donna* of the restaurant had to be the Maitre d', and Schleyn discovered Jean Drees, a 23-year-old Parisian genius working in the kitchens of the Washington hotel just across the street from the restaurant. Drees was a disciple of the legendary Escoffier who, together with César Ritz, a Swiss-born hotelier, had dominated the Edwardian scene, making the Savoy the most-sought after hotel in England.

The combination of Schleyn the host, the man who was reputed to check the credentials of every diner before accepting a table reservation, and Drees the chef that no diner ever saw, proved to be the perfect mix for creating a restaurant of such glamour and exclusivity that it achieved international acclaim and fame. London's gastronomic scene had for years been centred in the old hotels, such as the Ritz and the Savoy-group – the Connaught, Claridge's and the Berkeley. There were few restaurants which had the *chic* and romance of the great restaurants of Paris – Maxims, Tour d'Argent, and Lasserre, to name just three of the elite group recognised by Michelin with their top award of *trois étoiles* – three stars. The aim of Danny Brock was to rival them all. He had the right premises in the right location; had found the talent and, what is even more, possessed the financial resources to achieve his ambition.

After the austerity of the war years and the loss through bombing of many fashionable establishments that owed their origins to the plush days of the Edwardian era, London was ready to embrace a new Mirabelle. It did not take off at first like one of Brock's firework rockets, but spluttered rather like a damp squib. He was to tell me later-on that on the night after the glamorous opening party he came to the restaurant for dinner to find he was the only guest. Undismayed, he ate his dinner in solitary state and left, but not before handing over a £50 tip to the waiting staff. This then was the restaurant that from the late 1950s achieved such popularity that it was the first choice of any visiting American film star, was host to the Shah of Persia and all the remaining crowned heads of Europe and saw innumerable financial coups consummated over the consommé; the restaurant that would turn Rudolf Nureyev away because he was not wearing a tie and refuse entry to Sir Bernard Docker, the multi-millionaire Chairman of the Daimler Car Company because Lady Docker, accompanying him, was wearing a trouser suit.

Our business agent, James Smalley of Ackroyds, who had been instrumental in selling us the De Vere Hotel several months earlier, telephoned to say that Brock was now ready to talk to us. It appeared that Erwin Schleyn, to whom he had given a 49% interest in the restaurant company, had died suddenly the previous year. Probate had now been granted to his widow Cecilia, an elegant hostess who, with the able assistance of Louis Emmanueli, Erwin's reception head waiter, was managing the restaurant. I would have to negotiate with Stanley Rubinstein, the senior partner in the Gray's Inn law firm of Rubinstein Nash, to whom Arnold Goodman (later on to become the eminent and ennobled lawyer to the rich and the powerful) had been articled. We would be buying the whole of the issued share capital of Mirabelle Ltd., namely all the assets and liabilities of the company.

The major asset – its goodwill – was not shown on the balance sheet, but it was an intangible asset of immense value. The other assets were very visible: a restaurant that could seat 200 diners in great comfort with the tables spaced out at a discreet distance from one another; a restaurant that looked out onto its own garden and where, on fine days, the roof would be retracted electronically by the push of a button for dining under the stars. Only the best of Irish linen, silverware and Scandinavian glass was deemed good enough to show off the fine Royal Worcester china badged with the restaurant's logo.

The asset that, at first, was not prominent was the legendary wine cellar. Hidden away in caverns under pavements and in temperature controlled cabinets were stored wines to make even Bacchus drool with envy. There in total darkness nestled some 25,000 bottles, all chateau or domaine bottled, and thousands more were stored in bonded warehouses in London docks or held in warehouses in Bordeaux or in Beaune in Burgundy. This stock was to become the focal point of controversy in our negotiations and, failure to agree its value, to almost wreck the deal. It was recorded in the balance sheet at its historic cost price of £80,000, equivalent to £2 million today, and included wines of such great rarity as *Château Lafite* 1803 and *pre-phylloxera* clarets (wines that had been made before the *phylloxera* bug in the 1870s destroyed the French vineyards) of all the classified *Grand Crus*. Rubinstein wanted to increase the book value of the stock to a figure that would be midway between the original cost price and the cost of replacement. The vast majority of the exceptional wines had been purchased many years previously at very advantageous prices and I strenuously resisted Rubinstein's ploy.

Finally, having reached a compromise, the purchase price of the shares was agreed at £225,000. I will never forget the look on Stanley Rubinstein's face when his octogenarian client Danny Brock agreed to sell at this figure. Rising from his chair at the negotiating table, his finger pointing to the ground, he exclaimed, 'On your knees, Jackson. Do you realise you have won the jewel in the crown?'

The sale was completed on 8th November 1962 and made headline news in all the national newspapers. It was a real coup for De Vere, a small private company that very few people had heard of. It created considerable jealousy in the trade and there was no shortage of detractors who were convinced that we would debase the restaurant's quality and ruin the business. We did neither.

Until our acquisition of Mirabelle, I had operated from an office I had established in a building adjoining the De Vere hotel in Kensington. Our new purchase not only brought with it a 1955 Rolls-Royce (written down to £1 in the books), but a magnificent small Georgian building at No. 7 Queen Street, almost a stone's throw from the Mirabelle. Held on a long lease from the Prudential Assurance Company at a nominal fixed rent of £2,000 per annum, it made the ideal headquarters for our operations in the West End of London.

Taking our time, I instigated a long hard look at every aspect of the operation. The organisation of the kitchen under Drees, was on classical French lines. *Sous chefs*, or *chefs de partie*, with their *commis* cooks were responsible for different elements of the menu. There was the *saucier*, responsible for soups and a wide range of sauces; the larder chef for meats, game and poultry; the *poissonnier*, who took care of sea-food and the hors d'oeuvres; and the *patissier*, who enjoyed complete autonomy in his own small pastry kitchen away from the heat of the main ovens. All food was carried into the dining area on silver salvers and presented to the guest for approval. The present practice of plating food with the inevitability of its becoming tepid before reaching the diner was still, fortunately, many years away.

I was not yet qualified to make a critical appreciation of the way the kitchen was structured and run. I was content to find that every commodity bought was fresh and of the highest quality. No frozen foods were purchased, which resulted in the restaurant offering beans and peas only in the early months of the summer. But as an accountant I could not accept that our food cost in relationship to our menu prices should be as high as 60%, giving a gross profit of only 40%. I had to turn these figures round. I was soon to discover one of the main causes of the high food cost.

From time immemorial it had been endemic in high-class restaurants for tradesmen to bribe chefs and managers to buy from them. It was customary on a Friday for numerous brown envelopes to appear mysteriously in the kitchen or at the back door. In return, a chef would be expected to turn a blind eye to short deliveries, uncompetitive prices, even, ultimately, to inferior quality. It is on

187

record that in March 1898, César Ritz and Auguste Escoffier, probably the most celebrated *duo* ever to grace the English hotel and restaurant scene, were involved in a scandal which ended in dismissal by their employers the Savoy Hotel Company. The board of directors, after a searching investigation into the profit – or rather, lack of it – from their food and beverage operation announced in a statement to its shareholders that 'it had been their imperative duty to dismiss the Manager and the Chef from their service'. [*sic*]

In attempting to introduce new and better sources of supply for Mirabelle, I was encountering considerable resistance from the kitchen. My solution was to treble the chef's salary whilst making him aware of the fate that, 60 years earlier, had befallen his compatriot Escoffier, whose treatise *Guide Culinaire* served as Drees' bible. We now understood one another and were ready to enter into a new and profitable era together that was to last for 25 years.

19

Acquisitions and Losses

The year 1963 proved to be a momentous rather frenetic year, beginning only weeks after the purchase of Mirabelle. It started when Müller said to me, 'There is an auction tomorrow by Jones Lang Wootton in Grosvenor House. They will be selling properties owned by the Church Commissioners ... Let's go, as I'm interested in Television House in Kingsway.' Joined by Albert Berger, senior partner in the firm of estate agents Douglas Kershaw & Co., we took our seats under the crystal chandeliers in the ballroom of the hotel. Until I picked up the auction catalogue I knew nothing at all about Television House, which had previously been named Adastral House when it was occupied by the Royal Air Force. It was Lot No. 26, a property consisting of basement, ground, mezzanine and seven upper floors producing a rental income of £35,000 per annum. The photograph in the catalogue showed a most impressive building sited in Aldwych opposite Bush House. The Grosvenor House ballroom was packed, the auction, the first major sale to be made by the Commissioners, having attracted the attention of all the large property groups. The bidding opened at £450,000 and the auctioneer constantly implored buyers not to bid in hundreds. At one stage he remarked, 'Don't let anyone *dare* to bid in less than five thousands ... it saves my voice and your time.' As the price slowly rose, I could see Berger calculating the yield on his slide rule and whispering to Müller. Then up shot Müller's hand and he shouted, '£465,000'. The auctioneer's ivory gavel came down and De Vere had bought Television House ... a real feather in our cap although completely unrelated to our core business.

Müller and I left the ballroom and adjourned to the cloakrooms. Standing next to me in the urinal, he said with pride in his voice, 'What a wonderful buy, what a wonderful freehold.'

'Freehold, Mr Müller?' I exclaimed. 'We haven't bought the *freehold* – it's a lease. The London County Council own the freehold.' There was a shocked silence and, looking down, I could see his aim had altered and he was now splashing my shoes.

There was a reasonably satisfactory outcome to this impulse purchase some months later when I had convinced him that after tax the return on our investment would be minuscule and there was little chance that the LCC would ever sell us the freehold. I approached the Prudential, who were the underbidders, and was able to get them to buy it from us for the price we had paid plus the stamp duty and conveyancing costs. This *faux pas* served only to reinforce his determination to acquire, if at all possible, the freeholds of any properties in which we might be interested. He detested leaseholds.

Very little time was to elapse before we were back again facing an estate agent in the process of auctioning a portfolio of properties. This time the action took place at the London Auction Mart, a drab building in Queen Victoria Street in a bare soulless room, a far cry from the grandeur of the crystal chandeliers and plush carpets we had found in the Grosvenor House Hotel. The attraction to us on this occasion was a block of 12 large Victorian townhouses in Ashburn Place that was being sold by the Joan Campbell Estate, the owner of impressive chunks of South Kensington. The properties had the right to use the extensive communal private gardens which they overlooked and this land was included in the sale. As all the houses were coming to the end of their leases granted in 1866, they represented an interesting redevelopment proposition. I knew the area well as the head office of Spiers & Pond had been sited in Baileys Hotel, which was situated in a street adjoining Ashburn Place. The winning bid was ours.

Within two months of this purchase I happened to see an advertisement in the *Estates Gazette* placed by Cluttons, an old-established firm of estate agents, of the sale of the freehold interest in seven properties, mainly small guest houses and hotels, fronting onto the Cromwell Road and facing the new West London Air Terminal. On checking the location on an Ordnance Survey map, I was excited to find that when joined to the Ashburn Place properties that we had just bought, they formed a perfect 'L'. We were the logical buyers and we bought.

When travel literally 'took off' in the early fifties the air travel market was shared by two independent organisations. British European Airways (BEA) dominated flights within the UK as well as serving routes to the Continent, whilst British Overseas Aircraft Corporation (BOAC) took care of long-haul international flights. Heathrow was at an early stage of its vast development as an airport and the West London Air Terminal had been built to enable BEA passengers to deposit their luggage in central London and travel by shuttle coach to the airport. I envisaged a great opportunity to build a hotel on the land we had just acquired which would serve the air terminal by linking it with an underpass across Cromwell Road. I was greatly encouraged by the supportive attitude of the authorities, and preliminary discussions with our architects indicated that the site would enable us to develop a 400-bedroom hotel. The area which our properties occupied was about 2 acres, but this included Ashburn Gardens which, I soon discovered, was protected against development. London is blessed with many fine squares – gardens laid out for the exclusive use of residences that surround it and which individually have no private gardens. Amongst the better known ones and occupying land of enormous value are Berkeley Square, Hanover Square and Belgrave Square. They are protected from development by a statute entitled The London Preservation Squares Act of 1931, a copy of which I lost no time in obtaining and reading through from cover to cover. There, amongst the list of noble squares was our own modest Ashburn Gardens, as inviolate as Grosvenor Square, the grandest of them all.

Although there was still some 18 months to go before the leases ran out and we could contemplate building, there was a tremendous amount of preliminary work to be done. I resolved to see the owners of each of the residential properties personally and to negotiate their giving up vacant possession. First of all I had to convince them that not only did we have the intention of rebuilding, but we had the necessary finance available. Had I not been able to do this, they were entitled to seek protection under the Landlord and Tenant Acts and demand new leases. Most of the tenants were resigned to the situation but, as was only to be expected, a small minority of the commercial tenants endeavoured to capitalise on our desire to proceed with the minimum of delay.

One meeting I did not relish and which, after 35 years, still remains fresh in my memory, was an appointment to see the tenant of the largest house in the terrace – No. 23 Ashburn Place, the *Thai* Embassy. I was ushered in to see the Ambassador, an elderly, very quietly spoken man who, despite my unenviable mission, treated me with old-fashioned courtesy. I told him of our plans and indicated that in the proposed redevelopment we could incorporate a new embassy. He replied philosophically and in declining the offer said that his country had occupied the building for nearly a century and now wished to move to another part of London. I felt guilty at having to be the instrument of change, and in that large drawing room overlooking Ashburn Gardens I could sense myself being rebuked by the ghost of the King of Siam, if not of Yul Brynner.

Having finally secured vacant possession of all 19 properties, I learnt through the grapevine that BEA was considering relocating to Heathrow and eventually merging with BOAC to form British Airways. We went cold on our proposed scheme and decided to sell the sites. I contacted Stanley Grinstead, joint Managing Director of Grand Metropolitan Hotels, with whom I was friendly, and offered the site to them for twice the sum we had paid. They snapped it up and paid us £1 million. With a consortium of airlines, including KLM and Lufthansa, they built a monster hotel of 910 bedrooms which soared 27 storeys above a sadly reduced Ashburn Gardens. In recognition of the five members of the consortium who had financed the venture, the hotel was named The Penta, but in recent years it has been renamed The Forum. I am not so sure the ancient Romans would have approved.

In February, we made a bid for Overton (Holdings), a small

quoted restaurant group which owned Hatchett's in Piccadilly and two seafood restaurants, one in St James's Street close to St James's Palace and the other, with an adjoining shop selling wet fish, facing Victoria Station. In a heavy and important-looking gold frame hanging in the oyster bar was the Royal Warrant, appointing the proprietor a supplier of fish to Her Majesty Queen Elizabeth II. I was very proud of this signal honour but, sad to relate, in the next ten years we were called upon to supply only one pair of kippers to nearby Buckingham Palace.

The word 'restaurant' is derived, so the Oxford English Dictionary tells me, from the French word *restaurer* – to restore. In this sense Mirabelle always lived up to its definition. From the moment that an arriving customer handed over the keys to his car to the doorman until, several hours later, he came up again to street level to find his car waiting outside the front door with the engine running, the process of restoration was in full swing.

That the kitchen would produce superb cuisine was taken for granted. The flavour and seasoning would incorporate the customer's personal preferences and it would be served elegantly and, no matter how large the tables, the correct dish would be placed in front of each customer without the waiter having to enquire, for example, 'Who ordered the Dover sole?' That was the very least that a diner would expect from Mirabelle. The apparently effortless synchronisation was the result of a lifetime of experience on the part of the most competent and dedicated team of waiters I have ever come across. Almost to a man, they had been born in London of Italian parentage and had inherited the bonhomie and devotion to service that characterises the Italian restaurateur. To 'dress' the room, a job jealously guarded by the maitre d', was an important part of the game. Every regular customer had a preferred table which was reserved as soon as a booking was made. There was no necessity to ask how one liked their lamb or pheasant cooked, or should garlic be omitted from the recipe. A salad dressing would be built up ingredient by ingredient in view of the diner and a devotee of *steak tartare* would, during the course of its preparation, be offered a tasting of the seasoned chopped fillet of beef from a silver fork. The carving of a spit-roasted duckling or grouse at the table was transformed into a work of art. It was impossible for a spot on the freshly starched Irish linen tablecloth to escape the eagle eye of the station waiter who, almost unnoticed and with amazing dexterity, would cover it with a large crisply laundered serviette. Napkins would automatically be changed at every course.

Costa, the Greek head sommelier, was an authority on the restaurant's *carte des vins*. I am convinced that over the years he had tasted all 200 of the items listed and would discreetly guide the customer on his choice, marrying the wine with the food. The doyen of this team was the suave 30-year-old restaurant manager Louis Emmanuelli, who for years had been Erwin Schleyn's understudy. Not only would he greet every customer by name, except when it was just M'lord or M'lady, but they all had a smile for him. He was as much an ambassador for the restaurant as the chef.

We took over Mirabelle at the beginning of November 1962 and I began the task of gaining the confidence of a staff, made nervous by the change in ownership, by assuring them that our sole aim was to maintain its unique character and to build on its already formidable reputation. By Christmas Eve I felt I was winning the battle when, without prior warning, Louis dropped a bombshell. Asking for a meeting, he gave me a month's notice of his intention to leave our employment. It transpired that one of our customers, Mark Birley, during his frequent visits to Mirabelle had got Louis to agree to open his new discotheque in Berkeley Square, in the basement of the building occupied by the Clermont casino operated by John Aspinall. The nightclub was to be named after his wife Annabel.

I was not prepared to let Louis go without a fight to retain his services and I asked him to give me details of the remuneration package he had been offered. He was very forthcoming and for every element of it – salary, pension, motor car, clothing allowance, holidays and bonus – I offered an improvement on Birley's offer. I drew his attention to the fact that in a nightclub he would be working extremely unsocial hours and would become a night-bird, never getting home before four o'clock in the morning. Louis remained adamant, constantly repeating that he had given his word to Birley. I could not convince him that his loyalty and primary duty was to Mirabelle, his present employer, and not to Birley and the embryo Annabel's. To add further injury to insult he then gave me a list of the staff he would be taking with him to open the new venture. Apart from the kitchen, there was not one department where he had not enticed a senior member of staff to defect. The head cloakroom attendant was endowed with a prodigious memory; cloakroom tickets were unknown and there was never any need to ask a customer to identify his coat. He too was on Louis' list. At the time and for very many years thereafter I felt betrayed, even though John Wellesley and Victor Sonvico, Louis' very able deputies, quickly rebuilt the team and took the restaurant to new heights of excellence.

Annabel's duly opened and became an overnight success, with Louis Emmanuelli reigning there for 35 years. Visiting Mirabelle a few months ago I was astonished to see an older and now silver-haired Louis once again greeting guests on their arrival. Having retired from Annabel's, he had been invited to come back to the scene of his youthful success by Mirabelle's new owner, the celebrated master-chef Marco Pierre White. At long last I was able to exorcise the ghost of my past grievance as we embraced one another as friends.

By the end of March 1963 we had received 100% acceptance of our offer for the shares of Overton (Holdings) Ltd, which had been floated as a public company a few years previously but had failed to capture the imagination of the investing public. The total amount we had to spend to acquire the three very well known West End restaurants of Hatchett's, and the two Overton's was a trifle less than £200,000. Today that sum would be just sufficient to buy a small snack bar. Although our offer had become unconditional and De Vere now owned all the shares, we still had to go through the motions of holding the annual general meeting of the company which had been arranged to take place in the company's Hatchett's Restaurant in Piccadilly.

I took the chair, flanked on one side by the Company Secretary and on the other by Paul Kirby, a partner in Moore Stephens, Chartered Accountants, the auditors. This was the first of many occasions that I would preside over the AGM of a public company and I decided to make the most of my *debut*. Unfortunately for me, apart from a solitary newspaper reporter, we faced row upon row of empty seats, but I was determined to go through the agenda item by item. With no one voting other than myself and the Secretary, all the resolutions were passed unanimously! Mr Kirby, on being thanked for his attendance, casually asked whether De Vere would be interested in purchasing the five-star Royal Bath Hotel in Bournemouth, of which his firm were the auditors. I gulped and in a strangulated voice said, '*Yes*'.

The Royal Bath was the hotel of my youthful dreams. How many times during my teenage holidays had I gazed enviously at the advertisements for their tea dances in the magnificent ballroom; looked up admiringly at the low white-painted building with its conical roof-towers faced with lead and Welsh slate so redolent of a French château. Nestling in three acres of cliffside gardens with unobstructed sea-views stretching from Poole harbour in the west to the Isle of Wight in the east, it occupies a prestigious site in the very centre of Bournemouth. When the town was still just a collection of fishermen's cottages, the purpose-built hotel was first opened for business on Queen Victoria's Coronation day on 28th June 1838. It had over the years been host to a scintillating list of guests and boasted that the Empress Eugénie, wife of Napoleon III, had taken up residence there for several months. One room on the first floor was named the Benjamin Disraeli Suite, commemorating a Cabinet meeting convened there when Queen Victoria's favourite Prime Minister was holidaying in the resort and no doubt keeping in touch with his Sovereign residing in Osborne House on the Isle of Wight just a few miles away.

The owner of the hotel was a Mrs Phyllis Lee-Duncan, who had inherited it from her grandfather, Sir Merton Russell Cotes, a great benefactor of the town. He had, during the 1880s, built a residence in the grounds of the hotel which he filled with the spoils of his travels to the Orient. Presented to the townfolk of Bournemouth, it is now a museum with a collection of Pre-Raphaelite and other fine Victorian paintings. Whenever I am in Bournemouth I make a point of popping into the museum to feast my eyes on the paintings by Rosetti and Burne-Jones.

20

Seaside Visits

I had never met Phyllis Lee-Duncan before but I knew of her reputation. She was regarded as somewhat of an autocrat, having inherited the hotel in her youth and run it for 40 years. It had been the jewel in the family crown since 1876. There was one side of her character that I found disturbing, especially as I needed to negotiate directly with her. She was known to be an anti-Semite and the hotel was notorious for turning away Jewish customers. In the United States the hotel would have been described as 'restricted', where only WASPS (White Anglo-Saxon Protestants) were welcome. Anyone with the name of Cohen or Levy telephoning the Royal Bath for accommodation would be told that the hotel was full. Finding that this still allowed some of the 'chosen race' to filter through, correspondence would undergo a further test and a similar reply be sent to anyone with an address in the popular Jewish suburbs of north-west London. Today, with our racial discrimination laws in place, this conduct would constitute an indictable offence. In the early post-war era, with the Holocaust still heavy on the world's conscience, it surfaced publicly only when repeated rebukes in the House of Commons came from Barnett Janner (later Lord Janner), the Member of Parliament for Leicester West.

Lack of investment in recent years had seen the 120-bedroom hotel downgraded by the Automobile Association from five stars to four. What they could not take away was its great charm, the spaciousness of its lounges and its location in the very heart of Bournemouth, yet in a cliff-top setting amidst landscaped gardens with a Mediterranean feel.

I was ready to meet this ogre of an owner who, having become so dispirited with her lack of success in running the property as a hotel, had applied for and obtained planning consent to develop the site for a 16-storey block of luxury flats.

Paul Kirby was most helpful in breaking the ice in my first encounter with the lady. I cannot say that the two of us got on like a house on fire, but my worst fears proved unfounded. I could sense that she was resentful and reluctant to sell to someone who she feared might expose her professional shortcomings by making the hotel profitable once again. Our negotiations were brief and agreement was reached for De Vere to acquire the shares of the company for £285,000. The price was for the business as a going concern, to include all the fixtures and fittings other than the oil paintings and objets d'art, a schedule of these to be furnished to us at the time of completion, which we agreed would take place one month later on 1st July 1963. Having learnt from my experience several years previously when dealing with Mrs Amy Rose at the completion of the purchase of the Berners hotel, I was not surprised when Mrs Lee-Duncan told me that a small sailing yacht moored in the Hampshire harbour of Lymington was excluded from the sale despite it featuring in the company's balance sheet.

Armed with the mandatory banker's draft I arrived at the hotel, which, I confess, I had not previously inspected having held my initial meeting with Mrs Lee-Duncan in her private suite. I now asked to be shown around. My first impression was that the hotel was caught in a time-warp, somewhere between 1890 and 1910. The lobby was dominated by two figures in full suits of armour and the feel of high Victoriana was replicated in all the public areas. The lounges, overlooking the well maintained gardens, were of majestic proportions offering an exciting potential once the outmoded furniture had been replaced. The widest corridors I have ever encountered in a hotel were adorned by countless oil paintings in heavily carved Victorian gilt frames and mounts, and a favourite and frequently repeated decoration was the Grecian figures of the Three Graces, competently painted directly on to walls vying with ceiling paintings of Neptune arising from the ocean. In handing me a three-page inventory of the oil paintings,

Mrs Lee-Duncan explained that her grandfather Sir Merton Russell-Cotes had in the 1880s and 1890s given accommodation to numerous painters and had accepted some of their works in lieu of payment in cash. She proceeded to offer to sell us about 250 of these paintings together with 20 French *animalier* bronzes, for a total of £3,000. This was at a time when Victorian paintings were completely out of vogue, if not actually derided. My concept for the hotel was to bring the light and brilliance of the gardens and sea into every room and it was not difficult for me to refuse her offer. Had I accepted, we could, after just a few years, when Victorian painting came back into vogue, have sold the paintings and bronzes for more than we had paid for the entire freehold hotel. Within a week of completion the lady had had them removed but one marine oil painting, a very large canvas in a beechwood frame, was embedded in a wall. Valiant efforts to remove this painting proved unsuccessful and the fear of having to pay for making good any consequent damage to the wall outweighed her desire to deny us the painting. She decided to leave it behind.

From time to time I am overcome by a feeling of nostalgia for this great hotel and I pay a visit to the Royal Bath which had been restored to its five-star eminence within two years of our taking over. The hall porter opens the heavy plate glass doors leading to the reception and I look admiringly at the grand staircase at the bottom of which stood the two armoured knights in full battle-dress who had been the first to greet customers prior to 1963. I turn left past the lounge and, set in a small pool banked by flowers and ferns, I see the restored and gilded life-size sculpture of the Three Graces, the bestowers of charm and beauty. A stroll along the richly carpeted corridor, wide enough to drive a bus through, and to the right is the cocktail bar with its adjoining main dining room that can, in comfort, seat 300 guests. To my left is the grill room, now dedicated to Oscar Wilde, and ahead is a short flight of steps leading to the De Vere Suite, the hotel's ballroom. I mount the stairs and look back to the wall, where I feast my eyes on a majestic seascape framed in beechwood, permanently embedded

200

in the plaster wall. Painted and signed by the renowned marine artist Henry Moore, who was elected to the Royal Academy in 1895, it is in its natural habitat. A grin comes over my face and, if I'm not mistaken, it smiles back.

There must be something very special about Bournemouth that I find it such an attractive town. Could it be the ozone drifting in from the sea? Or the smell of the pinewoods which flourish all over the area? Or the high hedges of rhododendron growing wild along the broad avenues? For a city whose claim to fame or infamy only 160 years ago was its prominence as a smuggler's paradise, it has developed not only as England's premier seaside resort, but as a financial services centre of growing importance and a desirable venue for conferences and international conventions. I had been thinking long and hard about the strategy De Vere should follow in its expansion into the burgeoning leisure industry. Air travel and the popular ownership of motor cars had fundamentally changed the pattern of holidays. No longer would a family book into a hotel for a week or a fortnight's stay. In its place, the long weekend had arrived, bringing with it the urgent need to find new markets that would fill seaside bedrooms on weekdays. American resort hotels had pioneered the conference package and had prospered, and I decided that De Vere should follow the same route.

The ink on the share transfers signed by Mrs Lee-Duncan was barely dry when Knight Frank & Rutley, one of the leading agents in hotel properties, contacted us and offered the Dormy hotel in Ferndown, situated on the edge of the New Forest and only 6 miles from the Royal Bath Hotel. I drove down from London through Salisbury and Ringwood and on into Ferndown. Mr Dudley Beck, the owner, was waiting for me at the end of a long avenue of azaleas, hydrangeas and rhododendrons. Before taking me into the hotel he insisted on giving me a conducted tour of his Italianate gardens which, with the water garden, were the showpiece of the freehold estate of 10 acres. It was love at first sight. The country house, with its 50 bedrooms furnished and exquisitely maintained by the resident proprietors, fitted in admirably with my master-plan of developing as a leading player in the conference market. Dudley proved to be a kindred spirit; we were both of quick decision and we struck a deal almost immediately at £180,000.

Not unlike Mrs Lee-Duncan and, before her, Mrs Amy Rose, Dudley had one thing that he was excluding from the transaction. This time it was not a yacht or an old portable typewriter but a small terrace of bungalows he was in the process of building speculatively by direct labour, his own workforce. He had sited the bungalows at right angles to the hotel on part of the gardens that faced onto the main road running from Ferndown to Bournemouth. I was aware that in due course I would need to develop additional bedroom capacity as a 50-bedroom property would inhibit our ability to operate the hotel as a conference hotel alongside its traditional business. The houses had just been roofed in and plumbing and internal plastering was about to commence. 'How much, Mr Beck?' I asked.

'Let's say £15,000,' came the reply.

'Done,' said I, and with a shell building that I could convert into 12 additional en-suite bedrooms, I was well satisfied with my morning's work.

Exactly four weeks after buying the Royal Bath, we completed the purchase of the Dormy, with Dudley telling me that he had, after shaking hands on the deal, turned away three higher offers. I believed him.

During the four weeks before completion I had to appoint a Manager to replace the Becks, who would be departing on 1st August. I had my eye on the restaurant Manager of the Grosvenor House hotel in Park Lane. Rudolfo Sonvico was not a hotelier, his lineage being pure restaurants. One of three brothers, the eldest being Manager of the well-known seafood restaurant belonging to Madame Prunier in St James's Street and his younger brother Victor one of our Mirabelle Maitre d's, he was the very epitome of the perfect host. He was never content to just respond to a customer's requests, he anticipated them. Having spent most of his working life in the hothouse atmosphere of the West End, he yearned for a posting in the country and the Dormy was just made for him. He was about to start on the happiest and most fulfilled ten years of his life.

The hotel adjoined the Ferndown Golf Club, but as Dudley was not a golfer he had not kept abreast of developments at the club. The course was without guile and because of chronic under-investment was not in the top echelon of championship clubs. It was widely known as a 'customer' course, where it was easy to allow a potential customer or client to win the *game* and the host to win the *business*. The presiding Professional was the well-loved Percy Alliss, whose talented son Peter became a Ryder Cup player and a celebrated TV golf commentator. The club had fallen on hard times with a declining and aging membership, and the proprietor offered the course to us for £50,000. One did not need to be a golfer to recognise the potential that combined ownership of the club and hotel offered. I made the bid at the asking price but was thwarted at the eleventh hour by the club being purchased by its members. It would have made dining in the hotel's restaurant, overlooking the seventeenth green, even more enjoyable if it had become part of our estate. In the event I had to content myself with buying every house that came onto the market whose garden adjoined our land. Over the years, no less than six came into the fold.

Peter Alliss was instrumental in bringing many prestigious golfing events to the Ferndown course, with the Dormy hotel becoming one of the main benefactors. De Vere was thus able to enjoy the benefits that ownership would have brought, without the capital outlay. It certainly did no harm that Derek Silk appointed General Manager after Sonvico's retirement, whilst building up the hotel to its present eminence, was able to employ Peter's daughter as his secretary.

As 1963 drew to a close and whilst pausing only momentarily to catch our breath, we were able to announce the purchase of the Norfolk, a four-star hotel close to the Square in Bournemouth, an important step forward in our strategic plan to raise De Vere's profile in the conference trade in the city.

Earlier in these memoirs I described the Soho of my boyhood days and the manner in which it had evolved in its Bohemian fashion into London's restaurant centre. Close to Piccadilly and an integral part of theatreland, it was the first choice for a night out on the town. It would be a very unusual palate that could not be satisfied from the wide variety of ethnic cuisines on offer. This story is about Napoleon III and the part he played in one of Soho's most popular French restaurants – *Kettners*.

Mention the name Napoleon to the average Englishman (if there is such an individual) and he conjures up the picture of a jaunty 40-year-old Corsican, sporting a tricorn hat, one hand hidden in the breast of his uniform coat mounted on a magnificent white charger. He is either leading his victorious troops into battle, or in the vanguard of a dejected and beaten army retreating through the snow on the outskirts of Moscow. Bonaparte had three brothers, Joseph, Louis and Jerome who, before his defeat at Waterloo in 1815, he had made respectively Kings of Naples, Holland and Westphalia. A weakened France then entered a period of change and reform with a short-lived reign by Napoleon II, the son of Bonaparte and his second wife Marie Louise of Austria, who died in 1832 at the age of 21. The direct line of succession having been broken was there to be a third Napoleon? The mantle of Emperor was to fall on Louis' son who, returning from exile in the wake of the 1848 Revolution, was made Emperor as a result of a *coup d'état* in 1851. We can skate over the next 20 years until the Franco-Prussian War resulted in France's defeat and Napoleon's abdication. He chose England as his land of exile.

Napoleon III during his time at the Elysée Palace had employed a chef named Auguste Kettner, who had preceded his royal master to London and had opened a small restaurant in Romilly Street, in the heart of Soho, which prospered. His skills, however, were not restricted to his prowess in his kitchen. In 1877 he was prevailed upon by a literary luminary of the day, George Auguste Sala, to publish his own cookery book, which he named *Kettner's Book of the Table*, a first edition copy of which I was fortunate to find whilst rummaging in a bookshop in Charing Cross Road.

In January 1964 we were able to celebrate the purchase of

M. Kettner's old restaurant, much enlarged over the century that had passed since its foundation. It was patronised by a large clientele who appreciated the French provincial cooking in which it excelled. It was only to be expected that a restaurant of this age would have many legends, which included stories of romantic assignations in the *salles privées* on the first floor. One which I would not lightly dismiss involves Edward VII and Lily Langtry after her appearances at the Palace Theatre, only a stone's throw away. Dominating the cocktail bar was a full-length portrait of Auguste Kettner, which hangs there to this very day, serving to remind the current pizza-orientated clientele of the great days of Soho gastronomy.

We acquired the whole issued share capital of Kettners restaurant for the sum of £353,000. Once again we were the recipient of valuable hidden bounty. Not only had the vendor, Maurice Monnickendam, been able, during the war and the immediate post-war years to maintain the culinary reputation of the restaurant, but he had also used his skills and the very substantial profits he was making to build up large stocks of fine wines. I suspect that this was his way of sheltering his profits from EPT, the penal Excess Profits Tax which was levied at the rate of 100% on the profits of a business made during the State of Emergency, over and above the average it had earned before the outbreak of war.

Adjoining the restaurant on the corner of Soho's main street, Old Compton Street, he established a wine shop from which he sold his fine wines and the widest range of Scotch single-malt whiskies to be found in London. It was what lay under the floor of the restaurant and the wine shop that was startling. Cellar after cellar, with racks from floor to ceiling, was an Aladdin's cave of wine. If this was not bountiful enough, I discovered two basements in adjoining Frith Street which the company had rented and which were full of unopened wooden crates of wine packed from floor to the pavement flaps through which they had been lowered. But there was still more. In a bonded warehouse there was sufficient to start up an independent wine merchant's business. Going through the inventory, I noticed that we had 100 cases of Château

Margaux 1945 priced at ten shillings a bottle (50p). No doubt it was bought *en primeur* before this outstanding vintage was even bottled, soon after the war, at a time when the pound could buy a record number of French francs.

I suggested to my colleague Reginald Constable that we should draw a case from bond and sample it, more for enjoyment than to establish its value, although I was very keen to cash-in a major part of our newly acquired liquid wealth. The case was delivered to the restaurant and in the cellars I poured my very first tasting of a Château Margaux. I dispensed with the customary twirling of the glass that would enhance the bouquet, as well as the first cautious sip to be sucked slowly into the mouth. We both took a long swig of the deep purple liquid I had poured so carefully into our glasses so as not to disturb the sediment. Reg looked at me in dismay and grimaced; I was not so mannerly – I spat it all out. Its tannin content was pronounced and had the highest degree of acerbity I had ever experienced. I would be the first to admit that at the time my knowledge of fine wines was, at best, rudimentary. I instructed Reg to sell the whole parcel of wine and was pleased that we were able to do this at a price of £12 for a case of 12 bottles, double the figure shown in the inventory.

If only we had had the benefit of hindsight. We were unaware that the 1945 vintage in Bordeaux would be proclaimed as one of the top three vintages of the twentieth century and that Château Margaux loaded with tannin and acidity would not reach its peak until the years 1985 to 2005 – at least 20 years after our amateurish tasting and 60 years after the grapes had been harvested. In my humble opinion it is a wine that will go on improving year-on-year, keeping pace with its price; at auction today *one* case would probably fetch more than £12,000.

One of my scary moments in the war was lying 2 miles off Beachy Head for three interminable hours in the light of a full moon, waiting to escort a westbound convoy to the Bristol Channel. The sea, in as calm a mood as one could wish for, was turned into a silver mirror. It was an idyllic setting – a painted ship on a painted ocean. But I was not thinking romantically as our engines turned over just sufficiently to counter the flood tide and keep us in position for the rendezvous. On the bridge, searching the horizon through my night glasses for a sight of the convoy, I imagined I could see a periscope, or was it the fluorescent bow wave of an E boat speeding towards us at 40 knots, or even worse the trail of a torpedo? As I trained my binoculars towards the shore I picked up the lighthouse silhouetted against the white cliffs, its warning flashes long extinguished for the duration of the war.

The memory of that night came flooding back as I drove across the undulating South Downs on which grazed flocks of Sussex-bred sheep. A more peaceful and typically English landscape it would be impossible to conjure up. As I drove, I found myself singing aloud that immortal hymn 'Jerusalem' and the stirring words of William Blake:

> Bring me my bow of burning gold!
> Bring me my arrows of desire!
> Bring me my spear! O clouds unfold!
> Bring me my chariot of fire!
>
> I will not cease from Mental Fight,
> Nor shall my sword sleep in my hand,
> Till we have built Jerusalem,
> In England's green and pleasant Land.

My destination was the town of Eastbourne, a seaside resort of greater subtlety than Brighton, its brash neighbour to the west. The beach is of pebbles and shingle, not the fine sand of Bournemouth. The promenade, which extends for 2 miles from the Grand Hotel to the pier, is free of unsightly commercial development – no advertising hoardings, no amusement arcades, not even shops. In their place is a profusion of hotels, *pensions* and guest houses discreetly displaying their names on stucco and brick. I was in Eastbourne to buy the Cavendish hotel, a late-Victorian pile with a great reputation for comfort and personal service. It was owned by the last remaining members of the Pimm family who had invented Pimm's No. 1, the popular summer drink that looks like a fruit gardener's extravaganza – replete with borage, cucumber and mint all jostling for space in a glass tankard filled with sparkling lemonade mixed with the secret formula gin-based Pimm's essence. The Misses Pimm, two elderly spinsters, met me with their solicitor following a tour of inspection around the hotel. I had already seen the accounts and balance sheet and I was satisfied that the asking price of £100,000 was not out of the way. I was concerned that the hotel was leasehold, but the freehold belonged to the Chatsworth Estates, who also owned virtually every property along the promenade as well as great parts of the town of Eastbourne. The solicitor was reassuring, the reversion was a long way ahead and would see me out! The grandfather of the present Duke of Devonshire had granted a lease, when the hotel was built in 1882, for a term of 2,000 years at a fixed annual rent of £1. The purchase of the Cavendish introduced me to a new skill, the rebuilding of the entire east wing which had suffered a direct hit from a bomb jettisoned from a low-flying German Heinkel bomber. Having mastered the forms claiming war damage compensation, we were able to rebuild to a design that was sympathetic to the main building, 15 new bedrooms each with superb sea views through floor-to-ceiling picture windows. The acquisition of the Cavendish, the fifth in our growing chain of hotels, was a fitting conclusion to the year 1963.

21

Seeing Stars

As a result of our intensive acquisition programme over the past two years, we began to feel the strain on our personal cash resources. The time had now come to raise outside loan capital. Through our solicitors we had an introduction to Sir Kenneth Keith and Sir Robert Clark, respectively Chairman and Managing Director of Philip Hill, Higginson, Erlangers (renamed Hill Samuel after their amalgamation with the blue-blooded merchant bank of M. Samuel), which the previous year had taken over Mr Charles Clore's Investment Registry.

In Bob Clark, a former partner of the City solicitors Slaughter & May, I found an individual who had confidence in our business plan. Secured on our freehold hotels, a £1 million first mortgage debenture stock at $6^{3}/_{4}\%$ was arranged. Had we been a quoted company the coupon would have been shaved by $^{1}/_{2}\%$. I was later to find out that having a mortgage debenture was very much a mixed blessing. If we wished to sell one of the properties, not only did we have to secure permission from the trustees for the debenture holders, the Norwich Union, but we would have to hand over the proceeds of sale to them by way of reduction of the £1 million, despite the fact that the remaining portfolio of properties provided more than adequate cover for the full loan. It gave me a great deal of *schadenfreude* when, many years later, interest rates having soared, we were able to buy back the debenture at a substantial discount.

Once again we were in the market looking for suitable acquisitions. Our sights settled on the Abbey hotel in Great

Malvern. This would be a purchase which in culinary terms could not be regarded as an *entreé*, but rather a mere *soupçon* as Malvern, the home of the late great composer Elgar, was otherwise an undistinguished town. The hotel, almost an integral part of the adjoining Saxon church, was clad in Virginia creeper and surrounded by gardens at the foot of the forbidding Malvern hills. It was approached by a narrow road that ran through a mediaeval stone archway, giving the hotel the impression of great age. It had character, but was almost completely reliant for its business on parents visiting their offspring at the numerous private schools in the area. Invariably this trade was limited to weekends. The price was attractive, only £85,000 for a 60-bedroom hotel. We agreed to buy and soon exchanged contracts.

It was the August bank holiday when, with Reg Constable and our solicitor, we drove through the Cotswolds and nearby Worcester to hand over a banker's draft to the owner, Mr Manley, to complete our purchase. The vendor had already moved his personal effects out of the hotel and was about to leave, never to return, when I asked to see the Manager, Robert Cave-Brown-Cave, whom I had briefly met on my previous visit.

'Oh,' said Manley, 'he left when he heard I had sold the hotel.'

'And his wife?' I asked. (They had been joint managers.)

'She's gone with him,' replied Manley as he disappeared out of the door into the bright summer sunshine.

There we were with a hotel and no management. As the number of staff could be counted on both hands, I was lucky to catch sight of the cook slipping out of the kitchen back door. I asked her if she knew where the manager had fled.

'To Welshpool,' she said.

'Do you know whereabout in Welshpool I can find him?' I asked in desperation.

The lady thought it might be a pub but wasn't too sure which one Bob had gone to except that it was 'a very busy pub'.

Armed with this illuminating piece of intelligence, I turned to Arthur Krestin, our solicitor, and asked him whether, despite it being bank holiday, he would come with us to Welshpool. I made it clear that if he decided that he had had enough for one day, I would be pleased to run him to the station to catch the next train back to London. He seemed to be enjoying the bizarre situation that had unfolded in the past few hours and decided to see it through with us. Off we went to find Welshpool, some 50 miles away just inside the border with Wales. There is statistical support for the fact that August bank holidays, on average, tend to be wet, but I can vouch for the one in 1964 having been a scorcher. To further complicate the situation, it was market day in Welshpool and all public houses were packed to the doors. Every pub was 'a very busy one'. But luck was finally on our side and in the first one we entered I enquired if they had a new manager. 'Yes,' came the reply and within ten minutes I was talking to Cave-Brown-Cave and arranging to call back to see him when the pub closed for the afternoon.

We met and for several hours I extolled the virtues and rewards of loyalty and the goodies that awaited him and his wife if only they would return to the job they had just left. They asked for time to consider. I told them that this request was not unreasonable and I could give them half an hour to make their decision! They agreed to give two days' notice to their new employers and return to the Abbey, where ultimately they were to give 25 years' service to De Vere to our mutual satisfaction.

We returned to London after motoring nearly 400 miles. It was past midnight before I got home completely exhausted but feeling triumphant. Looking back, there had been one touch of humour in the negotiations that afternoon. As we had already established our central meat supplies from our own butchery in London's Smithfield market, one of my first questions to Cave-Brown-Cave was to enquire the name of the hotel's butcher in Malvern. 'We haven't got a butcher,' he said. 'Mr Manley drives over the border once a week into Wales and comes back with a rustled sheep in the boot of his car.'

The model democracy established in 1918 and led for 20 years by Thomas Masaryk, its first president, was shattered on that fateful day in March 1939 that Hitler annexed Bohemia and Moravia. The defeat of Nazi Germany, however, did not bring a restoration of a democratic Czechoslovakia. On the contrary, it became part of Russia's empire and communism took over.

In 1938 Leopold Müller, a Jew, had fled the country, fearful of Nazism. Ten years later Jaromir Vydra, a fervent Catholic, fled from the Communists by night from his home in Bratislava and after a tortuous three-day train journey through war-devastated Europe arrived, with his young Danish wife Rosie, in London. Taking over a small café in Wigmore Street, a road running parallel to Oxford Street, he established The Boulevard, a restaurant devoted to the cuisine of middle Europe and modelled on a Viennese coffee house. It was an instant success and became the favourite rendezvous for Austrian, Czech and Hungarian refugees. There they could indulge their yearning for the cuisine of their youth, for *Wiener schnitzel*, liver dumplings and goulash in its many permutations. Vydra with his undoubted talent for catering, acquired further restaurants in Mayfair. Attracting the attention of a small-time accountant, Adrian Jacobs, and despite the fact that his company was only making profits in the region of £40,000 per annum, he was induced to reverse the business into Hannans Land Ltd., a shell company that had retained its quotation on the London Stock Exchange. The change of name to Vydra Restaurants was not accompanied by a rise in profits, despite further expansion including an interest in The Normandie hotel in Knightsbridge. Their shares of two shillings each continued to trade at only three times their nominal value.

Müller suggested to me that Vydra Restaurants would be a good fit with our small but more up-market group of West End establishments, especially as we had begun to lay plans to float De Vere on the Stock Exchange. It was in early September of 1964 that we launched a bid of nine shillings per share, valuing the company at £500,000. With the benefit of hindsight we were soon to come to the conclusion that we had pitched our price too high and had grossly overpaid. Our offer, whilst unwelcome to Mr Vydra, was attractive to the other shareholders and by the end of the month we had won the day. We soon discovered that there was no infrastructure to the company – Mr Vydra was a one-man band.

He tried hard to work with Müller but there was a native antipathy between them which I put down to the inbred dislike of the Czechs for the Slovaks whom they considered to be mere peasants. Vydra was a Slovak and Müller a Czech and the battle lines had been drawn centuries before. As a condition of our offer was the retention of Jaromir Vydra as a director of the company, I took him under my wing and protection and thus saved many fights between the two.

The road that runs along the Embankment between Vauxhall and Chelsea bridges encompasses some very desirable residences, not least of which are the imposing pre-war blocks of apartments known as Dolphin Square. Across the road and with an unrivalled location on the Thames was the River Club, owned by Vydra Restaurants Ltd and now part of the De Vere group. Moored on the river bank and connected to the club by a short gangplank was an original Thames sailing barge, complete with her suite of brown canvas sails. These Thames barges had been the maids of all work carrying cargoes from the Thames estuary up to all the many docks that served the metropolis. In their heyday before the war they made a colourful contrast to the gloomy riverside warehouses and could be counted on the river in their hundreds. Ours had been refurbished and fitted up as a cocktail lounge. Anyone foolhardy enough to decide to take their dry martinis on the barge faced the hazard of the return journey up the gangway, which invariably took on an acute angle as the tide dropped. Not long after taking control, during a violent storm the mooring hawsers parted and the barge with its stock of liquor went racing down river on the ebb tide and was never seen again. The club had been unable to get it insured and to my amazement we had no insurance cover against personal accident. It was with a feeling of resignation that I accepted the inevitable: that the maritime aspect of the club had come to an ignominious conclusion. That, unfortunately was not the end of the story. We still owed over £5,000 to the firm who had fitted it up and the club had been resisting this claim for nearly a year on the grounds of poor workmanship. We had now lost the evidence and in due course had to pay up.

The River Club had a small casino attached to it which was open only to members. It was rented out to an Italian operator, and despite the watchful eye of the Gaming Board, I was concerned lest we should harbour a Mafia presence. Furthermore, the club did not fit into our organisation, was difficult to control and after several years of just breaking even, I welcomed an approach to buy the business.

The River Club, unlike most social clubs, did not belong to its members; it was in a category known as a Proprietary club. Whilst De Vere was free to dispose of it without reference to its clientele, it operated in a highly specialised and restricted market and as a business venture its appeal was limited to an established nightclub owner rather than to a restaurateur. Furthermore, the prospective buyer was most likely to be someone who was intimately acquainted with London's thriving night-life. Oscar Lerman fell into this category and had all the right credentials. He was gregarious; he had well-established connections with numerous nightclubbers; he was married to Jackie Collins the authoress, sister of Joan Collins the film and TV star; and what was most important to De Vere, he had the finance. He was introduced to Müller, who agreed to sell the club to Lerman. The golden rule of deal-making is secrecy, as so often the very hint or whisper of a deal is sufficient to bring in competition. The nightclub grapevine became the conduit for Lerman boasting, before any commitment had been signed, that he had bought the River Club. The message came over loud and clear to Harry Saltzman, a Canadian-born film producer and co-owner with Cubby Broccoli of the film rights of Ian Fleming's books. The duo, commencing with *Dr No*, had made a series of 17 James Bond films, blockbusters built around the character 007, and in the process had made very large fortunes for themselves and United Artists, their main backers.

Harry Saltzman approached Müller with a proposition. He would buy from us 50% of the River Club, undertake to refurbish the premises and with his personal involvement create a glittering membership of film stars and showbiz personalities. To us it sounded like a formula that could not fail. We could see no downside, only the prospect of sharing in the biggest success story

De Vere hotels and restaurants - as printed in the Report and Accounts for 1978

Maître chef Jean Drees, Sous chef 'Spike' and Patissier Robinson with Paul Bocuse and other eminent French chefs

Menu of Diner de Gala
with Maxim's

Diner

à l'occasion du Festival Gastronomique

Maxim's - Mirabelle

Londres

20 Mars 1980

The Mirabelle

BUCKINGHAM PALACE

17th June, 1981

Dear Mr Jackson

   The Duke of Edinburgh has asked me to thank
you very much for sending him a copy of your
"Cuisine Mirabelle". I must say it looks as
though there are some wonderful recipes.
His Royal Highness has asked me to tell you
how much he looks forward to trying some of them
out.

   We all had a delicious dinner at the Mirabelle
the other night. Thank you very much.

Yours sincerely

Robert Acland

Leslie Jackson, Esq.

IO DOWNING STREET

THE PRIME MINISTER   15 June 1984

Dear Mr Jackson,

   I hear that the Press Centre established by the Connaught
Rooms for the London Economic Summit was a great success.

   I am in no doubt that your contribution and that of your
staff was invaluable in ensuring that the Press Unit for the
Summit received almost no complaints - and much praise - about
the facilities.

   Please will you convey my appreciation to all your staff.

Yours sincerely

Margaret Thatcher

Leslie Jackson, Esq.

Violette Szabó G.C.
with husband Etienne

Tania wearing her Mother's medals
Jersey Liberation day 1995

of any nightclub of post-war years. The terms were agreed and the deal was sealed. Meanwhile Lerman was furious and threatened to sue. Harry Saltzman, although softly spoken, was a flamboyant character, cut in the mould of the archetypal Hollywood film director. Müller deputed me to work with him as he had already found that their temperaments were diametrically opposite and they would only come to blows.

Harry had insisted on having a free hand in the management and refurbishment and we had conceded this. I called on Harry in his office on the top floor of his small building at No. 3 South Audley Street, primarily to discuss the costs of his schemes. As I entered the room he was speaking into one of a battery of telephones and he beckoned me to sit down opposite him. I saw a big man with a shock of snow-white hair sitting in a large armchair upholstered in green leather, his red shirt opened at the neck, his shoeless feet resting on top of an enormous desk. I heard him say in a soft and silky voice, 'Listen to me, Zeffirelli. As I said, meet me at Rome's Ciampino airport tomorrow morning at ten o'clock and bring ten million lire...' Who could fail to be impressed?

After our discussion, he asked me what I was doing at the weekend and, if I was free, would I like to bring my wife and children to watch some films in his small preview cinema in the basement of his office building. It was there that he viewed the 'rushes' of the previous day's shooting of a James Bond film. I accepted, and Saturday afternoon saw us being shown into four of the ten cinema seats, with Harry telling us that he would be screening *Blazing Saddles*, a western comedy featuring Mel Brooks. For once neither Peggy nor our children, David and Judith, had any interest in watching the screen – the film was secondary to looking spellbound at the audience. Before the lights were switched off, Harry had introduced us to the other guests. Judy was sitting next to Peter Sellers and his two children. I sat next to Danny Kaye, who had just flown in from New York. He was casually dressed and, complaining that his feet hurt, removed his Timberland boots. I burst out laughing on hearing Rudolf Nureyev, sitting on the other side of Danny Kaye, say, 'You know, with feet like that I bet you could dance.' He said this in a deep voice with a heavy Russian accent whilst looking down at Danny Kaye's stockinged feet and maintaining an inscrutable look on his face. I was convinced that Nureyev was serious and I wondered if he realised he was talking to a dancer who could rival Fred Astaire.

Having tea after the film and chatting away with the stars, I learnt that Harry was planning to make an epic film of the life of Nijinsky, the legendary Russian ballet dancer, and had offered Nureyev a million dollars to star in it. I am sure he thought he could repeat the success of Moira Shearer's film *The Red Shoes*, but Harry never made the Nijinsky film and Nureyev didn't get the million dollars. Another studio took the chance, made the film and I believe lost money on it.

For a short while I was an accepted member of Harry's entourage, being invited to his magnificent house in Denham, close to the Pinewood Studios where the majority of the Bond films were made. Harry, of course, like all big film producers, was larger than life and always needed to have a crowd around him. He never carried any cash even when he went out to restaurants surrounded by up to ten of his 'court'. His paymaster was Bill Offner, a Polish ex-serviceman and a great friend of Benny Fisch, who, as a pilot in a Polish squadron, had flown Spitfires during the war. Benny, too, was 'in films' and had been trying for years but without success to raise the finance to produce a film. Unwittingly, Benny, an extremely amiable character, was to have a baneful influence on the River Club. He was married to a most attractive French lady who had a young brother reputed to have earned a great reputation in Paris as a chef. On Benny's recommendation Harry appointed him as chef-in-waiting to the refurbished River Club.

The scenario and screenplay now read as follows. Harry and De Vere were to be equal partners, but operationally Harry would be more equal than us. De Vere in fact would play the part of the sleeping partner and Harry would be responsible for the decor, staffing and day-to-day running. Out would go the casino, its place to be taken by a themed cocktail bar named The Opium Den. The builders of the James Bond extravaganza sets at Pinewood Studios would design the interior of the bar; lighting would be just sufficient to detect, through a permanent haze of incense, the Fu Manchu concept of a Shanghai dive. Customers would sit on bales bound in hessian and be served their drinks by Chinese waitresses dressed in traditional tight-fitting *cheongsams* slit to the thigh. The restaurant would serve food 'fit to die for', innovatively conceived, cooked to perfection and exquisitely presented by the maître chef de cuisine, Benny's brother-in-law. Everyone who was anyone in Hollywood and in the English film world would be queueing to join as members. Harry's enthusiasm was infectious; he was an extrovert character who exuded infallibility. All the same I was uneasy.

Like all film producers, Harry hated budgets, and he now applied his expertise in overspending to the club. I pleaded with him for restraint but he just went on spending. I did not like the new decor in the restaurant, which overlooked the Thames and which before Harry's arrival had been panelled out in magnificent mahogany. Harry's instructions were to paint it cream. To cap it all, he had discovered a Parisian nightclub manager who, I was told, resembled Salvador Dali with a ginger toupée. He invited him over to London and appointed him manager of the club.

As the opening date grew closer and Harry went ahead with the planning of a grand gala dinner, I came under increasing pressure from Müller to extricate ourselves from a disaster waiting to happen. I had to get Harry to buy our 50% holding; time was of the essence with the clock ticking away. I was in full agreement with Müller's assessment of the situation and immediately started to work on it. At first Harry was reluctant to put more of his own money into the project but I persevered. It was a close-run thing, and with only 48 hours to go before the opening night I managed to get the necessary share transfers signed and had banked Saltzman's draft.

As Harry had promised, cinema and show celebrities accepted his invitation to the gala opening and turned out in strength to experience the new River Club but there was no invitation for me. What no one knew was that the chef's experience was limited to working in one of the grand residences in Paris catering for dinner parties of up to 20 guests. He had never been faced with 150 diners all to be served at the same time. I was informed by a guest who had no other place to go to, that the dinner took four hours to serve. It was a disaster from which the club would never recover. Over the next two years, I understand it lost more than a million pounds and was finally sold to a club operating in Curzon Street. They renamed it 'The White Elephant on the River'.

I like my stories to have happy endings. In this idiom, Bill Offner teamed up with Oscar Lerman and a third partner named Johnny Gold and created the highly successful nightclub Tramp, in Jermyn Street.

The White Elephant on the River survived and boasted a large loyal membership.

Benny Fisch eventually secured his finance and went on to make what I consider to be one of the best World War II films ever screened. Starring Laurence Olivier it was a great box-office success and, whenever it is shown on TV, I invariably watch this celluloid masterpiece and never fail to marvel at the aerobatics of his film *The Battle of Britain*.

22

Going Public

On New Year's Day 1965 we were able to look back on four, often frenetic, years of building up De Vere. We now owned eight freehold hotels, including the five star Royal Bath, together with ten prominent West End restaurants, including our flagship the Mirabelle. Apart from the £1 million debenture, we had been able to finance the business from our personal resources and I had been able to maintain my 25% equity interest undiluted, but with difficulty. It is often reported today that the City is 'awash with money' with the presence of hundreds of foreign banks and venture capital boutiques vying with each other to lend. There was no such proliferation of money sources in the early sixties and the bankers' pre-war distrust of lending to the hotel industry still lingered on.

It was suggested that in Bank of America in the City I would find a listening ear. I made the journey to Moorgate but was not exactly received with open arms; the problem was the nature of the security I could offer against the personal loan I was seeking of £100,000 to enable me, as it expanded, to maintain my equity interest in De Vere. I offered my existing shareholding in the company, which they politely refused on the grounds that it was a minority interest in an unquoted company.

Müller was against any change in the *status quo* as a private company, and was happy to tag along with a 75% holding. I took the contrary view and knew that we could not make De Vere much bigger unless we 'went public'. Having already initiated preliminary discussions with Philip Hill, our merchant bankers, I was able finally to win over Bank of America by promising them that we would be seeking a quotation on the Stock Exchange in the Spring. I left their offices in Moorgate with the backing I had been seeking.

I have never considered myself a politically focused individual. As a young man, prior to the war and before being enfranchised, I would have described myself as a Socialist. I was very conscious of the wide gap in our society between the 'haves' and the 'have-nots' and if I had had the opportunity and the right motivation I might have done something positive, however small, in helping to close this gap. The war and the small part I played in it, latterly as a commissioned officer, exercised a strong influence on my attitude to the main political parties. Suffice it to say that when the election was called in May 1945 as Victory in Europe was being declared, I cast my vote for the first time for the man who more than any other single person had brought about the destruction of Nazi Germany. It came as a personal bombshell that there were two million more voters favouring Clement Attlee over Winston Churchill and, surprisingly, most of them were in the armed forces. Labour swept into power with a landslide majority in the House of Commons of 180 seats, its greatest triumph as a Parliamentary party. In 1951 the Conservatives, helped by my vote, were returned to power, until Labour under the leadership of Harold Wilson won the 1964 election and with a working majority in the House proclaimed its intention to shape a new and more égalitarian Britain.

In making our preparations for the flotation of De Vere I was apprehensive of a radical Budget from the newly elected Labour party which would affect investment sentiment adversely. Our concern must have been shared by several other businesses making haste to go public. In the week commencing 15th March 1965 there was an unprecedented number of six flotations. Apart from De Vere, I can recall Customagic, Brook Street Bureau and Photo-Me International, the latter being the only one to have remained independent and retained its stock market quotation.

Our prospectus looked most impressive. It was sponsored by the blue-blooded City names of Joseph Sebag & Co. as brokers, and Slaughter & May as solicitors. Of the new shares created, two million were offered to the public at 11s 6d ($57^{1}/_{2}$p) per share, the total proceeds being received by the company. Both Müller and I had, over the years, loaned money to the company, and these loans were to a great extent to be satisfied by the issue of new shares. To demonstrate our confidence in the company's future and to underscore our belief that the investing public were getting their shares at an attractive price, Müller and I capitalised our loans at the higher price of 12s 6d. The application lists opened at 10 a.m on Thursday 18th March 1965 and closed two minutes later with the offer being twice oversubscribed. To our dismay, and proving that the stock market can be very fickle, our price drifted downwards over the next few weeks to stand at 10 shillings (50p).

The Budget proved to be every bit as radical as the pundits had forecast. Capital Gains tax and Corporation tax were introduced for the first time and the Finance Act that followed had a clause that disallowed tax relief on entertaining in restaurants unless the individual entertained was a foreign customer from overseas! The impact on Mirabelle was immediate and was catastrophic on all restaurants previously enjoying a significant business-lunch trade. We looked upon this piece of legislation as class-motivated. It did not achieve the effect of increasing tax revenue or stopping any abuse of the system. On the contrary, the reaction from the City was for banks and companies to set up their own directors' dining rooms serving meals at a far greater cost than if they had continued to use restaurants.

My boyhood fascination with the Bible had instilled in me a life-long interest in the 'promised land' but it was not until the fateful day of 14th May 1948 that it turned into a love affair. It was on that day that the British Mandate for Palestine ended and Ben Gurion declared Israel's statehood. Like most love affairs, it has not run smoothly. Inevitably it has had its ups and downs and although one-sided, I feel that my affection has not altogether been

221

unrequited. The fledgling state was only eight years old when on TV and in the press I was to watch day after day the botch-up of the Suez Expedition that claimed so many victims and reputations, not least the career and health of Prime Minister Anthony Eden. It did, however, have the effect of forcing Nasser for the first time to grant free rights of passage through the Suez Canal to Israeli shipping. A few months later, on my very first visit to Israel, I experienced the thrill and excitement of a small crowd gathered on the foreshore as the first oil tanker to have run the gauntlet of the Red Sea berthed safely in the tiny and newly established port of Eilat.

The blocking of the Suez Canal by Nasser, contrary to international law, had been a body blow to the existence of the new state. It is ironic that Israel, a country only the size of Wales, is devoid of oil but its surrounding and hostile neighbours enjoy this vital commodity in abundance. There would be no oil-pipelines to Israel from Syria or Egypt, all imports would have to be brought in by sea from distant lands. I am reminded of the joke that, had Moses and the children of Israel after crossing the Red Sea, turned to the *right* instead of to the *left*, Israel would have got the oil and Egypt the oranges.

In 1957 I went up from Tel Aviv to Jerusalem, still a divided city. The road, tortuous and roughly hewn out of the mountainside, was littered with burnt-out trucks, evidence of the bitter struggle to raise the siege of the beleaguered city during the War of Independence. I stayed at the King David hotel, the former British army headquarters that had been blown up by the Haganah – the Jewish covert self-defence organisation, in July 1946. The hotel's garden was ringed with barbed wire and my bedroom overlooked no-man's land, the area annexed by the Jordanian army when the Kingdom of Jordan gained its *own* independence in 1946. Throughout the day and night sporadic sniping was commonplace and the feeling of being in a besieged city was still very palpable. The 'Wailing Wall', dating back to the Second Temple, the souk, the old Arab market, and the labyrinth of lanes that had made up the ancient Jewish quarter, were out of bounds, but the thrill of just being in the holy city was indescribable.

Peggy and I were staying in a hotel in Herzlia, some 10 miles to the north of Tel Aviv and we were driven up the coast to Caesarea. I was fascinated by the history of the place, learning that King Herod the Great had built the city and port, naming it after his lord and master Octavian who, after defeating Antony and Cleopatra at the battle of Actium, was given the title of Augustus Caesar by the Senate in Rome 27 years before the birth of Christ. There, amidst the sand dunes, I became witness to past empires and felt myself reliving three millennia. The almost perfect Roman amphitheatre is flanked by an aqueduct that had been built 2,000 years ago to carry fresh water down from the Carmel hills to service the new city. Side by side, a complete Crusader town had been excavated, one of the last outposts to fall before the ignominious collapse of the Crusades, which ended finally in 1291 with the departure from Acre, their last stronghold, about 30 miles to the north of Caesarea. All I had to do to unearth a piece of history was to dig my toes into the soft sand and reveal pieces of glass dating back to the Byzantine period. I could walk along the seashore after a storm and pick up early Judean and Roman coins, whilst hopping over fallen marble columns of exquisite Corinthian and Doric design. I was in my seventh heaven and made up my mind to build, one day, a home in Caesarea.

Returning to London, I involved myself in the Joint Palestine Appeal, a charity devoting its funds to the rescue and resettlement of Jews, not only those from Europe who had been rendered homeless by the war, but those who now faced persecution in Arab lands where they had lived for thousands of years.

Mention the year 1967 to me and I immediately recall six epoch-making days in June when I could think of little else than the battles raging in the Middle East; in the skies above the Negev desert, on the shores of the Red Sea and the Gulf of Aquaba, and the battle for Jerusalem.

Following the Anglo-French debacle in Suez, dominated by the unanswered question 'Was there collusion with Israel?', there had been an uneasy decade during which the Arab countries continued to deny Israel the right to exist and kept up a cross-border guerrilla war. Despite the Israel economy constantly teetering on the verge of collapse, the Ingathering of the Exiles, as the policy of immigration was called, grew in momentum. With the demise of Josef Stalin had come a gradual thawing in the Soviet attitude to Jewish emigration to Israel and from every neighbouring Arab country poured a stream of Jews underprivileged and frequently persecuted. The world watched with amazement at the enormity of the task of resettlement to which the Government of Israel had pledged themselves. To transport, house, educate, provide medical and social benefits and create employment for two million immigrants, thereby doubling the existing population, was a venture without precedent. Furthermore the majority of those of Arab origin had been living in a primitive environment little changed from those of Biblical times and knew nothing of Western customs or social behaviour. Israel had tied no strings to entry, but the infrastructure to enable the country to cope with the old, the sick and the poor had still to be created. Its aim was to weld the jetsam of countless countries into a nation with a common language and ideals. To undertake this whilst still at war with a hundred million Arabs is proof that the age of miracles had not passed. There had to be Divine Providence to make it all happen. By comparison, Gaza still under Egyptian occupation and control had been left to fester as one big Palestinian refugee slum living on the handouts of UNRRA (United Nations Relief and Rehabilitation Administration) whilst their Arab brothers squandered their oil billions on sophisticated weapons they hardly knew how to handle.

The detonator to the explosive atmosphere that had existed throughout May took the form of the closure of the Straits of Tiran to Israeli shipping and Nasser's expulsion of the UN Expeditionary Force. All the Arab armies were mobilising. Jordan had opened her borders to the entry of Saudi Arabian soldiers and welcomed a whole division of Iraqi troops backed by 150 tanks which, entering Jordan and moving to the border with Israel, was placed under the command of an Egyptian general. Even faraway Sudan and Algeria were sending military units to fight side by side with Egyptian troops. There was a beleaguered feeling in Israel compounded by the need to keep its army, consisting almost entirely of National Servicemen, in a state of battle readiness, to the detriment of the fragile economy.

It was against this backdrop of events that I received a telegram addressed to all chairmen of JPA (Joint Palestine Appeal) committees to attend an emergency meeting at Michael House in Baker Street, the head offices of Marks & Spencer. The meeting, presided over by Edward Sieff, Managing Director of M&S and national Chairman of the JPA, was packed with more than a hundred delegates from all over the country. We waited nervously whilst Teddy (as he was affectionately called) introduced the guest speaker, an Israeli General, the head of the Intelligence Corps of the IDF (the Israel Defence Force, as their army is known). He proceeded to give us an up-to-the-minute overview of the situation in Israel. He reported on the surprise arrival of King Hussein in Cairo the previous day to conclude a defence agreement with Nasser, with whom he had been at loggerheads for years. Russia was acting in a belligerent manner by stepping up arms shipments to Egypt, countered by the movement of the United States Sixth Fleet to the eastern Mediterranean. We had been following these reports in the newspapers and on the radio, but the purpose of our presence at the meeting that day was to demonstrate solidarity. The people of Israel, he told us, were not desperate, they knew that they had no choice but to fight. It would be a war they *had* to win, for the Arabs kept repeating that their aim was the annihilation of the State of Israel and their people 'to be thrown into the sea'. If Israel were to lose even a single battle, the war would be lost and she would cease to exist – the stakes could not be higher. Our task was to raise the maximum funds not only to help sustain the civil and social fabric of the country when it went to war, but to send a clear message to all those embattled in Israel that the whole Diaspora was behind them.

When the General sat down there was a complete and tangible silence for several minutes until it was broken only by the voice of a man who had been standing near the door at the back of the room.

'I pledge one million pounds,' he said. We sat there stunned. I

225

turned around just in time to see a very tall figure disappearing out of the door. It was Lord Rothschild.

Five days later, at 9.30 a.m. on Monday 5th June, I heard on the BBC that hostilities between Israel and all the Arab countries had broken out and that victory communiqués were being broadcast all morning by Cairo radio. By a strange coincidence the Annual General Meeting of Marks & Spencer had been convened at noon that day in the ballroom of the Grosvenor House Hotel and, despite the fact that I was not a shareholder, I gatecrashed the meeting. It was packed with happy shareholders evidently deriving great satisfaction from the directors reporting on the excellent progress made by the company during the financial year.

I was impatient for the meeting to end, when I bounded up to the top table and, addressing Teddy sitting amongst his co-directors, asked, 'What news is there?' He knew what I meant.

'We've knocked out their air force,' he replied. 'It's going to be all right.'

And so it proved to be. The incredible story of the Six Day War has been meticulously recorded in many books written by soldiers and airmen who fought in the war, as well as by countless historians and political commentators specialising in Middle Eastern affairs. The greatest loser was probably King Hussein, who, tricked into attacking Israel by misinformation fed to him by Nasser and threatened by him that Jordan would not otherwise share in the spoils of a defeated Israel, went to war, with disastrous consequences.

23

Grand Deals and Becoming a Gentleman Farmer

Arguably, Eastbourne's major claim to fame is its mention in the Domesday Book in 1086, and one could be forgiven for thinking that the present-day residents look as if they might be the original inhabitants. The success of the Cavendish Hotel, purchased three years previously, as well as our acquisition of the Queens Hotel, facing the pier, had whetted our appetite for a greater presence in the town and the obvious target was the Grand Hotel. Built in the golden era of Victorian hotels it dominated the western end of the promenade. Looking seaward from its open-air swimming pool, the first to be built as part of an English resort hotel, one could see the Martello Tower, one in the chain of defences erected along the south coast as a bulwark against invasion by Napoleon Bonaparte.

The Grand had acquired a well-earned reputation for those with a *penchant* for living in the grand manner. Together with The Royal Bath, The Imperial in Torquay and Gleneagles in Perthshire, it was one of the exclusive group of four luxury hotels awarded a five-star rating by the motoring organisations. It had 200 bedrooms and had led the hotel industry in changing its mainstream activity from its dependency on the fickle holidaymaker to the more consistent and lucrative conference trade. Proving remarkably successful, it was this aspect of its business that I found most attractive. I was anxious to acquire the know-how of the conference business and to apply it to our other resort hotels, at the same time strengthening the marketing of the two Eastbourne hotels we already owned. The development of many of the large Victorian hotels had been financed by local investors. The Grand was an exception and was quoted on the London Stock Exchange. The decision was taken to make an open bid for the whole company without building an initial share stake through purchases in the market.

So it was that on a sunny day shortly after the Easter bank holiday of 1967, Leopold Müller and I arrived at the hotel to lay an unconditional offer before the company's directors. We had valued the net assets of the business at a figure of £700,000 and accordingly offered nine shillings (45p) per share. This was initially rejected by the board but the addition of a further sixpence (£40,000) was sufficient to secure their agreement to recommend the offer to their shareholders, who accepted it unanimously.

The hotel was known to a very wide public, the majority of whom would otherwise have been hard-pressed to tell you where to find Eastbourne on the map. In the early days of radio, or 'wireless' as it was known, its acoustically perfect lounge had become the venue for light musical concerts, which blossomed into the hugely popular Palm Court orchestral concerts broadcast every Sunday evening under the leadership of the violinist Albert Sandler. The hotel had already established a long musical and theatrical tradition, Claude Debussy having written his symphony *La Mer* whilst staying there in 1905 with his mistress Emma Bardac, the wife of a well-known French financier.

The stories of notables and prominent personalities who regularly stayed at The Grand are legion, many of them reflecting their eccentricities and foibles. One that I enjoy recalling was about a Mr Myers, one of the last of a long line of 'permanent residents', who occupied a suite of three rooms at a cost to him of six guineas a day. Every morning until his ninetieth birthday, his chauffeur would forsake the Rolls-Royce and bring his master's horse to the front door of the hotel, where Mr Myers would be helped into the saddle. This being successfully accomplished, the chauffeur, clutching the bridle with one hand and a bag of carrots with the other, trotted sedately down the promenade, to the delight and amusement of the early promenaders.

Jack Cohen, the pioneer of the supermarket, would, year after

228

year, spend Christmas and Easter at The Grand, booking three suites for himself and his family. One year there was a problem with the booking and he telephoned me to ask if I would resolve the crisis, which I was able to do. Thereafter, he made it a habit to contact me in London to look after his reservations. One year, meeting him by chance at the hotel, he said, 'Why don't you sell me The Grand? I would like to buy it.'

Caught by surprise, I replied, 'You don't want to go into the hotel business, Jack. I should stick to supermarkets.'

He replied, 'Hotelkeeping? That's the last thing I would do. I would pull it down and build my largest Tesco store on the site.'

'But Jack,' I said, 'it's isolated, there are no shops within half a mile of The Grand.'

'That doesn't matter,' he replied. 'Everyone would find us and come to Tesco.'

With the more recent advent of out-of-town shopping he might well have been proved right. But the man whose motto had been 'pile it high and sell it cheap' and who was knighted for founding the largest chain of grocery supermarkets in the country was not allowed by his more sceptic board of directors to add The Grand to his many trophies.

With The Grand came two other properties. One was a small hotel in the Regency town of Royal Leamington Spa – the Manor House, most notable for the first game of *real* tennis, the Elizabethan version, having been played on its lawns. The other was a hotel in the process of being built at Kenilworth in Warwickshire, a small dormitory town of the close-by city of Coventry. With only about 15,000 inhabitants, Kenilworth was notable only for castles, one a vast ruin close to the hotel and the other, some 3 miles away, much grander and intact, the ancestral home of the Earls of Warwick and innumerable old master paintings, including a famous Holbein portrait of Henry VIII.

The hotel was being built by the Eastbourne firm of Llewellyn & Sons, whom I had regularly employed on repair work at the Cavendish after the winter gales. The construction had reached roof height and I arranged for the topping-out ceremony to be performed by Jimmy Hill, the Manager of Coventry City Football

Club, who was already a local celebrity. To the ceremony I invited the Chair of the Kenilworth Rural District Council and her committee. The ceremony consisted of hauling up a keg of beer by hand on to a flat roof and toasting the foreman, bricklayers and fellow craftsmen in pint tankards. Whilst on the roof, the Chairman took me aside and asked if I was happy with the building. I replied that my company had *inherited* the plans, but ideally I would have liked to have built the ballroom twice as large and to have been able to create a coffee shop on the ground floor. As soon as I had finished speaking, she beckoned to the other members of her council to join us whilst, at her request, I repeated my observations. Turning to me whilst her colleagues were nodding their heads, she said, 'Granted. Just get your architect to send in the drawings. I will approve them and send them on to the County for rubber-stamping.' No planning application ever had a speedier and more satisfactory outcome.

A few days before Christmas, we were ready for business and I invited the Earl of Warwick to perform the opening ceremony which involved cutting a ribbon stretched across the front door with a ceremonial sword. After three unsuccessful attempts it was left to a small pair of nail scissors to get us out of an embarrassing situation. I stood on the Welsh slate steps of the hotel facing our invited guests and several curious passers-by, and thanked his Lordship for honouring us with his presence and for naming the hotel after Simon de Montfort. I claimed that De Vere was not being foolhardy in building a £600,000 hotel in Kenilworth but was demonstrating its faith in the future of the small community. Perhaps I was being a little economical with the truth, as we had from the very beginning been apprehensive of making such a large investment without a proper feasibility study. We had to hope that this inheritance from the original Grand Hotel company, relying on its proximity to Coventry, would generate a thriving business. That is precisely what happened and within two years we were increasing the bedroom capacity of the de Montfort Hotel by 50%.

* * *

Great Queen Street, almost but not quite part of Covent Garden, starts at Kingsway in Holborn and runs westwards through to Bow Street, famous for the Bow Street Runners of old, and still with its magistrates' court. The Covent Garden of today bears no resemblance to that immortalised in the stage and screen musical *My Fair Lady*. Gone are the vast displays of fruit and vegetables and the flowers shipped in by air from every continent. The area, a honeycomb of cobbled streets and alleyways previously jammed with barrows from the early hours of the morning until dusk, has been transformed into one of London's major entertainment and tourist attractions, even surpassing Soho in the number and variety of its restaurants.

Great Queen Street is home to the Freemasons of England. A thoroughfare, otherwise undistinguished architecturally, is dominated by Freemason's Hall built in 1926 as a memorial to Freemasons who lost their lives in the Great War of 1914–18. It is a noble building, characteristically enshrining noble ideals to which I have been proud to subscribe for the whole of my adult life. Adjoining and linked into the hall is the Connaught Rooms, a complex of no less than 22 banqueting suites catering for every type of private and public function and ceremony.

As one of the largest catering businesses under one roof, I would often daydream of adding it to our group. Acting the part of Merlin it was its General Manager, Jimmy James, who brought my dream from fantasy to reality, and the plan was worked out, not in London, but in Copenhagen. He and I were guests of the Carlsberg Breweries, the only registered charity in the world that brews beer and lager. Their hospitality is legendary, and seemingly no expense was spared on this occasion to please their English customers. The smorgasbord buffets were such works of culinary art that it was almost an act of desecration to disturb the display of mounds of smoked salmon, herring in a dozen different sauces and bountiful bowls of caviare nestling on beds of crushed ice. Both Jimmy and I shared a love for catering and it was not long before he was extolling the virtues of the Connaught Rooms and its ability to serve upwards of 3,000 guests for dinner at one sitting. The more he talked about his work, the more enthusiastic I became to be his 'boss' and the owner of this unique business.

On my return to London, I was able to enthuse Müller, who gave me the green light to go ahead and acquire the company. I discovered that the business was the sole asset of Connaught Rooms Ltd., a company that had been formed at the turn of the century and was now quoted on the London Stock Exchange. Dealings in the shares were erratic. We started to buy through a nominee and within a few months had amassed more than 100,000 shares, representing about 10% of the issued share capital. Having decided that the time was now opportune to make our bid, I took steps to raise the necessary finance. Our first step was to see the merchant bankers Hambros, with whom Müller had, the previous year, deposited £1 million, and to arrange a back-to-back loan to support our offer. A meeting, which I felt would be no more than a formality, was hurriedly arranged with their deputy Chairman Charles Hambro.

We had no sooner taken our seats in their boardroom than I was passed a telephone to answer a call. I was perplexed because in the interest of confidentiality I had kept my visit to Hambros secret. The caller was Leonard Dennis, previously a co-director of Mirabelle and now responsible for operating Le Coq d'Or Restaurant, owned by Grand Metropolitan Hotels Ltd. He told me that his Chairman, Maxwell Joseph, had requested an urgent meeting with us that afternoon and he would come to our office. I asked him to explain the urgency and the reason for asking for a meeting. He told me that he could give no answers, but Joseph had impressed on him the need to meet us without delay. The telephone call, in the earshot of the bankers, was embarrassing me so I hastily, but reluctantly, agreed to meet Joseph that afternoon.

Charles Hambro listened to our request for a bridging loan and then inexplicably refused, saying that Müller's deposit was repayable only after six months' prior notice had been given. We could not believe our ears and sat there dumbfounded at the audacity of the banker.

After what seemed an eternity. Müller turned to me and asked, 'What shall we do now?'

232

'Let's go and see our *real* friends,' I replied.

We left the building and hailed a passing taxi, asking the driver to take us to 100 Bridge Street, the offices of Hill Samuel. We were received by Robert Clark, the Vice-Chairman, and within five minutes had secured the necessary financial backing and the assurance that they would be happy to act for us in the takeover.

Back at my office, we issued a press announcement of our offer for the shares of Connaught Rooms Ltd. and waited for Maxwell Joseph to arrive. He came alone and we were both reminded of his visit, 13 years previously, to our small office above the Chicken Inn in Haymarket. We had all come a long way since then, but Joseph had outstripped us and as an adversary and competitor he was a force to be reckoned with. He did not mince his words.

'I want you to withdraw your bid for Connaught Rooms. I believe you have about 100,000 shares and I have 112,600. You have bid ten shillings, I will bid eleven; unless I come in as an equal partner I will overbid you. I will leave the room to let you discuss it for five minutes. If you do not agree, I will proceed without you.'

I felt that we had had sufficient drama for one day so when he returned to the room we signified our agreement. We made it conditional on our having the day-to-day management, whilst Derek Taylor the talented Marketing and Sales Director of Grand Metropolitan would be responsible for promotion. I knew that this was not peace, only an armistice, but I was prepared to try and make it work. In our Annual Report for 1967 we announced our joint acquisition with Grand Met, 'of what is undoubtedly the finest banqueting centre in the Country'.

As soon as Müller was able to secure the release of his deposit with Hambros, he lent it to De Vere free of interest. A cynic would say that he was neither beneficent or charitable but was avoiding having to pay income tax on the investment income, which at that time was at the penal rate of 75%.

My first marital home had been in the north London suburb of Kinsgbury and by 1953 I was looking for a larger home. My

233

preference was to build a house to our own specifications, not too far from Kingsbury, where we had established a wide circle of friends, and near to the preparatory schools that our two children were attending. Wartime building restrictions were still in force and as the post-war housing boom had not yet got under way, I felt that I was looking for the proverbial needle in a haystack – a plot of land with the benefit of planning consent. In my small Triumph Mayflower car, I scoured the streets of Stanmore, Middlesex, a relatively undeveloped suburb with an unspoilt village atmosphere lying about 4 miles to the north of Kingsbury. My luck did not desert me and I spotted a builder's board on a former vegetable allotment off the London Road, which ran from Edgware to Uxbridge. The M1 and M25 motorways were not yet on the drawing board and London Road saw very little traffic and was well served by public transport, in particular the London Underground.

Mr Curton, who had established an enviable reputation as a local builder of quality homes, had acquired the vegetable allotments and had obtained planning consent for 14 detached houses. I was able to buy the last remaining plot, with a frontage of 60 feet and depth of 200 feet, just large enough to build our dream house. Mr Curton would sell the plot at £20 per foot frontage with a separate building agreement for him to build a five-bedroom house at a cost of £8,000. Buying the house in this manner resulted in a significant saving as the 2% *ad valorem* stamp duty was levied only on the land purchase, whilst the building agreement escaped with but a twopenny stamp. The finished house turned our dreams into reality, and for 34 years it proved to be a happy and secure haven for Peggy and our children to grow up in, and a refuge for me from the stress of an active business and social life.

Most of my ventures have had a fortuitous start. An example of this was my entry into the world of the land-owning gentry or, to be more exact, my arrival at its periphery. Three years after moving to Stanmore, I was walking along Denis Lane, then little more than a wide cart track, when I spotted an estate agent's board, faded and overgrown by a beech hedge, on which were still legible

234

the words '80 acres of Green Belt for sale'. I had just disposed of my small holding of shares in The Anglo Iranian Oil Company and I felt that this would be an ideal alternative investment to lock up for my, as yet unborn, grandchildren; a very long-term strategy, as the elder of my two children was still only eight years old. The local estate agent, Leslie Glover, was acting for the Warren House Estate, owned by the major landowner in the area, Sir John Fitzgerald, on whose quarter-of-an-acre site in London Road Mr Curton had built my home, which I had named *Devon Lodge* – both Peggy and our son David being Devonians by birth. The parcel of land was available for £500 per acre and I had no hesitation in purchasing the 80 acres for £40,000, having interested Müller in joining me in the venture as an equal partner.

Zoned in the county development plan as Green Belt, it was potentially the most attractive of residential developments imaginable. To the north were fields owned by the Greater London Council. The western, eastern and southern boundaries extended to, and almost merged with, the gardens of detached houses. The land sloped gently northwards to a point where one could look out over London and see the Post Office Tower, more than 10 miles away. In the south, standing at my farm gate, one looked down on the railway lines of Stanmore Underground Station, a distance of barely 200 yards. As events subsequently turned out, development might still be a century away.

We were in the middle of expanding our chain of chicken restaurants, which was regularly calling for a supply of 10,000 chickens a week. I conceived the idea of building broiler houses on the farmland and rearing our own strain of chickens, making us independent of the vagaries of Smithfield market. I was to discover, shortly after our purchase of the Warren House Estate, that recently-enacted legislation had designated chicken broiler houses as industrial units and not as agricultural buildings. Consequently as planning consent would be required and was unlikely to be granted without a fight (on which I was at the time unwilling to embark), I dropped the idea and let-off the fields for horse grazing on a short tenancy.

One of the roads bordering the estate, Stanmore Hill, which led up to the Common, featured several imposing homes set in their own grounds. One that I found very attractive was built to resemble a Spanish hacienda with a roof of glazed green tiles. It was owned by Max Bygraves, the very popular singer and radio and television star. It was, therefore, with a feeling of pleasurable anticipation that I received a telephone call from a lady inviting me to call and see Mr Bygraves at his farmhouse in Wood Lane on my northern boundary. He wanted to discuss renting my fields for fattening young cattle and preparing them for market.

I duly arrived and was received in a shabby farmhouse by Mrs Bygraves, a slightly built blonde, who asked me to wait whilst she called her husband from the byre. All this was far removed from what I was expecting and I was beginning to feel very uneasy when in strode a towering giant who had to stoop to clear the top of the doorway. My hand completely disappeared in his grip as he greeted me, as a neighbour, in a deep resonant voice that owed nothing to Stanmore in Middlesex but everything to Jamaica in the Caribbean. At no stretch of my imagination could I envisage him singing 'Tulips from Amsterdam', the tune that had made Max Bygraves world-famous. I tried to hide my mixture of surprise and disappointment and accepted his invitation to ride in his tractor and inspect the fields he was renting from the GLC. I sat beside him glancing surreptitiously at his head, which looked as if it had been carved out of a block of brown granite. During the ride he told me that he had been the Empire Heavyweight Boxing Champion in 1956 and 1957 and had fought Henry Cooper. I could not help feeling sorry for Henry Cooper.

Over the next decade we prepared several schemes to develop a minor part of the estate for residential purposes and, as a *quid pro quo* for getting planning consent, offered to build and maintain at our expense either an old people's home or a small school. The fields would be landscaped for use as public open space, and riding facilities and bridle paths would be created. These plans were discussed with Mr Foxley, the Chief Planning Officer and Architect of Harrow Borough Council. He was well disposed to us and could see merit in our proposals. On the other hand, he constantly recommended a delay in the submission of a formal planning application until the political climate in both Harrow and at the GLC was favourable to an encroachment into the Green Belt in our area. He argued that when the Tories ruled in Harrow, if they granted residential development, a Labour-led County Hall would, most likely, slap a compulsory purchase order on the land and build council houses. This would alter the balance of power by bringing into the area voters on the opposite side of the political spectrum. We were between a rock and a hard place.

In the run-up to the 1970 election I had worked for the Tory candidate who was fighting our constituency for the first time and I was delighted when a young Hugh Dykes was elected as Member of Parliament for Harrow East and we became friends. Hugh had been to Oxford and was working at Simon & Coates, who were my own stockbrokers. He was very popular in the constituency and a hard-working Member of Parliament, being appointed a Parliamentary Private Secretary in Edward Heath's Government. I took the opportunity, when he invited me to lunch with him one day at the House of Commons, to tell him of the *impasse* I had experienced over the years with the local planning authorities.

He expressed sympathy with my predicament and gave me his views on the vexed question, to build or not to build? I left the House with the impression that, whilst he personally would be in favour of selective development within the Metropolitan Green Belt, it was a political hot-potato and the Party line was to refuse any encroachment. It seemed to me that London's Green Belt was akin to a Crusader's wife's chastity belt – it was not to be tampered with.

My ownership of these 80 acres of England's green and pleasant land was becoming a financial burden. The economic crisis of 1974/5, with plummeting share prices and soaring interest rates, had placed a strain on my personal resources. It only needed the introduction in 1975 of the Development Land Tax and at the same time the enactment of the Community Land Act to finally convince me that all my efforts to retain and one day build on the Warren House Estate were futile and doomed to failure. The DLT was designed to tax away virtually the whole of any profit realised as a result of a change of use, whilst the Community Land Act required local authorities to acquire Green Belt land for future use but at *current-use* value – in my case the price that was applicable to parkland.

My experiences had finally led me to the conclusion that the provision of new housing was a political football – it had very little in common with *people* but everything to do with *votes*.

I asked Mr Foxley to arrange for a consultation with him and the chief valuer of the GLC at his office in Harrow Town Hall. In the discussion that ensued, I reviewed my 17 years of ownership and the frustrations I had experienced. I told the officers that I now wished to dispose of the land and would accept a price that would just clear a bank overdraft secured on the property. They asked me to quantify the figure and I replied '£75,000'. There were protestations on the part of the Chief Valuer, with both officers confirming that their respective councils had no budget for land purchase and for that matter any money at all but, personally, they were very much in favour of a purchase as my estate would unite with their own land to the north. On being pressed as to value, the Greater London Council valuer said, 'I would place a current use value on it of £400 per acre, but on the other hand I *could* justify a figure of £1,000 an acre having regard to one day, in the next millennium of course,some limited development being allowed.'

Faced with such arguments, I caved in. We finally shook hands on £75,000 and I ceased to be a gentleman farmer.

24

Tales of Three Cities

One of the most momentous happenings of our times, a century filled with more scientific discoveries, that one could class as miracles, than in the preceding two millennia, occurred on 17 December 1903. On that day the world shrank. On that day in the small town of Kitty Hawk in Virginia, USA (it is so small you would have difficulty in locating it on an atlas) the Wright brothers flew 300 yards and ushered in the era of the aeroplane. Before then, all international commerce had been sea-borne. Lines of communication had been the shipping lanes across the oceans; from there to the estuaries and rivers and finally to the centres of population. It was no accident that the capital city of most countries were sited and grew up on the banks of a major river, and London is a prime example of this development. Father Thames carried the argosies that created the wealth of England, and on the river bank in Westminster the seat of government was established.

All rivers run down to the sea and when they are tidal they can be complex and cause problems. I am unsure of the precise date that studies began dealing with the effect that tidal surges in the Thames might have on London. The findings were alarming, so much so that they were kept secret for years by successive governments for fear of creating a panic. It was calculated that the combination of a severe easterly gale on top of a high equinoctial flood tide would cause the Thames to overflow its banks and leave major parts of London under water. Westminster would be a prime victim of such a disaster and the Houses of Commons and the Lords rendered unusable. The solution to the problem lay in building a barrier to control any extreme changes in the level of the Thames. Greenwich was chosen for this engineering feat and top priority was given to the scheme in the knowledge that it would take several years to construct. Meanwhile an emergency plan had to be put in place to safeguard against the possibility of England being bereft of government!

Surveys of central London revealed that Holborn was above the level that the flood waters were likely to reach and the hunt for a suitable site began. It was, of course, out of the question to build a modern version of Noah's Ark as a temporary measure, but the Connaught Rooms provided a ready-made solution at minimal cost to the public purse with the 22 banqueting suites replicating, in the event of an emergency, the needs of the Commons and the Lords. But a seat of government without communication was unthinkable. Unlike Noah, Members of Parliament could not rely on relays of doves, so British Telecom was set to work and in 18 months had installed a sophisticated network of telephones equivalent to Connaught Rooms having 2,000 direct lines to the outside world.

We felt very patriotic in allowing British Telecom to pepper our walls with bore holes and to trail miles of cable under our floors. Even though the greater part of the work was done during the night, each morning a hectic clearing-up process was quickly under way to restore rooms for their designed function of hosting receptions and banquets. Feeling that we were discharging a civic duty, we did not claim compensation and, needless to say, none was offered. Our reward was still to come when, several years later, the Central Office of Information approached us to host the Press Centre for the London Economic Summit. The brief was to provide a 24-hour catering facility for some 3,000 international journalists and newscasters who would be covering the five-day G7 summit. Without any hesitation we told the COI that we could accept the challenge. The essential infrastructure was in place and we had the expertise. Discussions ensued on the detailed requirements of the hospitality that would be expected. The previous year the summit had been held in Los Angeles and catering had been on a lavish scale, with the US Government 'picking up the complete tab'. Negotiations between our General Manager, Arnold Perl, and the COI went on for months. At each session the original budget was revised *downwards* and menus trimmed. We were told that the PM, Margaret Thatcher was taking a personal interest in the arrangements and scrutinising every item of expense. Her final veto was to exclude the provision of wine and beer as a *freebie*, even embarrassing the departmental head who came to advise us of the decision.

For the five days of the summit, Connaught Rooms was in a state of siege. Each of our 300 staff had been interrogated by the security services. Rooms were checked daily by sniffer dogs and only accredited visitors could pass the armed guards in the entrance hall. The working sessions of the delegates took place at Lancaster House off Pall Mall, with the Finance Ministers and their advisers, at the end of each day, adjourning to Connaught Rooms. There they would be interrogated by reporters in the numerous soundproof recording studios we had set up, and broadcast by cable and satellite to the whole world. On the final day of the conference every participating Head of State gathered for a joint press conference and the issuance of a bulletin summarising their conclusions. As they arrived, I looked down the length of Great Queen Street and counted the number of marksmen on the rooftops of the buildings that faced us, with their sniper rifles fitted with telescopic sights trained on the Connaught Rooms entrance. I could not make up my mind whether this made me feel more secure or just threatened.

From our point of view the G7 Summit was a triumph and the Prime Minister sent me a personal letter to say that our contribution had been 'a great success'.

The Thames Barrier over the years has done its work well and there has been no flooding at Westminster. Of course, one can never be absolutely sure, but it should be of comfort to know that the Connaught Rooms with its 2,000 telephone lines stands ready to do its duty.

The early success of our new hotel the de Montfort in Kenilworth, together with the Manor House in Leamington Spa, had convinced me that we should build up a strategic presence in the Midlands. We had acquired, extremely cheaply, the small Manor Hotel in Meriden, a village midway between the sprawling cities of Birmingham and Coventry and known for little else other than the presence of the ailing Triumph motorcycle factory, which had lost out so badly to Japanese competition. The Manor afforded only basic accommodation, but being set in three acres of gardens on the fringe of the Coventry green belt, it had distinct expansion potential.

I was introduced to Ron Stone an architect with a small practice in Coventry who impressed me with his design concepts. Being a good salesman, it was not long before he was bringing me local development projects, all of which I rejected out of hand for their failure to meet the three prime criteria for a new hotel – location, location, location. Finally the day came when one did catch my imagination – to build alongside the new Coventry Cathedral that had arisen like a Phoenix from the wartime ashes of its blitzed predecessor. Coventry, a city of 300,000, its prosperity built on the booming motor car industry, had only one hotel worthy of the name – The Leofric. Originally designed as an office building, it was acquired by the brewers Ind Coope and Allsopp, and altered to become a hotel. It took its name from the Earl of Chester, an eleventh-century nobleman who achieved fame through his marriage to Lady Godiva, who, legend has it, rode naked through the streets of Coventry in order to obtain concessions from the King for the citizens of her city. Free of any competition, the hotel had been an overnight success and I could foresee the scope for an even bigger and better hotel which would carry the De Vere name.

The brief I gave to Ron Stone was exacting and daunting. He had to design a modern hotel adjacent to a cathedral that had achieved for its designer, Basil Spence, international acclaim and a knighthood. The cathedral housed the famous tapestry of Graham Sutherland, the sculpture of Jacob Epstein and the stained glass windows designed by John Piper. Arguably the biggest constraint I placed on Ron, was the financial budget and on this score I would not compromise. Much more was at stake than Stone's reputation. He had never designed a hotel before and he needed my input to make it work, particularly in the design of the kitchens, restaurants and banqueting areas. In promoting the project to my board, and particularly to my Chairman, who I knew had an almost pathological dislike of building because of his inability to read plans, I was taking a big personal gamble, the extent of which was to become very apparent in later years.

The expanding tourist industry was playing an increasingly major role in the country's economy. The one single factor that was inhibiting its growth was the dearth of modern hotels and the failure to replace those destroyed by bombing during the war. Recognising that the fundamental problem was the difficulty of securing finance for new projects, the government offered a cash grant of £1,000 per bedroom towards the cost of building. This incentive, coupled with the liberal income tax allowances on plant, furniture, fixtures and fittings, was large enough to persuade financial institutions to discard their old prejudice against providing hotel finance. A time limit to qualify for the grant was imposed and every project had to be commenced by 31st March 1973.

I was not prepared to take the scheme any further until we had secured affordable finance of at least one half of the budgeted cost. A fortunate introduction to the Finance Director of the Liverpool Victoria Friendly Society, who had been born in Coventry, resulted in their offering a fixed mortgage of £1.2 million on very favourable terms.

The site was owned by the Coventry City Corporation and a 99-year building lease was negotiated at an initial ground rent of £2,500 p.a. with reviews every 21 years. The corporation was very keen to see a hotel built on this prominent site, but at the last moment and literally minutes before I was due to sign the building lease I was having doubts as to the wisdom of committing ourselves to an expenditure of more than £2 million. Churchill Machine Tool Company, one of the major businesses in the city, was experiencing financial problems and on the point of closure. Wage rates at the Coventry motor works were the highest in the country and industrial unrest and strikes instigated by militant trade unions had become commonplace. I voiced my fears to the Town Clerk and asked him, point-blank, what would happen if the car factories at Ruyton were to close. He did not mince words and replied, 'Coventry would become a ghost town.'

With the agreement, imposingly sealed with large blobs of red wax and signed by the corporation in my hand, I asked the officers of the city who had collected to witness the signing, to withdraw from the room whilst I had a short consultation with my co-director, Reginald Constable. We debated the pros and cons, but the final argument that persuaded us to go ahead was the prospect of the new International Conference Centre being planned by Birmingham, which would in fact be closer to Coventry than to the city of Birmingham. A building contract was soon placed with Taylor Woodrow and work commenced on the construction of a four-star 220-bedroom hotel, with separate staff accommodation, at a fully furnished cost equivalent to £11,000 per bedroom.

I was very budget conscious, so as soon as we had accepted the builder's fixed-price contract and even before building had commenced, I placed fixed-price orders for 440 divan beds as well as 220 enamelled iron baths (not the fibreglass or plastic variety unfortunately so commonplace today). A firm price with our carpet manufacturers for the miles of carpets we would require was also agreed. In the event, inflation in the early 1970s started to accelerate and my action resulted in a significant saving.

One of the features I greatly admired in the new Coventry Cathedral was Sir Jacob Epstein's dramatic sculpture *St Michael and the Devil* which had been hung on the east wall. In the background, stood the ruins of the former cathedral that had been blitzed. It was the persistence of Sir Basil Spence, the cathedral architect, that secured the sculptural commission for Epstein. His proposal did not originally commend itself to the Reconstruction Committee, who objected, not to the choice of subject, but to the artist himself, saying, 'We cannot give it to Sir Jacob, after all he is a *Jew*.' Sir Basil's reply was, 'And so was Jesus', to which there was, of course, no answer.

I was determined to place some artefacts in the new hotel that would forge a link with the cathedral and I got in touch with Sir Jacob's widow, Lady Kathleen Epstein, who invited me to tea. I asked whether she could spare any sketches of the sculpture and her response exceeded all my expectations. She told me that she would consider letting us have on permanent loan a *maquette* of *St Michael and the Devil* but, unfortunately, although we met once again at her house, the offer did not materialise.

Etched into the transom windows around the cathedral is a series of angels, each one in a different but dramatic flying pose with outstretched wings. Learning that the studio of the artist was in Maida Vale, London, I called on John Hutton and was able to purchase several of his original sketches, which he had drawn in red chalk. I am very happy that whilst giving preference to the hotel, I purchased one to hang in my own home, where it is constantly admired.

In the late 1960s the economy began to expand and it was prudent to take a more optimistic view of the future. Consequently when a hotel project in Cambridge was brought to me by the well-known London architects Fitzroy Robinson & Partners, the board agreed to my going ahead with a feasibility study. Cambridge, renowned for its university, was the home of numerous scientific and high technology companies who were enthusiastic, when I approached them, to see De Vere build a prestige hotel in the city centre. I had recently visited a small hotel in the industrial town of Winterthur on the outskirts of Zurich and was impressed by the fact that local businesses had undertaken to provide some of the hotel's vital installations as a practical and living showroom for their products. In this way the hotel had been able to acquire, at minimal cost, stainless steel state-of-the-art kitchens, central heating plant and passenger lifts, and even its fine Swiss bedroom linen. I decided to try this approach out in Cambridge and it worked.

The site we had bought for our prospective hotel was close to Fitzwilliam College and opposite the county council offices. It comprised a garage and petrol filling station together with several small cottages, one housing a doctor's surgery, in all about an acre

245

and a half. Initially we only had vacant possession of the garage, and separate sets of negotiations had to be undertaken, in secret, to relocate or compensate the other tenants. Our architects, who had an office in the town, designed a 210 bedroom hotel which would have the potential of catering for college balls of up to 1,000 guests. Cambridge had seen no new hotel building for more than 50 years and there was a large unsatisfied demand for accommodation of the standard provided by the De Vere group. The site was large enough to take a mixed development and the city planning authority granted us an outline planning consent not only for the hotel but in addition, banking premises, 10,000 square feet of offices and a petrol station with car showrooms. We felt a sense of achievement and looked forward to providing the city with a superb hotel.

We had no sooner accepted the lowest tender and commenced work on the site so as to meet the government-grant deadline, when a bombshell burst. I received a telephone call from our architects telling me that the newly created Department of the Environment (formerly the Ministry of Town and Country Planning) was 'calling in the papers' with a view to holding a public enquiry into the development. The Secretary of State was Peter Walker, who had been a partner of Jim Slater in Slater Walker & Co., a publicly quoted finance house. Walker had four ministers to help run the department, and I ascertained that the person who was dealing with our case was Mr Graham Page. On getting in touch with him and expressing our dismay at the turn of events, I received his office's assurance that if we would drop the garage element there would be no need for an enquiry and the development could proceed. I agreed to do this and on asking when the papers would be 'released', was told 'in five days'. I did a quick calculation and mentioned a precise date, only to be told, 'No, that's not correct, we mean five "working" days'. Two months later, despite a weekly telephone call, I was still being fobbed off. In the meantime work on site had been halted.

In an endeavour to break the political deadlock, I invited David Lane (subsequently Sir David, chairman of the Race Relations Board) the sitting Member of Parliament for the City of

Cambridge and Francis Pym (later ennobled), the Government Chief Whip, who was the MP for the County of Cambridge, to a conference in my office. They expressed their dismay at this sudden and unexpected development and undertook to go as a joint delegation to see the Prime Minister at No. 10. A very embarrassed David Lane then reported back to me that Ted (Mr Edward Heath) had told them, 'I don't keep a dog and bark myself. Go and see Peter Walker.'

It was obvious that there were some powerful forces at work, and I warned David Lane that if we were not allowed to proceed with our building we would have no option but to sue the city for compensation to the tune of £500,000 – probably resulting in an increase of sixpence on the rates, an event which would have catastrophic repercussions for Cambridge's Tory representatives in the House of Commons.

A public enquiry was arranged by the ministry and De Vere engaged Sir Derek Walker-Smith, MP, a leading planning QC, together with Mr Alastair Dawson of Counsel to represent us. The hearing took five days and when the independent inspector's report was published it was a complete vindication of our scheme, which he recommended should go ahead. The ministry would not accept the inspector's findings and called for a second enquiry. I told all concerned that De Vere 'had had enough' and would be suing the city for compensation. Alarmed by the turn of events, the county authorities decided that provided we would support them they would fight and pay the costs of the second enquiry, which would be chaired by a different inspector. This was duly held some months later and on the third day, Counsel approached me with the news that the government would withdraw their appeal if we would agree on what he called 'a face-saving' formula. The formula the Minister proposed and we accepted was 'to reduce the number of bedrooms by five and to set back the top floor by eighteen inches'!

I experienced no sense of victory. I was just weary after having spent four years piecing together the site and fighting for the privilege of building a hotel that would be worthy of a city as important as Cambridge. I racked my brains to find a logical explanation for the cause of the trauma I had been forced to undergo. I asked myself the question 'Who is powerful enough to thwart such prominent MPs, one of whom was the Government Chief Whip?' Was I the latest victim of the battle that had been waged for centuries between Town and Gown? The Town had certainly been on my side, but who in the university had been my adversary? The conclusion I came to, and I admit that I was not able to substantiate it, was that my opponent was none other than the Master of Trinity College, the foremost and most influential of all Cambridge colleges, whose appointment is in the gift of the Prime Minister. If my surmise was correct, then that person's influence would have to extend to the inner sanctum of Whitehall. There was indeed a Master who fitted the description – Lord Butler, who, as R.A. Butler, had earned the soubriquet the 'best Prime Minister England *never* had'.

Over a year had passed since work had stopped on the hotel infrastructure and I sought assurances that the enforced delay had not made us ineligible for the grant of £1,000 per bedroom. Meanwhile, our quantity surveyors were busy getting a revised price from the builders. Having secured this, I had a board meeting convened to review the position in the light of an increase in the overall cost of almost £1 million. The majority of the board agreed with me that a De Vere hotel in Cambridge would still be viable, even at the increased cost, but Müller demurred and moved that the site be sold. I had long previously made it a policy that we should only proceed with projects on a unanimous vote in the boardroom and, acting on this principle, and with great sadness and reluctance, I told the board I would seek a buyer. I have never ceased to regret this decision and I am sure the city of Cambridge shares my disappointment.

Douglas January was the leading estate agent in the city and my instructions to him resulted in his finding a buyer within a week. I was so despondent that I did not bother to enquire his identity. My sole concern now was to pay off our professional team, the lawyers, architect, quantity surveyors and structural engineer, which left the company with a surplus of £350,000 whilst I was inconsolable at the missed opportunity.

Completion of the sale was due to take place towards the end of 1974. The due date having arrived and passed without any action, our solicitors issued a 28-day notice requiring specific performance on the part of the buyer. I was relieved when, two days before Christmas, I was told that the purchase consideration of £750,000 had been paid into De Vere's bank account. It had been touch-and-go, a fact that I only found out some two weeks later when the buyer was revealed as a company owned by a Mr William Stern, who had just claimed a place in the *Guinness Book of Records*, having gone bankrupt for over £100 million.

The sad ending to this story is that Cambridge has never acquired a much needed prestige hotel. Instead, after the site had lain derelict for seven years, the city was blessed, or cursed, with yet another monster office block. I can only surmise that Gown was able to claim one more victory in its centuries-old battle against Town – in this instance a *Pyrrhic* one.

25

The World in Recession

All world religions have their own special holy days and traditional festivals. Some days commemorate a unique historical milestone whilst others may celebrate the differing seasons of the year, such as springtime and harvest. Christians celebrate Christmas and Easter, the birth and the last days of Jesus Christ. Jews go back two further millennia in time and in the Festival of Passover, which frequently coincides with Easter, they recall the exodus of Moses and the children of Israel and their deliverance from slavery in Egypt. Moslems find many occasions to celebrate in the life of their prophet Mohammed, who in the seventh century AD, founded the Islamic faith. Their most holy festival is the month of Ramadan, when from sunrise to sunset devout Moslems must abstain from eating and drinking – and sex.

The year 1973 witnessed mounting tension in the areas occupied in the Six Day war. On the Golan Heights on the Syrian border, there had been constant violent clashes, including the shooting down in one encounter of 13 Syrian warplanes for the loss of one Israeli fighter. In the south along the Suez Canal, crossings by armed patrols by both sides to the conflict were a nightly occurrence. The Syrians, in concert with the Egyptians, both massively armed by the Russians with the latest weaponry, completed the planning in great detail for an all-out war, with the avowed intention of eliminating the State of Israel once and for all.

The date agreed upon by President Sadat of Egypt and President Assad of Syria for their attack was 6th October – a day of special significance to Moslems and to Jews. It was the tenth day of Ramadan, commemorating the preparations made by Mohammed in the year 623 for the battle of Badr which led to the conquest of Mecca. Code-named 'Badr', co-ordinated hostilities by the Syrians in the north and the Egyptians in the south were planned to commence at 2 p.m. There would be no declaration of war, all the Arab countries having been in a continuous state of war with Israel since its Declaration of Independence in 1948. To maintain the element of surprise the actual D-Day was a secret known only to the two Presidents and a handful of generals. The massive build-up of forces and military hardware on the banks of the Canal and on the Syrian border were played down as repetitions of frequently staged manoeuvres. In choosing Saturday 6th October with its Islamic significance as the day to attack, Sadat, the prime architect of the plan, knew that it was also the most holy day in the Jewish calendar. On that day synagogues throughout Israel would be packed and the Army as well as the population would be at prayer and fasting. It was Yom Kippur – the awesome Day of Atonement.

It is a fact of history that the commencement of hostilities *did* catch the Israelis by surprise and for the first two days the fate of the State hung in the balance. Syria committed 1,400 battle tanks, many of them the latest Russian T62, against the partially mobilised Israel Defence Force, who were outnumbered by five to one. In the south the Egyptians crossed the Suez Canal in force and overran the forward defence lines.

I heard the news whilst praying in my local synagogue and it swept through the congregation like a fireball. We now added the armed forces of Israel and the beleaguered citizens of that tiny country to our Day of Atonement prayers and supplications.

Not only did I have numerous friends in Israel, many of them of military age and no doubt already in action, but our daughter Judith was working as a teleprinter operator in the British Embassy in Tel Aviv. On Monday morning, with the war two days old, I made contact with Judy on our office teleprinter and she was able to give me assurances of her own safety. Several of my neighbours had relatives living in the war zone, and for the following two weeks, through my office teleprinter and that in

251

HM's Embassy in Tel Aviv, I became the conduit and the disseminator of up-to-the-minute news of the war.

From an independent source, I had confirmation of the unprecedented level of casualties incurred by the IDF in the early days of the onslaught as an outnumbered and only partially-ready army faced a Syrian force in tank battles as great as any fought in World War II. A close and very dear friend was the plastic surgeon Leo Bornstein, later to become professor of plastic surgery at the Tel Hashomer hospital in Tel Aviv. In-between operations he called me on Tuesday from a telephone in the military section of the Ram Bam hospital in Haifa in the north of Israel and close to the battlefield on the Lebanese and Syrian borders. He described the desperate battles that were going on only 30 miles away and the constant stream of casualties – in the main, tank crews with horrific burns – on which he had been operating non-stop for 72 hours. To illustrate how serious the situation was, he told me that the rabbinical authorities had, for the very first time ever, given permission for grafts to be taken from *cadavers* and had also authorised the use of pig skin.

It is a matter of history how, after the initial setbacks, the IDF counter-attacked and pushed the Syrians back (they had been supported by armoured divisions from Morocco, Iraq and Jordan). When a ceasefire was declared, the IDF had advanced to within artillery range of Damascus. On the southern front, the Egyptian Third Army was decimated and in bitter fighting the Israeli troops had crossed the canal and reached to within 50 miles of Cairo.

Israel had been saved. Hopefully *not* to have to fight another day.

The year 1973 had started inauspiciously, a setback in the economy having followed the freezing by the government of prices, dividends and rents the previous November. During that year I can recall only two favourable events affecting De Vere, and many adverse ones.

First the good news. The hotel in Coventry was completed more or less on time, despite its having been selected, at random, as one of the sites to be picketed during a national strike of building unions. This reprehensible and unjustifiable action brought building work to a halt for six weeks. When we finally opened we were very proud of the new addition to the group, in its prestigious location taking up one side of Cathedral Square. We knew that, given time to establish, the hotel would make a valuable contribution to the business and cultural life of the city. We had, however, experienced the greatest difficulty in booking conferences prior to the hotel's opening, despite having produced a brochure with colourful artist's impressions of the facilities and amenities that would be available. We had debated long and hard before printing the tariff and decided that the market would comfortably bear a charge of £7.50 per night inclusive of breakfast, service and the newly introduced VAT. Only two days before opening, and sensing a downturn in the market, I decided to reduce the price to £7.00 and I had all the literature reprinted. Even so, we had an uphill struggle to reach a room occupancy that ensured break-even.

In the Bournemouth area we had built up a dominant position in the conference and tourist sector of the market, with the group now comprising five major hotels. Early in March I answered a telephone call from a Mr Lionel Green who described himself as a residential property developer.

He quickly came to the point, saying, 'I want to buy the Branksome Towers Hotel and I will offer you £650,000.'

I replied, 'No thank you,' and hung up.

Moments later he came through again and said, 'I will increase my offer to £850,000.'

I replied, 'The hotel is not for sale,' and put the telephone down.

Two days later he telephoned again and I told him not to pester us as he would need to be speaking of a price in seven figures for my co-directors to show even the faintest interest in selling.

Without hesitation he said, 'All right then, £1,250,000.'

I now felt that this was an offer that I should bring to the notice of the board, convinced that they would find it one that they could not refuse.

Mr Green made only one condition, namely that he needed to

exchange contracts not later than the end of the month, 31st March 1973. The magic in this date lay in the fact that every outline permission for development that had previously been granted but not implemented would expire if, by that date, it had not been converted into a full consent. In concentrating our minds and energies in running the property as a hotel, we had overlooked the outline planning consent that a previous owner had obtained for the erection of 180 flats on one of the finest positions on the south coast of England, its ten-acre cliff-top site being covered with pines and firs that lined the pathways leading down to its own stretch of sandy beach.

We were only three weeks away from the deadline, with Easter intervening, and I felt sure he would be unable to comply. He was dismissive of my reservations, assuring me that he would make it; and he did.

We exchanged contracts, with deferred completion for 24th December to enable us to discharge our commitments for forward bookings. My most difficult task lay not in the boardroom, as my co-directors were delighted with the price that the telephone auction had produced, but with my loyal staff. I now had to break the news to my General Manager, John Welsh, who had devoted so many years to making the hotel a successful venture. He made me feel like Judas and, for that matter, so did many of our customers, many of whom had been patronising the hotel from childhood.

During the year that followed the sale, I met Green on several occasions. He would land his helicopter alongside the swimming pool, having had the hotel demolished very soon after completion. He would taunt me by boasting that he had been offered £4 million for the site, but could make a lot more money by developing. He intended to make a start as soon as Poole Corporation had agreed his latest amendments on siting and the height of the blocks of flats.

Two years passed and building had still not commenced when, to curb the inflation that was roaring away, interest rates were increased to an unprecedented level of 15%. The demand for flats in Bournemouth vanished overnight and Lionel Green never built on the site. Instead his company especially formed to purchase the hotel went into compulsory liquidation when his financiers, the County Bank, foreclosed on their loans, which had risen with accrued interest on the original purchase price to a sum in excess of £3 million.

The repercussions of the Yom Kippur war were manifold. Despite Syria having lost more than 80% of its armoured divisions and air force, a major defeat suffered by Iraq, and with Egypt looking at Israeli troops dug in on the west bank of the Suez Canal, the Arab states claimed the war as a historic victory for them. The Israeli euphoria that had followed the Six Day War in 1967 was not repeated in 1973, the country was in fact traumatised and confidence in its leadership had ebbed away when the realisation of the scale of the casualties it had suffered began to sink in. The course of the battle would have been so different had Golda Meir, the Prime Minister, and Moshe Dayan, the Minister of Defence, heeded the Army Intelligence reports that war was imminent and had ordered full mobilisation 48 hours earlier. Once again Israel was victorious but Arab honour had been restored by their having fought for a week longer than in 1967. Strategically and in terms of land, it was back to the *status quo*, but peace was as far away as ever.

To avenge themselves on the West and particularly on the United States for having supported Israel, the Arabs decided to use the oil weapon and cut back production. To further aggravate the situation, the Canal was blocked by mines and scores of sunken ships and it was to take many months before the waterway could be freely navigated by oil tankers.

Meanwhile, interest rates rose; the price of petrol soared and the seeds were sown for a rate of inflation that would run into double figures. Tourism was badly hit and De Vere's profits nose-dived as costs, particularly wages, rose to a level where they could not be covered by higher tariffs. It had been my policy to review our charges on a bi-annual basis, but with inflation in 1974 running at 16%, it became necessary to revise them quarterly. Fixing the

255

selling price of our hotel rooms did not follow some intricate mathematical formula. Because the hotels were individual and not standardised, we did this in consultation with each hotel manager. It was a delicate balancing act of keeping track of the competition and then fixing the rate at what we felt the market could bear. With the world going into recession, the fear was that price increases would prove counter-productive, bringing increased pressure on 'bottom line' profits.

With Leopold Müller and myself holding in excess of 50% of the company's share capital we had every incentive to support the company financially. We both waived the dividends on our shareholdings and for many years Müller lent the company £1 million interest-free, which provided a support to our cash flow in a period of rapid expansion. Our directors' fees were modest, I paid the annual premiums on my personal pension and even the Daimler motor car that I drove had been bought from my own pocket. There certainly was no 'fat cat' lifestyle in our boardroom, none of the golden perks that today are a common feature of quoted companies – golden helloes, golden handcuffs, golden handshakes share options and bonuses that in their sheer size border on the obscene, especially as there is a total failure to punish *failure*.

Industrial unrest at the end of 1973, resulting in the advent of the 'three-day-working week', conspired to create a depressed business background. Piles of rubbish lay uncollected in the streets of London and press reports of long delays in getting people buried made lurid newspaper headlines abroad which proved fatal to tourism. The FTSE 100 stock market index (known as 'the Footsie'), a sensitive sensor of contemporary events, drifted from a peak of almost 600 and continued to fall over the next two years, losing 80% of its value in the process.

It was the most serious and dramatic bear market since the Wall Street crash of 1929 and precipitated a crisis amongst secondary banks, who were only saved from drowning by the inspired launching by the Bank of England of a 'lifeboat'. The downturn in the stock market had an early impact on us both as Müller had arranged to purchase a personal portfolio of 'blue chip' shares and

256

had borrowed £1 million from Hill Samuel for this purpose. The loan was guaranteed by both of us on a joint-and-several basis and, as was usual in this type of transaction, the bankers required the loan to be covered by shares having a market value equivalent to 125% of the money borrowed. As the stock market fell, so our collateral had to be topped up. I was soon under financial strain but was reluctant to sell any of my De Vere shares, whilst recognising the danger should the stock market continue to fall. As I had entered into the arrangement on the urging of Müller, I asked him and the bank to release me from my personal guarantee, which they agreed to do. The transaction had been entirely speculative and we had got our timing wrong, but we were soon to face a further and more serious dilemma. De Vere shares had reached a peak of 234p, possibly because it had been leaked that I was talking to the Chairman of the Rank Organisation, Sir John Davis, and Alastair Dawson, his Managing Director who were interested in making an offer for the company. Our shares now began to fall in line with the market and Müller decided to use all his resources to support the price. Experience soon taught me that in a prolonged bear market you cannot buck the trend. By aggressive buying, however, he was partially successful and over the next two years had bought De Vere shares all the way down to a price of 67p, at a personal cost of more than £3 million and in the process increased his holding to more than 60%, a position which he had not sought and with which he did not feel comfortable.

Many entrepreneurial chairmen of quoted companies were in the same predicament and not a few in peril of losing all that they had worked for. Maxwell Joseph, through his company Grand Metropolitan Hotels, had prospered since our first meeting in 1954 when he proposed joining forces with us and boasted that he could invest £10,000. He had a buccaneering style, whilst ours was cautious. Needless to say that when we were in competition for an acquisition he invariably outbid us. I can cite several companies, including Express Dairies and Mecca, where our own negotiations were so advanced, with Walter Nell the President of Express Dairies on the one hand and Eric Morley, Managing Director of

Mecca on the other, that press releases had been drafted announcing our agreed bids, only to find Max intervening and overbidding us. Perhaps it is true that only the brave deserve the fair.

Grand Metropolitan's entry into the big league came when they launched a bid, backed by Warburgs the merchant bankers, to take over Watneys, England's third largest brewer, with more than 7,000 public houses. The idea originated from Joseph's fertile brain and even his two very able joint Managing Directors, fellow chartered accountants Stanley Grinstead and Ernest Sharp, were taken by surprise. On going to Joseph's office shortly afterwards to discuss the acquisition from Grand Metropolitan of their 50% holding in Connaught Rooms Ltd., I was told by his secretary that she had helped her boss work out the Watney scheme 'on the back of an envelope'. The reaction of the Watney board to the all-paper bid was extremely hostile and a bitter battle ensued, with the brewery trade unions joining in the fray to 'see off' the minnow which was trying to swallow their whale. It was reported that Max borrowed heavily to support his company's share price, to make the deal more attractive to the Watney shareholders, and after a hard fight, won the day. Having acquired Truman Hanbury Buxton, the London brewers in Brick Lane only a few months earlier, he had at one stroke propelled his company to the top of the brewery sector.

The fall in the stock market by the end of 1975 decimated the share price of Grand Metropolitan which must have left Max with a great headache and huge personal borrowings. He managed to ride the storm and when he died some ten years later, he had been knighted and had earned the esteem of the City, having built up a multi-billion pound company virtually from scratch. No one regretted his passing more than I, as we had become staunch friends, despite our business rivalry in the early and formative years of our careers.

It was in 1948, when I was initiated into the restaurant business with the acquisition of the Chicken Inn at the top of Haymarket, that I became conscious of being literally surrounded by restaurants owned by a Mr Charles Forte who, even in those early days, had acquired dominant sites in the West End of London. On the opposite side of the Haymarket I looked over to the offices of D. & J. Levy, one of the area's leading estate agents. It was only natural that when I formulated the plan to expand the Chicken Inn concept into a chain of West End restaurants I should contact them. Over the years I persistently asked them to offer sites to us but without success. I soon came to the conclusion that their first choice was Mr Forte and if he showed interest, Chicken Inns could whistle in the wind. I followed Charles Forte's progress with a keen eye and with considerable admiration. Deal followed deal, commencing with Rainbow Corner in Shaftesbury Avenue, famous during the war as *the* rendezvous for the American forces in London. He bought the Criterion in Piccadilly Circus – a building erected at the turn of the nineteenth century by my old company Spiers & Pond. Standing at the Eros statue, the island at the hub of Piccadilly Circus, and looking up at the roof of the Criterion building, one can still see the intertwined letters S & P.

In 1962, Mr Forte took his company to the stock market for the same reason that three years later De Vere, a more modest flotation, decided that a Stock Exchange quotation was essential if one wanted to expand in the capital-intensive world of hotels. The Forte group offered 40% of their shares to the public and at the offer price the whole company was capitalised at £4 million, a figure that rose rapidly as the market responded with enthusiasm.

A major milestone in the Forte story was the merger in 1970 with Trust Houses Ltd. Renamed Trust House Forte Ltd., they acquired national coverage and were recognised as the leading hotel and catering group of the country. Allied Breweries, who, many years previously as Ind Coope & Allsopp had helped Charles Forte buy the Criterion, now made an unwelcome bid for the company at 164p per share. This valued the business at £128 million, about half the price that Charles felt it was worth. He strenuously opposed the bid. Part of his strategy was to buy his company's shares in the market, thus denying Allied the opportunity of building up a cheap stake. His faith and confidence in his company was absolute and he had no hesitation in committing his substantial family fortune to this end. Before the closing date of the offer and to ensure the success of his company's defence, he found it necessary to borrow, on personal guarantees, a further £10 million. Allied's hostile bid failed dismally, a tribute to the dedication, commitment and fighting spirit of the Forte family and their shareholders. Charles was left with personal borrowings which, at the time, were only a relatively small percentage of the total value of his shareholdings. The effect of the recession of 1973/5 is amply illustrated by the performance of Trusthouse Forte shares.

By the end of December 1974 they had dropped to 40p, only a quarter of the price offered by Allied Breweries two years earlier and almost an eighth of the value placed on them by Charles who, in common with so many tycoons who had supported their companies, had problems. With the recovery in the stock market Fortes surged ahead and, 20 years later, Britain's most successful hotel company, under the Chairmanship of Sir Rocco Forte, commanded a market capitalisation in excess of £3 billion!

26

Heard on the Grapevine

The grapevine is a wonderful plant. It takes root in almost any soil and he who cultivates it with care can reap a rich harvest; to another its yield can best be described as sour grapes. If questioned after a successful business coup many an entrepreneur would confess that he first heard of it 'on the grapevine'. The winner enjoys the sweetness akin to a Château d'Yquem, the loser is left with the bitter taste of wine vinegar. I recall two such deals, the first involving a most desirable group of hotels and the other an individual hotel of such excellence that it deservedly falls into the category 'a hotel to die for'.

In my youth I could never have imagined an England without *Joe Lyons*. Founded at the end of Queen Victoria's reign by a Mr Salmon and a Mr Gluckstein, J. Lyons & Co. Ltd. had for nearly a century been synonymous with excellence in many comestibles. Their teas and coffees were market leaders, their bakeries turned out the country's favourite Swiss roll, whilst their ice cream – Lyonsmaid – had no peer. If trading in these commodities was still insufficient to establish them as a household name, their activities included a chain of tea-shops and a group of 34 hotels. Established before the First World War with the development of The Regent Palace in Piccadilly Circus, The Strand Palace opposite The Savoy and The Cumberland at Marble Arch, the generations of Salmons and Glucksteins had built a unique chain of London and regional hotels that was the envy of the hospitality industry.

Their acquisitive eye fell on De Vere and I found myself making frequent visits to their headquarters at Cadby Hall, close to

London's Olympia, and discussing a merger with the Lyons hotel division. I escorted the chairman, Geoffrey Salmon (a grandson of one of the founders of the company), on a clandestine tour of our group. He was impressed. I was attracted to being taken over by Lyons by reason of an undertaking given to me by their chairman that I would be called upon to occupy a major executive role in their merged hotel and catering division with a seat on their board. I cleared my negotiations with Leopold Müller, who, as controlling shareholder, could sanction or frustrate any deal. He indicated that a price of 240p would be acceptable to him for his stake in the company. The Stock Exchange would require the same offer to be extended to the minority shareholders within a period of three months.

Having secured my chairman's agreement in principle, I met with Geoffrey and one of his co-directors at their head office. To demonstrate their seriousness and keenness to proceed he showed me a press announcement that they had drafted and which if approved by De Vere they would release that afternoon. I was surprised by the speed at which events were now moving. I carefully read the report and asked if I could adjourn to another room so that I could telephone Müller and clear it with him. I returned crestfallen and embarrassed to inform them that they would need to increase the price by 25p per share to get my chairman's irrevocable acceptance. They demurred and I left Cadby Hall, never to return.

Several years later, having experienced difficult trading conditions during the slump of 1974/5 they made a grave error of judgment in electing to borrow in Swiss francs at a much lower rate of interest than that prevailing in the UK, only to see sterling undergo a major devaluation. Lyons decided to bail themselves out of trouble by disposing of their chain of hotels. With hindsight, I am convinced that they would have been better off if they had, instead, sold their American ice cream business, Baskin-Robbins, and used the dollar proceeds to clear their Swiss loans.

On the grapevine I heard of their intention to sell the hotels and informed Müller. He found the prospect of us buying them out, instead of *vice versa*, irresistible. The hotel that he declared he would give his eye-teeth to acquire was The Cumberland at Marble Arch. For many years after his arrival in London following his escape from Czechoslovakia he had been an habitué of The Cumberland Lounge, which every day was thronged with refugees from Nazi oppression, and which served as a substitute for a typical Viennese coffee house. I agreed to contact Lyons and find out what they had in mind.

Having unilaterally been responsible for aborting our merger talks some years previously, I was apprehensive of the response I would receive from Mr Salmon. I telephoned and asked him if he would confirm the report that Lyons would sell their hotels. To my astonishment he was remarkably friendly and confirmed that they *were* in negotiation. I then asked if they would sell The Cumberland to us. He replied that the hotels were for sale as a group and we could not 'cherry pick'. On being advised of the global price they were asking for the group, I told him that I would discuss it with my chairman and come back to him. Several days passed before I telephoned again, only to be informed that Geoffrey was out of town but I could speak to Neil Salmon, the Deputy Chairman, who had been kept informed of my earlier discussion. Neil told me that negotiations with another group were well advanced, but if we were prepared to take on The Tower Hotel as part of the package (which the other party had refused) they would give De Vere preference.

In many respects, Lyons were pioneers and never afraid of being the first in the field. They had been the first in England to identify the potential of the computer and had placed considerable resources into developing Leo, the name they gave to their first commercial computer system. The funds they had available might well have been insufficient to finance the fast-moving concept, and after a few years they had to withdraw from the venture.

It was Lyons who were amongst the first to see the potential in the reclamation of London's derelict dockyards and embarked on building an 800-bedroom hotel in St Katharine's dock on a superb site overlooking Tower Bridge. The interior designer of this major hotel, Peter Glynn-Smith, had over the years been involved in several schemes for De Vere and we had become good friends. He arranged an inspection of the hotel, only for me to experience great difficulty in getting to the hotel's entrance. It was still surrounded by derelict Victorian warehouses adjacent to the abandoned Royal Mint building. However, the views from the hotel over the Thames were spectacular, but in the absence of any form of public transport and its remoteness from theatreland, I could not see it becoming a favourite haunt of the tourist or the preferred location for conferences. My fears were well grounded and the hotel had for several years suffered substantial trading losses, with occupancy levels well below 50%. It was against this adverse background that we had to make a judgment and we decided not to go ahead. Somewhat in desperation and being convinced that there was no trade buyer around for The Tower Hotel, Lyons proceeded to sell the rest of the group to our adversary-of-old, Sir Charles Forte, on extremely generous terms. Lyons were left to shoulder the burden of The Tower for several years more, until a white knight in the form of Scottish & Newcastle Breweries came to the rescue. Subsequent experience has fully vindicated Lyons' foresight in building The Tower Hotel. The error they made was to develop too early, proving the point that with hotels it does not pay to be a pioneer.

The West End is second only to the City of London in being the most valuable real estate in the United Kingdom. Arguably the biggest landlord is the Crown, owning amongst many locations, the whole of Regent Street and Piccadilly Circus. Not far behind, in valuable holdings, must surely be the Grosvenor Estate, the fiefdom of the Duke of Westminster, with major chunks of Belgravia and Mayfair. In a minor league is Earl Cadogan, his properties around Knightsbridge being in a very fashionable part of the metropolis. Cadogan Place, a veritable oasis in a gridlocked neighbourhood, is the setting for one of my most admired London hotels – The Carlton Towers, built by an American hotel corporation. I attended its formal opening, I believe in 1960, and applauded the owners' foresight in commissioning the Polish artist Felix Topolski to decorate the lobby and the Rib Room restaurant with murals of London scenes. I have been entertained there frequently and, of all the other hotels in London, it was my wife's preferred venue for her Ladies' Night dinner when I was elected Master of my Masonic lodge – the Lodge of Tranquillity, founded in 1787.

Through the grapevine I learnt that the hotel was for sale but, as no English agent had been instructed, I was at a loss to know how to start negotiations. One of my closest friends was Milton Garner, an attorney living in Philadelphia who also had the advantage of having stayed at the hotel during one of his frequent trips to Europe. I called and told him that we would like to buy the Sonesta Towers Hotel, formerly called The Carlton Towers. He did not prevaricate and quickly said, 'Then you must get in touch with Sonnabend, he's the owner.'

I replied, 'But how can I get hold of him?'

Milton told me, 'Leave it to me, I will call you in half an hour.'

As good as his word, within half an hour I was speaking long-distance with Mr Sonnabend in Boston. I told him of our interest and he asked me how much we would pay for the hotel. I was caught unprepared to quote a figure, having expected him to name a price on which we could negotiate once I had been put in possession of all the relevant details. I had no knowledge of the hotel's trading performance or the terms of the lease under which the property was held from the Cadogan Estate. I knew that it comprised 220 luxury bedrooms, restaurants and banqueting facilities, including a penthouse entertaining suite with scenic views over the Square and down to Chelsea and the Thames. In addition there was a tower block of apartments developed jointly with the hotel, and if they too formed part of the sale I was at a loss to know how to value them.

I said, 'Mr Sonnabend, you will have to help me to assess a price that will be mutually acceptable.'

He replied, 'What return would you be expecting on your investment?'

I thought quickly and related it to the optimum yield I was endeavouring to squeeze out of De Vere. 'About 8%,' I said.

'After taxes, I presume?' said the voice at the other end of the line.

I could hardly believe my luck, as I had really meant a gross return of 8%. I swallowed and said, 'Yes of course, and I am prepared to fly to Boston today.'

He then disclosed that I had caught him at a very delicate stage of negotiations that he was having with an English group who, at that very moment, were in an adjoining room. He then promised to 'come back to me' if his discussions came to naught.

Earlier in these memoirs I recalled how, as a youth in the years immediately after the First World War, I roamed the streets of Soho, having made the area my own personal playground. Running through the western part of this cosmopolitan district is Brewer Street, and I can still conjure up that at one end of the long street, there was a Marks & Spencer store with its fascia reading 'Penny Bazaar'. Those were the days when Woolworths traded as the 3d (threepenny) and 6d (sixpenny) stores with their boast 'Nothing over sixpence'.

Running north from Piccadilly Circus was Windmill Street, always thronged with peripatetic musicians waiting with their musical instruments to be picked up by agents to form, or fill vacancies in, orchestras and dance bands. The small theatre halfway up the street was later to become famous during the Blitz by using the slogan 'we never closed'. As Windmill Street crossed Brewer Street its name changed to Lexington Street, and on the corner stood a garage notable for a steeply winding ramp leading to the car park on the upper floors. Private cars in those days were few and the garage forecourt catered in the main for fleets of black taxicabs, the natural successors to the hansom cabs that plied for lucrative trade in the heart of theatreland. Forty years on and, incongruously, Lexington garage was now to play a part in my life.

The two brothers Chinn, both very astute, the elder a solicitor and the other a businessman (later to become a dear friend as he worked assiduously for charitable causes in which I too was involved), saw in the early post-war years an opportunity to acquire a small almost moribund company quoted on the London

Stock Exchange called Lex Garages. The two entrepreneurs expanded the company by acquiring motor car distribution agencies, the most prominent one being the United Kingdom distributorship for the Swedish car manufacturer Volvo. The company prospered and, looking for diversification, selected the hotel industry. Our company was at the final stage of developing the De Montfort hotel in Kenilworth when the local authority governing Stratford-on-Avon, only 12 miles from Kenilworth and our other hotel in Leamington Spa, invited tenders for a site on the banks of the river Avon, facing the Shakespeare Memorial theatre. It was an idyllic location for a hotel and I mentally conjured up visions of bedrooms and restaurants themed around Shakespearean characters and plays.

We bid for the site but lost out to Lex. A redbrick hotel not unlike an army barracks was duly built, spoiling a unique vista and location. To my surprise there was apparently a change of heart on the part of the Lex board when, at an early stage in the building process, they decided not to operate the hotel but to lease it to the Hilton organisation, who furnished it in sombre colours and dark woods which no doubt made a visiting American feel at home, being sure that if he wasn't in Milwaukee, it had to be Kalamazoo. I assumed that Lex had gone cold on their hotel aspirations. My assumption might have been correct so far as the Chinn brothers were concerned, but there was now a new force in their boardroom in the presence of Trevor Chinn, Rosser's son, one of the newly emerging breed of thrusting, skilled and highly motivated business managers with a business-school background.

I never heard from Sonnabend, but two days after my telephone call to him in Boston, I learned from the *Financial Times* that the Sonesta Tower had been sold to the Lex Group. Having pulled off this coup, and although they went on to develop a hotel at London's Heathrow airport, Lex subsequently concentrated their expansion on their core business of motor cars, electronics and engineering. The question that still remains unanswered is that had I been entirely open with Sonnabend that we would buy on a *before* tax yield of 8%, would De Vere have carried the day?

So much for the grapevine. In these two instances I seem to

have got to the vineyard just too late – the grapes had already been picked and the vendage completed.

Mirabelle, the jewel in the crown of London restaurants, had earned an international reputation. It was on the 'must visit' list of every gastronome and sophisticated traveller, particularly American celebrities. The *livre d'or*, the autograph book maintained by the manager, contains the signatures of all the great stars of stage and screen in the three post-war decades. Maria Callas signed after a night at Covent Garden singing *Medea*; Pietro Annigoni too, whilst in London to paint his dramatic romanticised portrait of the young Queen Elizabeth; Humphrey Bogart and Lauren Bacall; whilst Zero Mostel takes up two whole pages with hysterical drivel about his Aunt Feige; Maurice Chevalier and Jean Cocteau; Charlie Chaplin and Grace Kelly; David Niven; Laurence Olivier and Sir Alec Guinness. Nureyev, soon after his arrival in London after defecting from his Russian corps de ballet, would no doubt have signed had he not been refused admission on entering the restaurant because he was wearing a leather 'bomber' jacket and was tieless.

Nubar Gulbenkian – Mister Five Per Cent – slept at the Ritz but ate at Mirabelle. Paul Getty, who had possibly an exaggerated reputation for meanness, would examine his bill meticulously and check the addition. King Hussein of Jordan's bodyguard would leave his pistol in the care of the cloakroom attendant and sit his royal master with his back to a wall whilst he took up a position at an opposite table where he could observe everyone entering from the cocktail bar. I am only 5 foot 4 inches and I was delighted to see, when I spoke to the King, that I almost towered over him. Princess Margaret loved to come during the game season, enjoying the way Chef Jean Drees prepared her grouse.

I was present in the restaurant when Aristotle Onassis dined with his son Alexander on the night before the young man was killed piloting his own aircraft; his father always maintained that it was not an accident but that his son was murdered.

I recall an occasion, about 11 p.m., when I telephoned John

Wellesley to enquire how busy dinner had been that evening, only for him to tell me, 'I have a table of Kings and Queens.'

My rejoinder was, 'John, don't tell me you are playing poker?'

'Of course not,' said the unflappable Wellesley, 'we have got the Kings and Queens of Norway, Holland, Denmark and Greece.' They were in London for the wedding of Princess Alexandra to Angus Ogilvy.

Lunching in the restaurant one Friday I noticed a table with ten guests at the far end of the room and was told that the Shah of Persia's brother had telephoned from New York the previous day, making a booking for the royal party who would be in transit to Teheran. Ten days later the Shah, who had only recently celebrated the 2,000th anniversary of the founding of his dynasty (the Pahlavi) and who was one of the last omnipotent monarchs of modern times, was forced to abdicate and to flee for his life, together with his family and court including, no doubt, the lunchtime guests I saw on that fateful Friday.

Membership of the organisation Traditions et Qualité, based in Paris, was probably the ultimate accolade granted to the leading independently-owned restaurants of Europe, many of them already distinguished by the award of three Michelin stars. Mirabelle was one of the founding associates and for nearly two decades the only British member, until it was joined by Le Gavroche, the restaurant founded in 1967 by two of England's greatest chefs, the illustrious Roux brothers, Albert and Michel. The annual general meeting of the association was an event which an associate could miss only at his peril, it being followed in the evening by a *dîner de gala* hosted by one of the members at his own restaurant. Invariably the opportunity was taken to show off to his peers the culinary excellence of his establishment, which resulted in his choosing a menu that those present could not fail to remember as a unique gastronomic experience.

I still chuckle over the dinner in the celebrated three-star Parisian restaurant Taillevant, whose wine list included such rare vintages as Château Lafite Rothschild 1846. Peggy and I were staying at the hotel Plaza Athénée, in the fashionable Avenue Montaigne, close to the Champs Elysée. Before leaving for Paris I had asked the maître chef of Mirabelle, Jean Drees, what he would like me to bring him back from Paris. As it was late autumn he said, 'A kilo of truffles.' Saturday morning found us in the Place de la Madeleine spending an hour in Fauchon's, established in 1886 and one of the finest grocery stores to be found anywhere, admiring the selection of the world's finest produce and the display of unusual tropical fruits and vegetables.

Walking across the square, we entered the portals of Maison de la Truffe, to be greeted by the pungent earthy smell of this highly sought after culinary fungus. In a French kitchen truffles are used as a seasoning ingredient imparting a very special flavour to a sauce, but we had customers who would order a whole truffle cooked in champagne and thinly sliced. Nonchalantly, I told the shop assistant I wanted to buy a kilo of truffles and would she put some out for me to select, knowing that as a natural product they came in different shapes, sizes and weights. I selected a few from those rooted up by the specially trained boars in the forests of Périgord in south-western France. Asking her to weigh them I enquired, '*Combien?*' The price was so staggering that I asked her to repeat it in case she was quoting me in the old francs that were in circulation before the devaluation of the previous year. As an accountant, I was already working out how much we would need to sell one truffle for, the size of a walnut and weighing only a couple of ounces. My mental arithmetic convinced me to stick to caviare – it was much cheaper. I paid by traveller's cheques and took my trophy purchase back to the hotel, where I placed the carrier bag in the wardrobe. This proved to be a monumental blunder as when we came to change to go out to dinner our clothes were saturated with its earthy aroma which no amount of spraying of Peggy's Chanel No. 5 could neutralise.

Arriving at Taillevent, a former ambassadorial residence, we were warmly greeted by the proprietor, M. Vrinat, who had closed his restaurant for the night for the exclusive use of his fellow members of Traditions et Qualité. On sitting down, in front of each diner was an outsize Limoges dinner plate covered by a folded serviette which, on being removed with a theatrical gesture by the waiter, revealed the menu for the evening. It had been fired into the fine plate in gold leaf. My pleasure at this unusual presentation quickly dissipated as I read through the six-course banquet that awaited us. I turned to Peggy and said, 'We are in trouble.'

To which she replied, 'What's the problem?'

I answered, 'You will find out soon enough.'

In the multi-racial and multi-cultural society we have become I have found the creation of a menu that will please everyone's tastes and offend none is extremely difficult. As a Jew who still observes whenever possible the dietary laws of the religion, I do not eat shellfish or the many variants of pork. To my consternation I was now looking at a menu composed by the Patron which incorporated many specialities of the house, including *fruits de mer*, *homard cardinal* and *cochon de lait*. Disaster had struck and I had to think quickly and find excuses that would not embarrass us or upset our host. When we refused the first two courses of oysters and assorted shellfish and the delectable-looking lobster served with a *mornay* sauce, I explained to a very concerned Monsieur Vrinat that we had an allergy to seafood. Resourcefully, he quickly substituted fillets of Dover sole Caprice which, to cover our own embarrassment, we went overboard in complimenting as being absolutely divine. It was obvious that the pièce de résistance was to be the *cochon de lait* – sucking pig. The presentation was theatrical. The restaurant lights were dimmed and three pairs of waiters entered the room in procession carrying on their shoulders small hammocks in each of which nestled a little piglet. With an apple impaled on a sword running the length of their body and flames shooting from the mouth, the piglets were paraded around the room to the applause of all the guests, including Peggy and myself. We had no intention of sampling the delicacy but we just had to applaud the nice touch of theatre. The piglets were carved in the room. Peggy and I settled for an *omelette aux fines herbes*!

27

Collecting Silver, Paintings – and a Chequebook

Throughout my life I have been a collector. Like many schoolboys of my era, I started with cigarette cards, those attractive and informative slips of cardboard to be found in every packet of cigarettes. The aim was to make up a complete set, usually of 50 cards, often a difficult task only achievable by swapping duplicates with one's friends, which served to enhance the pleasure derived from the hobby. Cars and footballers, ships and film stars, statesmen and aeroplanes and countless other series all featured in my collection. As I think of the cards I recall the names of the popular brands of cigarettes most of them now confined to oblivion, or should I say the ashtray of history. Never having been addicted to the 'weed' does not affect my fondness for all the different brands which I now recall with a strong feeling of nostalgia. There was Passing Cloud, De Reszke, Black Cat, Gold Flake, Players, Senior Service, du Maurier and Woodbines all selling for one hundreth of the price of cigarettes today.

In middle age I was introduced to the world of silver-collecting by my cousin David Orgel, one of America's leading antique silver dealers, and I became an ardent admirer of the work of the Georgian silversmiths. David had been responsible for encouraging and helping his friend Arthur Gilbert of Los Angeles to build a world-class collection of silver, which together with his collection of gold and silver boxes and micro-mosaics recently valued in excess of £75 million, is rivalled in range and quality only by those to be found in the *Hermitage* in St Petersburg. Sir Arthur has now donated his collections to Britain and they are housed in a gallery specially built for this purpose in Somerset House in the Strand. My ambition was on a much more modest scale and David recommended that I concentrate on Paul Storr and Hester Bateman, two of the most sought-after exponents of this *genre*.

Paul Storr's work appealed to me immensely, so much so that I made a close study of the career of this outstanding craftsman. He was born in 1771 in the reign of George III, his life spanning three kings. He died during the early years of Queen Victoria's reign at the age of 73, having over the years been commissioned by all three monarchs to supply cutlery and decorative silver to the royal households. It was also the custom for the City of London and Lloyds to make presentations of silver plate to commemorate special occasions; Nelson's victories at the Battle of the Nile in 1798 and the Battle of Copenhagen three years later were the occasion for gifts to Nelson of some splendid and monumental silver table-settings and ornaments. One of my prize pieces was a set of four large salt-cellars embossed with the coat-of-arms of the Prince Regent. Ten generations of silver cleaners had failed to obliterate the cartouche engraved with the Prince of Wales's feathers and the motto '*Ich Dien*'.

Paul de Lamerie, who died 20 years before the birth of Storr, is acclaimed as the greatest of the Georgian silversmiths, but his work was beyond the budget I had set to embark on this most enjoyable hobby. However Hester Bateman, the doyenne of a family of silversmiths and collected with great enthusiasm by the Americans, offered a far less expensive alternative and her silver teapots, wine labels and pierced sweet baskets of classical design and engraving graced my collection.

I next turned to books. For many years each Christmas I wandered into *The Times* bookshop, then established in Wigmore Street in London's West End, and treated myself to £100 worth of books, many of them printed on hand-made paper and bound in superb hand-crafted leather bindings. In this haphazard and fortuitous way I acquired many first editions, including Dickens' *Pickwick Papers* and *Nicholas Nickleby* as well as *Alice's Adventures in Wonderland* and the sister book, *Through the*

Looking Glass. Books illustrated by W. Heath Robinson, René Bull, Edmund Dulac and, most of all, by Arthur Rackham are today still giving me lots of pleasure. They adorn my bookshelves and I frequently take them down to browse through and enjoy the sensuous smoothness of their silken calf and morocco covers.

I started to frequent the antiquarian book fairs and to build a collection of early eighteenth century and nineteenth century cookery books. Helped by Arnold Whitaker Oxford's 'bibliography of English cookery books published between 1500 and 1850', I started to buy cookery books and manuscripts, many 200 and 300 years old, and several editions of Hannah Glass's classic *The Art of Cookery Made Plain and Easy* first published in 1747 'price three shillings stitched and five shillings bound'. My copy of the fourth edition, published in 1751, is actually signed by the author in sepia-coloured ink 'H. Glass'. Her book was so popular that it was repeatedly reprinted up to the year 1803. I also acquired from Heywood Hill, the antiquarian bookseller in Curzon Street, a first edition of the famous *Beeton Book of Household Management* edited by Mrs Isabella Beeton and published in 1861. It has gone into dozens of editions and is still being reprinted to this very day.

At one book fair I was approached by a dealer who knew of my interest in old cookery books and I was able to buy two morocco covered books containing the daily menus written up by the royal chefs. The cover of the first being blocked in gold letters is inscribed 'Buckingham Palace – 1912'. Presented by the head chef each day to the monarch for approval, virtually every page is annotated with remarks written in pencil by Queen Mary. Frequently she deletes certain courses and makes substitutes, sometimes with comments like 'the King only likes small trout'. From her numerous observations I gained the impression that she was very food conscious and had an extensive knowledge of fine cuisine.

The second one is from Sandringham and gives the daily hunting menus – '*Déjeuners de chasse*' – during the autumn of 1936. The one for 19th October carries the pencilled initials 'ER', denoting the approval of King Edward VIII.

Many years after I had acquired these two royal menu books, I was browsing through the catalogue of a Parisian auction house when I noticed that in a sale of cookery books there was one lot which comprised 50 original menus from royal palaces, the royal yacht *Victoria and Albert* and houses of the aristocracy. I placed a postal bid of 1,000 francs in the hope that the collection might contain examples of those in the 1912 Buckingham Palace book. My hunch paid off and I found that I had become the proud possessor of three gold embossed Buckingham Palace menus each printed for a State dinner, which matched those hand-written by the chef in my Buckingham Palace menu book. Metaphorically speaking, I now had the bit between my teeth and by getting in touch with the royal archivist at Windsor Castle I learned that the royal chef was a Frenchman – Monsieur Auguste Cédard. The archivist was able to give me a specimen of Cédard's handwriting, together with the history of his service in the royal Household from the beginning of the 1900s until his retirement more than 30 years later. She also gave me a facsimile of Queen Mary's handwriting which exactly matched her entries in the 1912 menu book. It is lucky breaks such as this one that are the essence of collecting and give the collector the greatest thrill.

Whilst my collection of books takes pride of place in my affections, it is closely followed by my paintings and in particular my Victorian marine water-colours. The unplanned acquisition of one particular oil painting was to lead to a friendship with the painter, an episode in my life on which I now look back with nostalgia.

Peggy and I were spending a winter week-end at our Grand Hotel in Eastbourne and I decided that a new pair of shoes would not come amiss. Finding a shoe shop in the High Street and glancing at the specimens displayed in the window, my attention was distracted by a painting displayed on an easel in the shop next door.

Stacy-Marks' art gallery had been established in Eastbourne for very many years and had a lineage going back to the Victorian artist Henry Stacy-Marks. He first exhibited at the Royal Academy in 1853 as a young artist of 24 and was elected an Academician in 1878. The gallery specialised in Old Master landscapes and portraits whilst not neglecting and sponsoring living artists. The canvas that had caught my eye and which dominated the window was well-known to me. I felt sure that I had seen it in the National Gallery and on many occasions as a framed print. I stood spellbound in front of the window, totally floodlit by a battery of halogen lamps which picked out the vibrant colours of the full-length figure of a Burmese dancing girl set in a heavily carved gold frame. Could this possibly be the original or was it an enlarged print? The only way in which I could find out was to go into the shop, which we both proceeded to do.

Selling paintings in a gallery has a lot in common with selling sleek, glossy new cars in a dealer's showroom. The customer is cosseted from the moment he expresses interest and the maximum of charm exudes from the sales assistant. 'Of course we can take the Kelly out of the window for you to examine, sir,' gushed the urbane young man, and within a minute we were both deeply seated in Louis XVI armchairs gazing in rapture at the stunning original painting of *Saw Ohn Nyun in a Yellow Tamein*. It was love at first sight and I enquired the price of this painting by Gerald Kelly of his Burmese model. Mr Stacy-Marks breathed deeply and began a discourse on the provenance of the painting, during the course of which he explained that they were selling it on commission for a lady who had had it in the family for many years. It was the first time it had come onto the open market. They could sell it for 3,500 guineas. This time it was I who breathed deeply. I looked at Peggy, then at the young man and, in a strangulated voice, almost a whisper, I said, 'Would you take £3,250?'

Haughtily he replied,

'I'm sorry, sir, we always sell in guineas ... we *buy* in pounds.'

'Then 3,250 guineas,' said I, and so by adding 3,250 shillings or £162, the picture became mine.

I forgot all about buying the shoes and could not wait until, two weeks later, the gallery delivered the painting to my home in Stanmore. It was a large painting measuring 40 inches by 32 inches and I hung it in the dining room, where, by sheer coincidence the walls, which were surmounted by a plaster frieze of acanthus leaves picked out in gold leaf, toned in with the identical lime-green colour of the painting's background. My wife and I were enchanted.

On being told that Sir Gerald Kelly, now an octogenarian, was living in London, I wrote to tell him how much pleasure his painting was giving us and that we would be happy if he could visit our home and see how we had hung and lit it. Alternatively, we would be delighted if he and Lady Kelly would be our guests for lunch at the Mirabelle. He chose the latter course and with hardly concealed excitement we greeted Gerald and his wife in the cocktail bar. A short Irishman with a puckish face and eyes twinkling through his spectacles, he proved to be the perfect lunchtime guest, and then and there we forged a friendship that lasted until his death at the age of 92.

Sir Gerald at the time was the most celebrated living English artist. A past and exceedingly popular President of the Royal Academy, he had been invested by King George VI as a Knight Commander of the Victorian Order on completion of the state portraits of the King and Queen Elizabeth which are now hung in Windsor Castle. His painting career commenced in Paris in 1901, where he met many of the Impressionists, including Monet, Cézanne, Renoir and Degas.

I became a regular visitor to his home and studio at 117 Gloucester Place, a road that runs parallel to Baker Street, in London's West End. We talked about wine and restaurants – Sir Gerald was a *bon viveur* and had built up a very esoteric wine cellar. He was fond of showing me his vast collection of Japanese prints, which he stored in large mahogany plan chests. He gave me free range of his studio and would accompany me around it explaining the canvases, talking about the sitters and how he was fascinated and often defeated by hands, which he found the most difficult part of the body to draw. One large canvas had been divided by a ruler into innumerable squares on which, in charcoal, he had drawn a hand resting on a marble pedestal.

As I was visiting him for tea one Saturday afternoon he said, 'I would like to make you a gift, Leslie. Walk around the studio and pick out anything you like.'

I was lost for words and mumbled something like, 'I can't do that, Gerald, it would be taking advantage.'

'Nonsense,' he replied. 'Please me, and do it.'

So I walked around, past portraits of Somerset Maugham, sketches of King George VI, uncompleted paintings and drawings, numerous portraits of his favourite model, Jane, his wife for more than 50 years. I felt embarrassed as I knew Sir Gerald wanted me to take him literally when he had said 'pick out anything you like', and I felt I could not take advantage of his kindness. I eventually chose a still life of oriental fruits in a bowl which he had painted on his first visit to Burma in 1908 and which was probably the most modest of all the works I had found hung on the walls or stacked around on the floor. He praised my choice and insisted on personally wrapping up the painting for me in sheets of *The Times* newspaper.

I have always promised myself that I would visit his memorial tablet placed close to the grave of Sir Joshua Reynolds in the crypt of St Paul's Cathedral. My friend, too, was a great man.

With more than two million individuals working in its hotels and restaurants, the catering industry is the largest employer in the country. The industry is very fragmented, hotels ranging in size and quality of operation from the humble bed and breakfast boarding house to the 750-room five-star international hotel. Restaurants range from small fast-food operations to Michelin starred haunts of the rich; from works canteens to corporate hospitality tents at Ascot and Wimbledon. It has traditionally been considered a low-pay industry. To help those who at one time or another have served in the industry and subsequently found themselves in need, a very worthy charity has been active since its foundation in 1847 when it operated under the quaint name of 'The London Coffee and Eating House Keeper's Benevolent Association for Decayed Members, their Widows and Orphans'. Dickensian days behind it, progress dictated a change of name to 'The Hotel and Catering Benevolent Association' (the HCBA).

When Sir Lindsay Ring, a former Lord Mayor of London, invited me to join the Grand Council of the HCBA, of which he was Treasurer, I was glad of the opportunity to give something back to an industry that had given me such a pleasurable and successful career. In due course I was appointed President, succeeding in that office such stalwarts as Lord Forte and Sir Maxwell Joseph. It was during my Presidency that I was asked to be the guest of honour at the annual banquet of the Food and Cookery Society. The Society, formed in the latter part of the nineteenth century, has traditionally been presided over by the Master of the Queen's Household, and I received a letter from Vice-Admiral Sir Peter Ashmore, KCVO, DSC, inviting me to meet him in his office in Buckingham Palace to discuss the keynote speech which I would be delivering at the forthcoming banquet. The man I was to meet had been born into a naval family, both his father and his brother having been admirals. Sir Peter had had a distinguished war service and as a 20-year old sub-lieutenant serving in the destroyer HMS *Kipling* had been awarded the Distinguished Service Cross for his services at Crete and a Mention in Despatches for his part in the destruction of a U-boat. He survived the sinking of his destroyer by enemy aircraft in May 1942 and in the light cruiser *Royalist* had participated in air attacks on the German battleship *Tirpitz*.

I was somewhat apprehensive but unnecessarily so, as he exuded great charm, and any qualms I might have had in working with such a high-ranking naval officer were quickly dispersed. Whilst giving me a tour of part of the Palace he explained the functions of the Master of the Household, who was responsible for the smooth running of all the royal palaces. Whenever the Queen and the Duke of Edinburgh made a state visit abroad, Sir Peter would lead an advance party several weeks beforehand and meticulously plan the event and put in place all the *minutiae* of a very complex tour. He had just returned from India, which had taxed to the limit his ingenuity and expertise in organising the royal visit.

On returning to my office, taking the relevant notes out of my briefcase to dictate a memorandum of the meeting, I was appalled to find that amongst my papers was Sir Peter's personal chequebook, which I had inadvertently picked up from his desk, along with several other documents. I telephoned him immediately, jocularly pleading with him not to punish me by making me 'walk

279

the plank' or have me incarcerated in the Tower of London. Fortunately he laughed off my mistake and I ensured that he was reunited with his chequebook within the hour.

28

Ventures into the Media

When at the turn of the century the Marchese Guglielmo Marconi chose England rather than his native Italy to continue his experiments with radio waves and succeeded in sending a radio signal from the Isle of Wight to Cornwall, a distance of 200 miles, I wonder if he could have foreseen the revolution in communications that would develop out of his early work. The telephone, television, radio and, more recently, the ability to receive pictures of planets in outer space, like Saturn a billion miles away, are but a random selection of the miracles of our century that owe their origin to his genius. Some 30 years later on, as a ten-year-old, before the days of the radio valve and later the printed circuit, I built a wireless set for a few shillings, consisting mainly of a crystal and a 'whisker' as fine as a human hair. Wearing earphones, and providing I was successful in twiddling with the whisker to make a good contact with the crystal, I was able to pluck out of the ether the sounds of 2LO broadcasting from Savoy Hill. By no stretch of my imagination could I then have foreseen a personal involvement with 'wireless' but that was 40 years into the future and resulted from my eye catching a small announcement in the *Bournemouth Evening News* of the formation, under the leadership of Lord Stokes, of a consortium to bid for one of the new local commercial radio licences.

The licence was to cover the counties of Hampshire and Dorset, and Donald Stokes invited me to join the board of a newly formed company that, in competition with four other consortia, would be bidding for the licence. We won, and named the radio station

'2CR' – Two Counties Radio. Contrary to the experience of other commercial radio stations, ours was profitable from day one – a success I attribute to the sagacity and charismatic leadership of our Chairman. I had previously met Donald through my business interests in the Midlands, particularly in Coventry, and now that I was working with him in the radio business we became good friends. When he came to the mandatory retiring age set by the Independent Radio Authority, I was elected by the board to succeed him as Chairman of Two Counties Radio Ltd.

I had great admiration for Donald's business acumen and enterprise. He was a Plymothian, and as I was stationed there during the war I had got to know his family whilst he was fighting in the Western Desert and in Italy. Demobilised as a Lieutenant-Colonel, he resumed his career with Leyland Motors, the company he had joined as an apprentice straight from Blundell School, rising to become their Sales Director. In this capacity he achieved national fame when he insisted on selling fleets of buses to Castro's Cuba against the wishes of the British Government. Cuba had been a pre-war customer of Leyland and Donald's loyalties now were firstly to his company and then to their customers. Castro, the arch communist, who was being treated as a pariah by the United States, badly needed friends and in appreciation of his steadfastness Donald became the recipient of Cuba's bounty in the form of a gift each Christmas of a casket of the finest Havana cigars, the size that Winston Churchill was fond of ... 7 inches! His company rewarded him by promotion to the Chair of British Leyland Corporation, and the government, recognising that after all 'business is business', followed by bestowing on him a knighthood. It must be unique in English corporate history for an engineering apprentice to progress through the numerous ranks of a company to become the Chairman of one of Britain's major industrial concerns. He was lukewarm to Prime Minister Harold Wilson's plan to put together the greater part of the British motor industry under one umbrella and float it on the London Stock Exchange. Donald was raised to the peerage and elected President of the company but the company failed to achieve its grandiose conceptual plan and was eventually liquidated.

Having been appointed to the Chair of Two Counties Radio Ltd., I was conscious of the fact that, as a private company without a stock market quotation but with a hundred small shareholders, there was no means of assessing the true value of our shares and consequently we might fall victim to a predator seeking to acquire a controlling interest on the cheap. I looked around for another commercial radio company with which we could merge and my attention was drawn to Radio 210, broadcasting in the Reading and Basingstoke areas, which was similar in size to 2CR. The first and major hurdle to overcome was to get the consent to a merger from the Independent Broadcasting Authority. This was uncharted territory as, except when a station had fallen on hard times and required a white knight to bail it out, the Authority had never allowed a merger of two stations. I telephoned Richard Palmer, the Chairman of Radio 210, and asked if we could meet. 'What for?' he asked. 'To merge our two companies,' I replied. He agreed that the two companies would make an ideal fit and we composed a letter to the Director of Radio setting out our preliminary thoughts and invited him to meet us for lunch at Mirabelle to discuss the matter in greater detail.

The meeting went well and consent was soon given to the merger. I formed a company which we called CRH Ltd. (Combined Radio Holdings), in which the shareholders of 2CR and 210 took an equal number of shares. In recognition of the ownership of its freehold broadcasting station, shareholders of Two Counties Radio Ltd. were rewarded with a short-dated debenture stock at an attractive rate of interest. Within 18 months CRH Ltd. had been merged with GWR Plc (Great Western Radio), a company quoted on the London Stock Exchange and broadcasting from Bristol and Swindon. In this rather roundabout way I managed to secure a quotation for the original 2CR shares and in the process had increased the value of the shareholders' original investment eightfold. GWR Ltd. has gone from strength to strength and, second only to the BBC, it is now the largest commercial radio broadcaster in the country, owning some 32 local commercial radio stations, including the outstandingly successful Classic FM which broadcasts nationally. Determined to remain in the vanguard of this fast expanding medium, the company is now pioneering digital radio in the commercial sector ... a far cry from my crystal wireless set.

One of the locations in the film *Gigi*, immortalised by the French actor Maurice Chevalier and his co-star Lesley Caron, is Maxim's, one of Paris's most celebrated restaurants. Opened in 1893 in the Rue Royale, it is decorated and furnished in the style known as Grande Époque, and its original interior is now subject to a French Government preservation order. As it was a fellow member with Mirabelle of Traditions et Qualité, I asked the owner, M. Vaudable, if he would participate in the tradition we had established some years previously of inviting a famous European restaurant to join us in a gastronomic week at Mirabelle. Amongst previous Parisian restaurants which had accepted my invitation (all having been awarded three Michelin stars) had been the Tour d'Argent, reputedly founded in 1582 and occupying a dramatic site on the River Seine opposite Notre Dame Cathedral. This legendary restaurant, owned by jet-setting Claude Terrail, was popular with many of our own clientele. Another participant had been the fashionable Restaurant Lassere, situated in the heart of Paris in the Avenue Franklin Roosevelt. One of the features of its interior is a retractable roof, which, like that at Mirabelle, enables guests on warm summer nights to dine under the stars. René Lassere presided over his eponymous restaurant and its Escoffier-inspired cuisine with loving care and had sent his son to work for a year in the Mirabelle kitchens.

These visits necessarily called for a great deal of detailed planning on the part of Mirabelle. Unlike my French counterparts, I was not prepared to leave anything to chance and my patience was frequently taxed to the limit in trying to reconcile and sometimes placate Gallic susceptibilities.

M. Vaudable expressed his pleasure and willingness to bring Maxim's to London and in March 1980 we launched a Mirabelle/Maxim week. Several of his chefs, accompanied by his Maitre d', arrived to work with our own staff in replicating the

Parisian Maxim's in Mirabelle's dining room. Large canvas screens, skilfully painted, depicted Maxim's Grand Époque interiors, and completely transformed the Curzon Street restaurant ... a Gallic influence pervaded every part of our operation. The Maxim's staff worked amicably with our own under the watchful eye of their Restaurant Manager, who the previous year had master-minded and run the multi-million-pound catering arrangements for the ill-fated Shah of Persia's party to celebrate the 2,000th anniversary of the founding of his dynasty.

To promote the Anglo-French event our public relations team went into overdrive. I asked that representative food and restaurant critics be invited to lunch, and for them to ensure that the list included Quentin Crewe, who could be accompanied by a guest of his choice. I hoped that another visit to Mirabelle would reverse the *animus* he had previously shown when dining with us some years previously. Until he arrived in the cocktail bar in a wheelchair, I had not realised that he was a paraplegic, and being concerned I went over to him, introduced myself and asked if he would like me to wheel his chair to a table in the bar and to join him for a drink. He declined the offer, saying that he would be joined by his guest Bernard Levin, who at the time was a columnist at *The Times*. I told John Wellesley to seat them in due course at a table for two and I went off and joined a table which included Sheila Black of *The Financial Times*, Alan Coren, the Editor of *Punch*, Marika Hanbury-Tennison, a well-loved and highly regarded food writer and wife of the explorer, and M. Vaudable. Lunch having finished, all at the table complimented the owner of Maxim's on a superb repast and I returned to my office at three o'clock.

That evening I telephoned Victor Sonvico, our joint Maitre d', to ask if he had any observations to make on Quentin Crewe's table. He told me that they must have enjoyed their meal immensely, having been the last to leave the restaurant shortly after 5 p.m after repeatedly calling for more bread rolls to mop up gravy and sauces and polishing off three bottles of wine. I relaxed and looked forward to a thank-you letter from either or both of them. None came but in the next issue of *Harper's and Queen*,

Quentin resumed the war of words, starting his article with the phrase, 'If there is one thing I cannot stand, it is being patronised.' He then went on to criticise everything except the condiments on the table. Initially I was furious at his boorish behaviour; this soon passed when the success of the Week was dramatically illustrated in the record turnover recorded.

This is an appropriate stage in my memoirs to record my debut as a writer. During the war, as a diversification from my activities as a minesweeping commander, I wrote poetry and some short stories drawing on my experiences of serving on a deep-sea trawler built to *fish* for fish but converted on the outbreak of hostilities to *fish* for submarines. My literary efforts were never published but, although written nearly 60 years ago, they still seem fresh to me and have the power vividly to invoke those desperate times when I just lived from day-to-day.

My appearance in print came, as many of my experiences in life have, by accident. I took a call one day in my office from a gentleman who explained that he was the owner of a colour library and wished to include in his inventory a photograph of an exotic-looking *gateau*. Could Mirabelle help him? He informed me that a colour library resembled a normal library except that instead of books they stored thousands of photographic negatives covering every conceivable subject and place. For a fee they would hire out a colour transparency to publishers of books, calendars, greeting cards and brochures, whilst retaining the copyright of the film. I was intrigued by what he told me and suggested a meeting at which I asked if instead of taking a single photograph he would be interested in publishing an illustrated Mirabelle cookery book. He responded positively and I set to work on it.

My first step was to get Chef Jean Drees enthusiastic about the project. In true Gallic style he immediately dashed my hopes to the ground saying that he had never ever written his recipes down and did not feel like doing it now at his age; the average housewife he avowed, would never have the patience or the understanding to reproduce his style of cuisine and in any case he was far too busy on the stove to contemplate spending hours in his office. I resorted to flattery and cajoled him by telling him that he owed it to future generations of *epicures*. I flattered him by saying that he would be joining the ranks of other famous author-chefs, including his idols, Escoffier and Carême. I told him he need not write, he could dictate the recipes and we would help him with the conversion of quantities into avoirdupois – long before metrication he was using kilos and litres instead of pounds and pints. I felt I was fighting a losing battle until one day he telephoned to say that he had spoken it over with his wife and Madame had told him to do it. I asked him to work on Robinson, our pastry chef, and get him to co-operate. He too needed encouragement, expressing reluctance to reveal his closely guarded secret recipes.

The next hurdle was to find someone in the media with a good literary style and a love of cooking. The answer to this problem lay in Sheila Black, an outstanding journalist whose charm would draw the best out of two still hesitant chefs. By enlisting Anthony Hern, the wine critic of the *Evening Standard*, I felt I now had a team that could produce a stunning cookery book, to which I gave the name *Cuisine Mirabelle*. When proposing the venture to Colour Library International, little did I appreciate the magnitude of the task of publishing a cookery book: the long photographic sessions, the interminable weeks spent composing and then correcting proofs and liaising with the printers.

Shortly before Christmas 1979 and after two years of effort it was over and it only remained for me to write a foreword, which I reproduce hereunder:

The ancient Egyptians have recorded their recipes in hiero-glyphic writing and the earliest manuscript devoted to cookery is attributed to Apicius and was printed as long ago as 1497. Since then every aspect of the Art would appear to have been covered from haute cuisine to microwave. As cookery books compare only with the Bible in the number that have been published, I feel somewhat apprehensive in adding further to the vast Bibliography devoted to the art of the kitchen.

I must confess that I have long had the urge to introduce to an even wider public, two of the great chefs of post-war England. The reader is taken through the lens of Neil Sutherland's camera, into the kitchens of Maître Chef des Cuisines Jean Drees and Chef-Patissier Edward Robinson who, after much urging, have for the first time in their long careers, revealed their most closely guarded recipes. I hope, as a result, 'Cuisine Mirabelle' will open up new vistas to the discriminating hostess. Sheila Black and Anthony Hern have impressed their literary virtuosity on this book and clothed it with abounding interest. To all these very talented people, my grateful thanks.

29

Bid Farewell

Tempus fugit, time flies. Leopold Müller, who in 1981 had celebrated his eightieth birthday, had for many years delegated to me complete control of the day-to-day-operation of the group, which included presiding over the company's annual general meetings. Because of his advancing age and the onset of Parkinson's disease, the future of De Vere had become a frequently recurring topic of conversation between us. By nature a wheeler-dealer, Müller was looking forward to making one final deal, the biggest of his long life, by selling off his controlling 51% interest in the company. I, too, was seeking the same end-play but for entirely different reasons. From the very commencement of the company more than 20 years previously and its successful progress since, the problem of where to place his controlling stake had never been far from my thoughts. His insistence on maintaining his holding intact had seriously affected our expansion as we were precluded from using our highly-rated shares for acquisitions because this would have diluted his 50% holding. I was aware that on Müller's demise the death duties on his estate made it a virtual certainty that our company would be the object of an auction. I would not then be in a position to choose the successor – the Executors would be duty bound to accept the highest price they could get for his shareholding without regard to the intentions of the buyer. I was fearful of the Group, so skilfully and successfully put together over two decades, passing into the hands of an asset stripper and I felt that I was the protector of the jobs of my staff, numbering more than 2,000, many of whom were known to me personally, having shown their dedication to the De Vere philosophy of *'operating hotels and restaurants of distinction'*.

Over the years I had instituted a series of discussions with other companies in our industry with a view to amalgamation, but the price set by Müller for his controlling stake invariably proved too high, except in one case where *pride* and not *price* was the determining factor in aborting a merger which I thought was 'made in heaven' – De Vere and Savoy.

At no stretch of the imagination could a young Auguste Escoffier have ever dreamt, as he cooked for the army officers at General Headquarters in the garrison town of Metz during the Franco-Prussian War of 1870, that one day he would preside over the kitchens in the most prestigious hotels of London. His first career was in association with César Ritz and commenced in 1889 at the newly built Savoy Hotel. Despite its grandeur and the lavish expenditure of its founder Richard D'Oyly Carte it failed to 'take off' until Escoffier took over the kitchens and Ritz the general management. Together the pair turned the Savoy into a hotel that has remained a paradigm for hotels until this very day.

Throughout the twentieth century the Savoy group has rarely been out of the news headlines because of the underlying value of its real estate despite its dismal trading record. After World War Two the Company attracted the attention of property magnates such as Harold Samuel (Lord Samuel of Land Securities), Jack Cotton and Charles Clore of City Centre Properties and even of the Kuwait Investment Office. Maxwell Joseph cast covetous eyes on their London hotels, which included the Connaught, Claridges, and the Berkeley, wishing to incorporate them into his Grand Metropolitan Hotels group. After acquiring a significant shareholding he bailed out, defeated by the complex capital structure whereby the relatively small number of 'B' shares (controlled by the directors and their friends) enjoyed 40 times the voting power of the 'A' shares which were held by the public at large. Added to this formidable defence against a take-over bid, and *any* bid was considered from the very outset as being a hostile one, there was the aloofness, bordering on outright hostility, of the Chairman Sir Hugh Wontner to overtures from whatever source.

My interest in the Savoy group was kindled by the continuing controversy surrounding the company, which surfaced at their Annual General Meetings. These began to mirror the wars of the Danizigers versus the Daniels (Zena and her father) in the early 1960s. These made newspaper headlines and invariably flared up at the Extraordinary General Meetings of Gordon Hotels which were held at The Mayfair Hotel, the flagship of the company which, like the Savoy, had been founded in the golden years for hotels at the end of the Victorian era.

Over lunch one day at the Mirabelle with the local directors of Barclays Bank Pall Mall district, I asked how I could get an introduction to Sir Hugh Wontner. Christopher Norman-Butler, whose father had been the General Manager of Martins Bank at the time it was taken over by Barclays, offered to set up a meeting for me as the Savoy Group was one of his customers and he knew Sir Hugh well. In the event it was to a suite in Claridges that I was invited to meet Sir Anthony Hornby, a former senior partner of stockbrokers Cazenove and now Deputy Chairman of the Savoy Group. I outlined my plan for a merger of equals. Our profits were similar and we shared the same philosophy – the pursuit of excellence in hotel-keeping. In addition to the Mirabelle we owned two five-star hotels and other upmarket hotel and restaurant properties. I thought I had made out a good case for the initiation of negotiations and Sir Anthony promised to report to Wontner. I did not have long to wait and had my answer the very next day. 'Sir Hugh was perfectly happy with his group; he did not seek to expand his company, and would we please go away.'

For several years I maintained contact through Giles Shepard, the Savoy Managing Director, whose ambitions included reigning over an enlarged Savoy group and who was in principle keen to see our two companies merge. Repeated requests to meet Wontner fell on stony ground. He had first been appointed Managing Director as long ago as 1941 and had served as Lord Mayor of London. A self-appointed autocrat and a snob he felt his position in the company was unassailable until Sir Charles Forte arrived

291

on the scene. Charles had the reputation of never buying shares in a company that he wished to acquire, prior to making his bid, and was known never to make a bid against a hostile board. The Savoy became an obsession with him and he changed his strategy. He proceeded to build up a commanding shareholding that gave his company virtual ownership of Savoy but with insufficient votes to take control. The difference was very narrow, so much so that Wontner felt threatened.

One day, out of the blue, I received a telephone call from Giles to the effect that his Chairman would now like to see me and how soon could I arrange this? I replied, 'I will come right away' and within half an hour I was sitting in a very small office at No. 1 Savoy Hill talking to Wontner – something I had yearned to do for more than five years. Wontner had asked me to come alone and had told Giles, after the introductions had been made, to leave us whilst I outlined my scheme to merge as equal partners. He told me that he was 'under great pressure from the Forte people' and I noted the strain that this must be placing on his normally laid-back and disinterested manner. He was 'ready to agree the plan' until I mentioned that Müller would want to receive a significant proportion of his shares in the 'B' category – those that outvoted the 'A' shares by 40 to one. Wontner asked 'How old is your Mr Leopold Müller?' 'He has just celebrated his eightieth birthday,' I replied. Wontner said, 'And what will happen to these "B" shares when he dies? We will be back in the same position as we are today.' I could offer no solution to the problem and I knew that that was the end of the Savoy saga so far as De Vere was concerned.

I had got to know Derek Palmar, Chairman of Bass the brewers, when he was on the Board of Hill Samuel. I got him interested in De Vere and Bass bought a million shares but stopped short of making a take-over bid, telling me, 'De Vere is a good company, but at the price you are asking the arithmetic just does not add up.'

Isaac Wolfson of Great Universal Stores expressed keen interest. He had earlier on been instrumental in financing Maxwell Joseph to buy the Mount Royal Hotel at Marble Arch. Our negotiations conducted over a whole year were very friendly and personal. Finally leaving it to his son Leonard to make a decision a price was offered which was so derisory that I ceased calling at Universal House in Tottenham Court Road where Sir Isaac, although still Chairman of GUS, had given up effective running of the company to his son and heir.

Cyril Stein, Chairman of Ladbrokes the betting and casino business, was keen to use his company's powerful cash flow to build up a hotel division that would improve the quality of Ladbrokes' earnings and diversify their business away from their traditional gambling activities. It was in the days before he bought-up the Hilton chain of hotels but I still found it strange that he turned down the opportunity to acquire De Vere because 'it was too up-market'.

Sir Maxwell Joseph had a personal vendetta with my Chairman which I found impossible to reverse and Lord Forte, whilst making encouraging noises and telling me that I would 'be treated as one of the family', was looking to buy at a bargain-basement price.

Lord Pritchard, who I had first got to know when he was Chairman of Allied Breweries, was interested as a diversification for the tobacco group Rothmans International, of which he was non-executive Chairman.

I flew to Zurich to conduct negotiations with the bankers Julius Baer acting for Mövenpick, who were contemplating a deal that would tie us both in with the Swiss food giant Nestlé.

A last-minute hike by Müller in the price he would accept scuppered my talks with J. Lyons & Company.

A newspaper leak of negotiations with Sir John Davis of the Rank organisation suffered the same fate as did earlier discussions with Sir John Reid of EMI, whilst discussions with Lord Sainsbury never proceeded beyond two visits to their headquarters near London Bridge – I can still recall the all-pervading smell of cheese maturing in their warehouse below.

I had very serious but protracted negotiations with Sir Gordon White who, with his partner Sir James Hanson (they were both ennobled later on by Mrs Thatcher's government), had founded the highly successful conglomerate The Hanson Group. The intermediary in our discussions was Greg Hutchings, who was to leave shortly after our negotiations were finally broken off to found the equally successful conglomerate Tomkins, whose range of interests stretched from guns (Smith and Wesson) to Hovis bread.

It seemed that we were destined always to be the 'bridesmaid but never the blushing bride' until early in January 1984 I received a telephone call from Paul Nicholson, who introduced himself as Chairman of Vaux Breweries of Sunderland. He asked if he could meet me as a matter of urgency and I invited him to see me the next day, a Saturday, at my home in Stanmore. He explained that they were a long-established firm of regional brewers; their Swallow Hotels division would like to expand and De Vere's four-star hotels would be an ideal fit. Our luxury five-star hotels, The Royal Bath in Bournemouth and The Grand in Eastbourne, would be excluded and Müller and I would be given first refusal on their acquisition. We did not discuss price and I told him I would report our discussion to my chairman. During the middle of the following week a letter was delivered to me by hand from Andrew Thomas, Deputy Chairman of the Warrington brewers Greenall Whitley, expressing *their* interest in making an offer for the company and asking for a meeting.

I immediately thought of the expression that 'it never rains but it pours' and I started on a cloak-and-dagger operation setting up a series of separate meetings limited to myself and the chief executives of each of the two brewery companies. Müller was excited but realised that in his poor state of health he would not be able to participate actively in the negotiations. Both companies were regional breweries of similar size and each one was anxious to impress on me that not only were their intentions honourable but that they would guarantee continuity of De Vere policy. There would be no redundancies – an assurance that is usually given by a predator with tongue-in-cheek. I was now in the enviable position of having two ardent suitors and I had to perform a balancing act with both parties. I endeavoured to keep my two sets of discussions in watertight compartments, or in present-day parlance, separated by 'a Chinese wall'. One day Christopher Hatton, Chairman of Greenalls, asked me point blank, 'Are we in contention with another party?', when I had to admit, without naming them, that that was indeed the case. Greenalls were represented by Warburgs, Vaux, by Morgan Grenfall and we had retained our old friends Hill Samuel as merchant bankers, but *I* was 'calling the shots'.

It was interesting to analyse the thought processes of the two rival chairmen and the brief and cursory manner in which they both appeared to carry out their due diligence of our company. Hatton was a solicitor by profession and insisted on sending a team of lawyers from his law firm in Warrington to inspect the title deeds of all our hotels to ascertain whether they were in fact freehold and unencumbered. Nicholson, a chartered accountant, had an entirely different approach. He was obsessed with the tax implications of a buy-out and the need to get his shareholders' approval at an extraordinary general meeting to sanction the purchase. They were both bidding the same price. Each man wanted an option on Müller's holding but he steadfastly refused to entertain such an idea and was adamant that he wanted an outright sale.

The die was cast in Greenall's favour when Hatton sent Müller a personal letter offering a small improvement on his earlier price, an offer that was to be open for his irrevocable acceptance within seven days. He indicated that as his company did not wish to be in the London restaurant business, Greenalls would give us first refusal to buy back the restaurant division. This comprised Mirabelle, the two Overton restaurants and the Connaught Rooms. Müller, in a state of great excitement, called me to his office and told me to telephone Hatton and to tell him that he did not *need* seven days. He would accept the offer for his personal shareholding provided the deal was done before the end of banking hours that same day (28th June 1984) and the money paid over in exchange for his share certificates. Knowing that with Müller's mercurial temperament this was the only way a deal would ever be done, I picked up the telephone and called Warrington. It was ten o'clock in the morning. I told Hatton that I was closeted with Müller and other members of the board and my Chairman would accept his offer but that the money had to be in Müller's hand not later than 3.30 p.m that day. Hatton exploded, saying that he was in Cheshire not in London and how did I think he could raise that kind of money in a couple of hours and fly down to London to conclude the deal? I told Hatton that unless he could work the miracle, he could forget the deal. Hatton asked for an hour's grace.

Half an hour later the telephone rang and I picked up the receiver. Hatton was on the line. Using his influence as a local director of National Westminster Bank, he had been promised the necessary funds. I told him that I would arrange for the completion to take place at the head office of Barclays Bank at 54 Lombard Street in the City of London and to meet us there with a banker's draft at 3 p.m. I then telephoned Alan Tritton, one of the main board directors of Barclays, with whom I was on friendly terms, and explained the situation to him. I asked if he would provide us with a room in the bank to carry out the transaction and to get Müller's share certificates released from the custody of their nominee company in whose name they were registered. He agreed. It was not long before I received a call from the nominee company saying that they required at least 48 hours to carry out the necessary paperwork. I replied, 'You have got 48 minutes; just get on with it.'

Just before three o'clock Müller, in an invalid's wheelchair, was being pushed across the vast white marbled floor of the bank to join me standing at the nearest lift to take us to the first floor, where we were joined by a flustered Christopher Hatton. The atmosphere in the room was electric and I could hardly believe that Müller at this final hour would not change his mind and refuse to sell, or at least try and raise the *ante*. With Müller's certificates in my hand, I asked him to sign the share transfers. I then asked to see the banker's draft and for ten seconds held a sum of more than £22 million in my hand before simultaneously passing the cheque to Müller and the signed share transfers to the Greenall representatives. In less than five minutes a business partnership that had lasted against all the odds for almost 40 years came to a close and I did not know whether to cry or shout 'hurrah'.

* * *

296

Many years later I was asked by his solicitor, 'was Müller really aware of what he was doing? After all, he was in his eighty-third year. Had he not "lost his marbles"?'

In reply I quoted Müller's last remark to the Director of Barclays Bank who, on being handed the cheque, had turned to Müller and said, 'Yes, Mr Müller, in accordance with your instructions we will place it on a seven-day-notice deposit in your name.'

As quick as lightning Müller had replied, 'You will do no such thing. I don't want to have to give you seven days' notice. What *I* want is a seven-day *fixed-deposit* and *then* I will tell you if I want it renewed.'

Now do you think he had lost his marbles?

INDEX

301